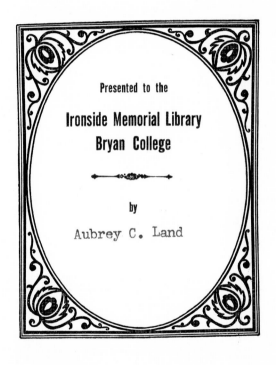

BLACKS IN THE NEW WORLD

August Meier, Series Editor

Freedmen, Philanthropy, and Fraud

Freedmen, Philanthropy, and Fraud

A History of the Freedman's Savings Bank

Carl R. Osthaus

UNIVERSITY OF ILLINOIS PRESS

Urbana Chicago London

LIBRARY OF CONGRESS CATALOGING IN PUBLICATION DATA

Osthaus, Carl R
    Freedmen, philanthropy, and fraud.

    (Blacks in the new world)
    Bibliography: p.
    Includes index.
    1. Freedman's Savings and Trust Company, Washington,
D. C.–History. I. Title. II. Series.
HG2613.W34F85   332.2'1'09753   75–23214
ISBN 0–252–00305–5

For my parents
and in memory of
Donna Arlina Norton

Acknowledgments

One satisfaction in completing this work is having the opportunity to acknowledge those who gave of their time and expertise. I am especially grateful to my mentor, Professor John Hope Franklin, who first suggested this topic and guided my efforts in the early months of research and writing. Professor Gerald C. Heberle of Oakland University attacked my wandering prose with enthusiasm and corrected many a stylistic error. Professors August Meier of Kent State University and William S. McFeely of Mount Holyoke College offered valuable suggestions and gave my work detailed criticism throughout the long process from dissertation to completed manuscript. Their criticisms are now an indispensable part of my education. I also benefited from Professor Weldon Welfling's suggestions on the history of savings banks and from the encouragement of my Oakland University colleague, W. Patrick Strauss. Because of what I like to call my independent streak (but which may actually be an innate perversity), I did not always follow the advice of these historians, and therefore I specifically absolve them from responsibility for any mistakes contained herein.

The National Archives, the Library of Congress, and Bowdoin College Library provided expert guidance and crucial services in locating material on the Freedman's Bank and the missionary community. I owe special thanks to Oakland University for a travel grant which enabled me to complete my research, and to Dr. Clifton Johnson, director of the Amistad Research Center, for locating and making available Freedman's Bank letters in the papers of the American Missionary Association. I am indebted to Mrs. James Edwards, who took responsibility for arranging the tables, and to Marian Wilson, whose literary skill and mastery of the arcana of footnotes and bibliography immeasurably eased the burden of preparing and revising the manuscript. Finally, I owe a great debt to my wife, Lorraine Norton Osthaus, whose patience and encouragement helped transform a potential endurance test into a labor of love.

Contents

Tables

Abbreviations

AMA = Archives of the American Missionary Association, Amistad Research Center, Dillard University, New Orleans

BRFAL = Records of the Bureau of Refugees, Freedmen and Abandoned Lands, National Archives, Record Group 105

FS&T Co. = Records of the Freedman's Savings and Trust Company, National Archives, Record Group 101

NA = National Archives

RG = Record Group

Bank Letters, BRFAL = John W. Alvord's letters relating to the Freedman's Bank, BRFAL, NA, RG 105

Committee on FA, NA, RG 233 = Committee on Freedmen's Affairs, National Freedman's Savings and Trust Company, Legislative Records, NA, RG 233

Journal = Journal of the Board of Trustees, FS&T Co., NA, RG 101

Minutes A or Minutes B = Minutes of the Agency Committee, Book A or Book B, FS&T Co., NA, RG 101

Minutes A or Minutes B, Finance Committee = Minutes of the Finance Committee, Book A or Book B, FS&T Co., NA, RG 101

1

A Practical Philanthropy

The Freedman's Savings and Trust Company, chartered on March 3, 1865, was an attempt by Reconstruction America to mold ex-slaves into middle-class citizens. As an economic institution for aiding freedmen in the post–Civil War period, it worked to develop concepts of industry and thrift. Its achievements are noteworthy. Thriving branch banks in a score of southern cities emphasized that progress was being made along the economic path "up from slavery." Adequate leadership and management and a modest amount of governmental supervision and encouragement would have provided a wellspring of black economic progress a hundred years ago. However, the Bank failed in 1874, and with it died the hopes and faith of thousands.

As Frederick Douglass once observed, the Freedman's Bank was the black man's cow but the white man's milk.[1] For a brief period the freedmen, with their many small deposits, had made the Bank a success, but the benefits went to white speculators and real estate dealers in Washington. To a certain degree, then, the Bank provides a case study in the perversion of a philanthropic crusade into a speculative venture. The failure wiped out nine years of fruitful growth, and the legend of the Bank—how blacks were swindled and how they lost their meager savings—lived on for thirty or forty years.

The beginning was auspicious. On January 27, 1865, while the Union and Confederate armies fought before Richmond, twenty-two New York businessmen, philanthropists, and humanitarians met in the directors' room of the American Exchange Bank to discuss the establishment of a savings institution for Negro soldiers. It was the Reverend John W. Alvord, teacher, Congregational minister, and long-time abo-

1. Frederick Douglass to Gerrit Smith, July 3, 1874, Smith MSS, Syracuse University Library.

litionist, who had summoned this gathering of prominent New Yorkers, which included Peter Cooper and William Cullen Bryant.[2] Having just returned from Savannah, where he had been doing charitable work among the Union soldiers, Alvord described the problems newly freed slaves and soldiers experienced in handling the substantial sums of money they received as pay and bounty for enlisting in the service. He related how some black soldiers had placed their $75,000 in bounty money in one general's hands for safekeeping, having no other place of safety for it. Other soldiers, he reported, simply squandered their money as fast as they got their hands on it. What the ex-slaves needed, Alvord stressed, was a secure place of deposit.[3]

There was nothing very original about this presentation. As soon as free Negroes and ex-slaves had begun to enter the army, sympathetic officers and missionaries had discovered that an organization was needed to help them save their money. For both black and white troops, pay-day was a time of reckless extravagance when gamblers, prostitutes, and confidence men descended on the camps to fleece the troopers. Even some unscrupulous officers joined the raid, "borrowing" money from their soldiers—one fellow being so well organized as to send two men around for the "loan" every payday.[4] To prevent this, Union officials had tried an allotment system to enable men from certain northern states to have deductions from their pay sent monthly to designated relatives or banks. The plan had some success with New York and Massachusetts regiments, but few other states established it. Furthermore, many black soldiers distrusted white officials and white banks; something more than the allotment system was needed to encourage them to save money.[5]

Alvord told the meeting about a more ambitious and more practical

2. Journal, January 27, 1865; U.S., Congress, Senate, *Report of the Comptroller of the Currency upon the Condition of the Savings Banks of the District of Columbia*, 42nd Cong., 3rd sess., 1873, Senate Miscellaneous Document No. 88, p. 6; *New Era* (Washington), March 31, 1870, p. 3. See Appendix A for a list of those attending the meeting.

3. *New Era*, March 31, 1870, p. 3. It was renamed *New National Era* in September, 1870, when Frederick Douglass became part owner and editor-in-chief. He served as editor until April, 1873, when his sons Lewis and Frederick took over. Then for a brief period the paper was titled *New National Era and Citizen*, but soon the editors restored the paper's former name, *New National Era*.

4. "The South as It Is," *Nation*, I, 25 (December 21, 1865), 779; U.S., Congress, House, *Freedmen's Bureau*, 39th Cong., 1st sess., 1866, House Executive Document No. 70, pp. 348–349.

5. *The Charter and By-Laws of the Freedman's Savings and Trust Company* (pamphlet), 1872, p. 9; Abram L. Harris, *The Negro as Capitalist* (Philadelphia: American Academy of Political and Social Science, 1936), p. 26; Thomas P. Jackson to John W. Alvord, June 5, 1865, Bank Letters, BRFAL.

venture in South Carolina. At Beaufort, General Rufus Saxton had announced by public circular on August 27, 1864, the creation of the Beaufort Military Savings Bank. The circular declared that, with the current high cotton prices and large bounty payment, it was the duty of the humblest person to save for his future well-being. Directing the teachers and superintendents of schools to explain the details of his circular, Saxton proceeded to appoint two officers and a civilian to organize the new savings bank. It was to be a secure place of deposit, yield a fair rate of interest, and support the government by investing in United States bonds. Negro soldiers and a few civilians responded with enthusiasm. One year after its inception the South Carolina Freedman's Savings Bank (as the military bank came to be called) held in its safe $180,000—almost exclusively the money of people who a few months previously had been propertyless slaves.[6]

General Benjamin Butler established a similar bank in Norfolk, as did General Nathaniel Banks in Louisiana. Smaller than the Beaufort organization, the Norfolk bank began in the fall of 1864 and by mid–1865 held almost $8,000 belonging to 180 black depositors.[7] In Louisiana in 1864, General Banks established a "Free Labor Bank . . . for the deposit of all accumulated wages and other savings." The bank provided useful service to thousands of Negro soldiers and freedmen who worked on the plantations seized by the government.[8]

Alvord's New York businessmen and philanthropists resolved to take up this program of promoting thrift among the Negroes, and they voted unanimously for the creation of a savings bank. It seemed "not only practicable," said one member, "but very important, to establish, as a benevolent institution, a National Freedmans Trust Company, to receive these funds and become a safe depository for the future earnings of this people."[9] The permanent civilian bank was obviously intended to supersede such temporary military banks as General Saxton's; indeed, the New Yorkers probably hoped to receive the funds of the military banks as working capital to start out with.

The New York group moved quickly to translate its decision into action. At a second meeting, on February 1, 1865, a committee brought

6. C. A. Woodward, *Savings Banks: Their Origin, Progress and Utility, with a History of the National Savings Bank for Colored People* (Cleveland: Fairbanks, Benedict & Co., 1869), p. 56, appendix, pp. 95–98; George Washington Williams, *History of the Negro Race in America from 1619 to 1880* (New York: G. P. Putnam's Sons, 1883), II, 403; "South as It Is," p. 779.

7. *New Era*, March 31, 1870, p. 3; Woodward, *Savings Banks*, p. 56.

8. Nathaniel P. Banks, *Emancipated Labor in Louisiana* (New York: n.p., 1865), appendix, p. 37; Harris, *Negro as Capitalist*, p. 27; *New York Times*, February 11, 1864, p. 4.

9. Journal, January 27, 1865.

forth a tentative act of incorporation which was ordered to be printed for distribution and discussion at the next meeting.[10] At this third meeting, five days later, the trustees decided to send John Alvord and the Reverend George Whipple, the corresponding secretary of the American Missionary Association, to Washington to discuss plans with government officials and with Chief Justice Salmon Chase, who at one time had had a great interest in a savings bank of this nature. It was felt, as Alvord later stated, that the founders could obtain a charter from Congress which "would be far better" than one from the New York legislature.[11] On February 15, at the fourth meeting of the New York group, Whipple reported that important cabinet members and congressmen had given their hearty approval, for they thought it important to make the bank a national rather than a state institution. For this purpose Senator Henry Wilson of Massachusetts had already introduced a bill containing the substance of the New York meeting's tentative act of incorporation. Encouraged by this success, the founders resolved that Whipple and Alvord should return to Washington to lobby for the bill.[12]

On March 2, 1865, the day before the second session of the Thirty-eighth Congress was to adjourn, Charles Sumner of Massachusetts brought the bill before the Senate. Sumner assured his colleagues that the act of incorporation established an ordinary savings bank with no special privileges. Charles Buckalew of Pennsylvania added that the charter was in proper form, but questioned whether Congress should establish such an institution outside the District of Columbia. James A. McDougall of California objected to the whole "scheme," while Lazarus Powell of Kentucky declared that the bill established "a kind of roving commission for these persons to establish a savings bank in any part of the United States." Powell thought the bill wholly unconstitutional; Congress did not have the right to establish a savings bank outside the District. Immediately Sumner consented to limit the corporation to Washington, and the bill was so amended in the title and the first section. The bill was then passed and sent to the House.[13]

At nine o'clock on the last evening of the session, while an anxious Alvord watched from the gallery, Thomas Eliot of Massachusetts moved to suspend the House rules to permit discussion of the Senate bill. John

10. *Ibid.*, February 1, 1865.
11. *Ibid.*, February 6, 1865; *New Era*, March 31, 1870, p. 3. It is interesting that Saxton, Banks, and Butler, the army officers who founded the first Negro military banks, were all Massachusetts men; yet in the organization of the Bank, like the Bureau, New York was more important than Boston.
12. Journal, February 15, 1865.
13. U.S., *Congressional Globe*, 38th Cong., 2nd sess., March 2, 1865, p. 1311; *New Era*, March 31, 1870, p. 3.

Ganson of New York asked where the corporation was to be located, to which Eliot replied, "In Washington." As it was not so stated in the bill, the House voted to insert the words "in Washington city, District of Columbia" in the first section. Ganson next inquired whether the trustees should include some person from the District. Eliot suggested Chief Justice Chase, and an amendment adding Chase's name passed without dissent. The House then passed the bill.[14]

"In the last days of the session," the *Nation* later reported, "many things are done which were not supposed to be done, and, conversely, it would seem that some things are supposed to be done which were never in fact accomplished."[15] Although passed unanimously in their respective houses, the Senate amendment to alter the title to limit the corporation to the District of Columbia and the House amendment to add Chief Justice Chase to the group of incorporators never received the consent of both houses, nor were they the subject of a conference. In the confusion of the last few days of the session, these two amendments slipped from the enrolled bill, and the Senate's original bill became law. These errors led to future uncertainty and trouble. Unquestionably the trustees' desire to aid the freedmen of the South implied a far-reaching institution; and, according to Alvord and Whipple, high government officials, including senators and representatives, thought the concern should be national. But when Congress voted, it definitely intended to limit the corporation, as it stated once in the body of the first section.

An Act to Incorporate the Freedman's Savings and Trust Company became law on March 3, 1865. The act declared that "the general business and object of the corporation hereby created shall be to receive on deposit such sums of money as may, from time to time, be offered therefor, by or on behalf of persons heretofore held in slavery in the United States, or their descendants, and investing the same in the stocks, bonds, Treasury notes, or other securities of the United States."[16] The Freedman's Savings and Trust Company was thus a simple mutual savings bank established for the benefit of black people. It was a nonprofit concern which had no stockholders; all the assets of the Bank were owned by the depositors in proportion to the deposits of each. The Freedman's Bank would receive the deposits of the freedmen, invest everything except a sizable available fund (for transacting business and for insurance against unusual demands by depositors) in government securities, and return all the profits to the freedmen in the form

14. U.S., *Congressional Globe*, 38th Cong., 2nd sess., March 3, 1865, p. 1403.
15. "The Story of the Freedman's Bank," *Nation*, XX, 511 (April 15, 1875), 253.
16. U.S., *Statutes at Large*, XIII, 511.

of interest. The trustees were to regulate all the bank's activities. The charter implied that no loans would be made, and, especially in the last three sections, emphasized safeguards: no trustee could receive any payment or emolument for his services; bank officers and agents must give such security as the trustees would require for the proper conduct of their duties; and the books of the company were to be open for inspection and examination to such persons as Congress would appoint.[17]

The strongest feature of the charter was the board of fifty trustees, composed entirely of "patriotic and philanthropic citizens." It would be difficult to find in 1865 a group of men better known for their business and financial acumen, antislavery principles, and philanthropic efforts. Synonymous with business success and the reform spirit, their names read like an abbreviated who's who of American life. This list of outstanding Americans was led by Peter Cooper, manufacturer, inventor, and philanthropist, and William Cullen Bryant, poet and abolitionist editor of the New York *Evening Post*. At the time of the Bank's founding, Bryant's name took precedence in New York's civic, social, and charitable movements. Other trustees who assured financial respectability in the highest circles were the Honorable William Claflin, congressman and future governor of Massachusetts, founder and president of a Boston national bank and organizer of the New England Trust Company and Five Cent Savings Bank; George S. Coe, New York financier, president of the American Exchange Bank, and probably this country's best-read authority on financial matters; Francis R. Cope, successful merchant and director of many banks and insurance companies; and Edward Harris, Rhode Island woolen manufacturer and president of the People's Savings Bank. John M. Forbes and A. A. Low, who both made fortunes in the China trade and financed railroad ventures, excelled not only as businessmen but also as leaders in the war effort. Forbes, a staunch Republican who was president of the New England Loyal Publication Society, had worked with the abolitionist governor John Andrew and had helped to organize Negro regiments. Low, who had been president of the Union Defense Committee of New York City, became in 1865 or 1866 a member of the American Freedmen's Union Committee, which was designed to ameliorate conditions of white and black refugees in the South. Many other trustees were renowned for their humanitarian and philanthropic activities. For example, Samuel Gridley Howe, educator and abolitionist, had devoted his life to charitable work, especially to the improvement of the blind. During the war he had served on the

17. *Ibid.*, pp. 511, 513.

U.S. Sanitary Commission and on a special congressional committee on the conditions of the freedmen. C. R. Robert, merchant, railroad president, and superintendent of Presbyterian Sunday schools, donated much of his fortune to schools and charities, especially to Hamilton College and Auburn Theological Seminary. Antislavery and abolitionist principles were well represented by almost all of the trustees, but especially by Gerrit Smith, Stephen Colwell, the Reverend John Morgan Walden, and Levi Coffin, who, along with several others, were already or were shortly to become members and officers in the various missionary societies and freedmen's aid groups in the South. Smith, a wealthy New York landowner—along with Bank trustees Samuel Gridley Howe and George L. Stearns, an independently wealthy abolitionist who had recruited black soldiers during the war—had helped finance John Brown's raid on Harpers Ferry. Colwell, a lawyer, iron manufacturer, and railroad director, had served on the U.S. Sanitary Commission and was a founder of the Union League. Methodist minister John Walden had proved his antislavery credentials in Kansas by publishing a free-soil paper and attending five free-soil conventions. During the war he was personally responsible for recruiting two Union regiments. Levi Coffin was a leading figure in the Underground Railroad.[18]

The reputations and positions of the trustees had facilitated congressional assent to the charter, and any prospective depositor could take comfort in their reputation for integrity. Superficially the plans for the Bank seemed sound. Writing in 1878, four years after the failure, banking expert Emerson Keyes asserted that to "those not familiar with Savings Bank charters, and the forms under which dangerous powers are conferred in very innocent phrase, there seemed to be nothing objectionable in the original act of incorporation." But as an authority on banking, Keyes realized that the hidden weaknesses were very real. Prospective depositors and those who voted for the act of incorporation might well have wondered whether such busy trustees would take an active interest in the Bank.[19] The trustees were not required to give any

18. *Ibid.*, pp. 510–511; *Dictionary of American Biography*, III, 200–205; IV, 79–80, 110–111, 268–269, 327, 409–410; VI, 507–508; XI, 444–446; XVII, 543–544; *National Cyclopedia of American Biography*, II, 353; VIII, 372; X, 492; XII, 99, 496; Henry Lee Swint, *The Northern Teacher in the South, 1862–1870* (Nashville: Vanderbilt University Press, 1941), appendix, pp. 145, 148, 149, 150, 157, 163, 168, and *passim*; James M. McPherson, *The Struggle for Equality* (Princeton: Princeton University Press, 1964), pp. 5, 6; Stephen B. Oates, *To Purge This Land with Blood* (New York: Harper & Row, 1970).

19. Emerson Willard Keyes, *A History of Savings Banks in the United States* (New York: Bradford Rhodes, 1876, 1878), II, 558–560. Keyes's two-volume study is an exhaustive treatment of the theory and history of savings banks in the first three-quarters of the nineteenth century. For a recent history of savings banks, see

security for the faithful discharge of their trust, which was a weakness of all savings banks in this era.[20] Not one of the original trustees was a Negro, and, since Chief Justice Chase was omitted, none of the trustees resided in Washington, the city in which the Bank was supposedly located. There was no explicit provision for regular inspections. The provisions concerning the available fund, which could be as much as one-third of the total deposits, were also somewhat disquieting to those familiar with the history of savings banks, for they knew that available funds frequently became unavailable. Recognizing the charter's inadequacies—which, with hindsight, was so easy—Keyes nevertheless concluded that the wise and beneficent purposes of the founders would have secured favorable action for a measure far more objectionable.[21]

From an economic viewpoint, the creation of a simple savings bank for people just released from bondage and in need of every necessity of life might appear paradoxical. It seems evident that a bank for capital accumulation and investment in the black community would have been far more beneficial.[22] But those who conceived and created the Freedman's Bank were limited by the historical experience and social values of nineteenth-century America. To some extent they were the captives of their own abolitionist propaganda, which had condemned the South's "peculiar institution" because it stripped Negroes of their freedom and left them in utter dependence and ignorance. Presumably the ex-slaves, now free to do as they pleased, might sink deep into poverty and degradation through their own improvidence unless something was done to educate them in the habits of work, thrift, and self-sufficiency. They would have to fend for themselves in the face of increased white hostility in the South, for, though Radical Reconstruction was still in the future, the free black men in 1865 appeared to be a fundamental threat to southern society and the symbol of southern defeat.[23] Moreover, the freedmen might become millstones around the neck of a country already burdened with reconstructing itself from a tragic civil war. For the founders of the Bank, the reformation of the

Weldon Welfling, *Mutual Savings Banks: The Evolution of a Financial Intermediary* (Cleveland: Case Western Reserve University Press, 1968).

20. Albert S. Bolles, *Bank Officers: Their Authority, Duty and Liability* (New York: Homans Publishing Co., 1890), p. 338.

21. Keyes, *History of Savings Banks*, II, 558–560.

22. In a brief discussion of the Freedman's Savings Bank, Mauris L. P. Emeka, in *Black Banks, Past and Present* (Kansas City, Mo.: By the Author, 1971), stresses the Bank's inability to aid in capital accumulation and investment in the black community.

23. John Hope Franklin, *From Slavery to Freedom*, 3rd ed. rev. (New York: Alfred A. Knopf, 1967), pp. 306–307.

Negroes' economic character was essential not only for the welfare of the freedmen but also for the survival of the country.[24]

In creating a mutual savings bank for freedmen, the founders were merely applying a remedy which seemed to have worked well in training the workingmen of the North in self-discipline. The first savings banks in the North were benevolent and philanthropic efforts of the rich and influential to aid the worthy poor. Although considered by some critics as simply charitable institutions, a kind of soup kitchen for the poor, most reformers recognized them as financial assistance to the honest, hard-working laborer to help himself—to save, to escape the threat of want, and perhaps even to find material security. Savings institutions instilled and encouraged thrift and industry, surviving only if their depositors acquired these virtues. Thus they appealed to the sense of dignity, independence, pride, and self-respect.[25] They rested on the presumption that *"some, many, perhaps a majority of mankind, would prefer honest independence, the result of industry, to beggarly dependence, the consequence of idleness; that they would be frugal rather than wasteful, if the savings of frugality could be carefully garnered for the time of need; that they would guard against vicious indulgence rather than steep themselves in drink, if there was the incentive of accumulation held out as the sure reward of self-denial."*[26] Up to the 1860's these banks had established an enviable record for safety, especially in comparison with American commercial banks, and most believed they had succeeded in benefiting the laboring population financially and morally. Said Alvord on one occasion, "Pauperism can be brought to a close; the freedmen made self-supporting and prosperous, paying for their educational and Christian institutions, and helping to bear the burdens of government. . . . That which savings banks have done for the working men of the north it is presumed they are capable of doing for these laborers."[27]

The founders of the Freedman's Bank intended to bring former slaves into the mainstream of working-class America, but they had to proceed cautiously. Trustees of savings banks typically provided advice and guidance, but no more, for the conventional wisdom dictated that giving too much aid to the needy merely pauperized them further. Mid-nineteenth-century America believed in self-help, and most citizens

24. *New York Times*, February 25, 1865, p. 4.
25. Keyes, *History of Savings Banks*, I, 2–24 and *passim*; II, 566.
26. *Ibid.*, I, 13.
27. U.S., Congress, House, *Freedmen's Bureau*, 39th Cong., 1st sess., 1866, House Executive Document No. 70, p. 349.

and even many reformers, as one historian described them, were "hag-ridden" by the fear of contributing to pauperism. Said one almoner, " 'I can ruin the best family in Boston by giving them a cord of food [*sic*] in the wrong way.' " Indeed, this charge was leveled at the relief and rehabilitation programs of the Freedmen's Bureau, even though the commissioner, General Oliver Otis Howard, had instructed his workers to help only the "absolutely necessitous and destitute."[28] The Freed-man's Savings Bank would not be a charity; it would give away nothing. On the contrary, it would encourage diligence and combat poverty. As the *New York Times* suggested, the Bank would be "a cheap, valuable and welcome boon for the freedmen for whose benefit it is designed."[29] Just as the Freedmen's Bureau would seek to satisfy the ex-slaves' need for land, education, and immediate relief, and the Christian missionaries would care for the reformation of their souls, the Freedman's Bank would instill economic morals and social values in the Negroes. Ob-viously, to men like Alvord, a lending bank extending credit to the freedmen before they had received such training in self-discipline would be unthinkable.

On March 16, 1865, John W. Alvord presented to the board of trustees a certified copy of the Act to Incorporate the Freedman's Sav-ings and Trust Company.[30] Over the next few months a small coterie of trustees translated the charter into a functioning concern by electing officers and selecting agents, establishing a home office in New York City, and expanding into the South—all this without any immediate funds. They also added an extensive list of bylaws, established branches, and took initial steps toward encouraging black leadership at the branches. Four months after its creation, the Freedman's Savings and Trust Company, an "ordinary savings bank," had some extraordinary features.

Significant changes began to occur in the Bank's management before the end of March. Seven of the most influential trustees, including Peter Cooper, Edward Atkinson, A. A. Low, and Gerrit Smith, resigned for reasons unknown.[31] Apparently no one had previously sought their consent to serve on the board. This untoward event, which suggests that the trustees were intended as mere window dressing rather than

28. Robert H. Bremner, *American Philanthropy* (Chicago: University of Chicago Press, 1960), pp. 79–102 *passim*, esp. pp. 86, 90.

29. February 25, 1865, p. 4.

30. Journal, March 16, 1865.

31. *Ibid.*, March 30, 1865. A search of the papers of these men has failed to re-veal the reasons for their resignations.

as active advisers, at once forced the trustees to provide for the election of new members. Elaborating upon the company's rules in a series of bylaws, the trustees decided that vacancies were to be filled by an affirmative vote of ten and, surprisingly, that as few as nine out of the entire membership of fifty would constitute a quorum for the transaction of business.[32]

In drawing up the bylaws, the trustees distributed important powers among several elective committees which theoretically would be supervised by the entire board. The subject of investments was placed in the hands of a five-member Finance Committee, where a quorum of three members could decide on the sale or transfer of securities. Another committee of immense importance was the Agency Committee. Composed of seven members, it was to appoint, control, and remove all agents of the Bank and supervise all the business of such agents "at any other place than the office where its principal business is located." Implicit in the creation of this committee was the trustees' intention of establishing interstate branches to reach vast numbers of ex-slaves. A three-member Examining Committee was to inspect the books, accounts, securities, and business of the Bank and report to the entire board, thus giving the trustees an additional measure for the Bank's safety. Finally, the trustees made plans for an Education and Improvement Committee which would decide in what ways the Bank's excess profits might benefit the freedmen, for already they had extravagant hopes.[33]

With hindsight, it is clear that these provisions and the early resignation and replacement of respected trustees should have raised a disturbing possibility—that control over every aspect of the Bank might fall to men who were not noted for their integrity and financial acumen. If a majority of the trustees neglected the Bank (as in practice they did), then as few as nine members might direct its affairs; from these nine members the committees would probably be drawn. Thus, instead of a diffusion of power among fifty trustees, the bylaws authorized a potential concentration of power. In March and April, 1865, no one perceived or predicted this course, but this was actually what happened. The board of trustees became relatively inactive if not indifferent, while individual officers, and to a lesser extent the small Agency

---

32. *Freedman's Savings and Trust Company* (pamphlet), 1865, pp. 13, 15.

33. *Ibid.*, pp. 16–17. One wonders about the legality of spending the "excess profits" in this manner. Theoretically, all profits above expenses were to be returned to the depositors as interest. The question, of course, only arises in theory, for there were never any "excess profits."

Committee, came to direct the company's affairs. Later, in 1870, the Bank's actuary and a three-member Finance Committee assumed all fiscal responsibility and effected a radical change in the Bank's course.

In early April the trustees elected to the presidency William A. Booth, president of the American Tract Society and a prominent New York merchant, banker, and philanthropist. Mahlon T. Hewitt, the proprietor of a New York City clothing firm and an agent of the American Union Commission, was elected first vice-president, while the position of second vice-president went to Walter L. Griffith, president of the Home Life Insurance Company. John Alvord was elected corresponding secretary.[34] The president's principal duties were to preside at the monthly meetings of the board and sit as a member ex officio of the committees. Nominally he had little power, but in practice he could wield considerable influence through persuasion and moral leadership. Much depended on his personality. President Booth actually served mainly as window dressing, as did Griffith, the second vice-president, who seems to have been given no official functions.[35] The actual management of the Bank in the first two years fell largely to Hewitt and Alvord. Hewitt, as first vice-president, was given general supervision and control. He became the directing force at the home office, making, with the board of trustees' consent (which was largely pro forma), most of the crucial financial decisions. In 1866 he became president. Hewitt worked closely with Alvord, the corresponding secretary, who was charged with managing the Bank's business outside the central office.[36]

The first branches of the Freedman's Bank—and, indeed, the early success of the entire organization—owe much to the work of John W. Alvord. Born in Connecticut in 1808, Alvord attended public school and became a teacher at the age of seventeen. For a short while he worked in a mercantile house in Savannah, and then returned north to study for the ministry. He dedicated his life to the goal of helping suffering humanity, but he seems to have been too restless to content himself with any specific job for long. He became an agent of the American Sunday School Union and worked at establishing Sabbath schools and libraries. In 1833 he attended Lane Seminary in Ohio, studying under Dr. Lyman Beecher, and the next year he participated in the Lane rebellion over the slavery issue. Alvord stood with those newly converted

34. Journal, April 4, 1865; *National Cyclopedia of American Biography*, X, 382; U.S., War Department, *The War of the Rebellion: A Compilation of the Official Records of the Union and Confederate Armies* (Washington, 1880–1901), ser. 1, XLVII, 711; *Trow's New York City Directory*, 1863, LXXVI, 398; *Freedman's Savings and Trust Company* (pamphlet), 1865, p. 5.

35. *Freedman's Savings and Trust Company* (pamphlet), 1865, pp. 14–15.

36. *Ibid.*; see below, ch. 2.

abolitionists who refused, in the face of demands by a conservative board of trustees, to disband their abolition society and cease discussing slavery. During the next few years he seldom strayed from the anti-slavery fight: he worked for an antislavery society in northern Ohio, faced mobs on lecture tours, and assisted fugitive slaves, meanwhile graduating in the first class at Oberlin. For a time thereafter he was superintendent of six Negro schools in Cincinnati. Later, prevented by illness from going to Africa as a missionary, he became associate pastor in Congregational churches in Stamford and Boston. In 1851 he traveled throughout Europe to restore his health and returned the next year to become secretary of the American Tract Society of Boston. When the Civil War commenced, Alvord headed immediately for Washington. There he directed the circulation of books and pamphlets among Union soldiers, a job which eventually entailed following the troops and working near the battlefields and in the hospitals. When General Sherman entered Savannah, Alvord followed to begin educational work among the freedmen. In 1865, after a varied career as minister, teacher, lecturer, abolitionist, temperance advocate, and sometime businessman—ample, if superficial, qualifications for the activities he was about to undertake—Alvord became superintendent of schools and finances for the Freedmen's Bureau and, simultaneously, corresponding secretary of the Freedman's Savings and Trust Company. While still employed by the Bureau, he became vice-president of the Bank in 1867, and then president in 1868.[37]

In 1865 and 1866 Alvord, with some help from Hewitt, directed the Bank's wide-ranging correspondence and traveled throughout the South, establishing branches and arranging for the employment of cashiers. His contacts with the mission community served him well in these activities. Although his actions were subject to the approval of the trustees on the Agency Committee, they were seldom overruled—for Alvord was the man most familiar with conditions in the South and was, after all, the Bank's founder. Informally, Alvord offered advice

37. *New National Era*, March 28, 1872, p. 1. There is relatively little published material on Alvord's career, yet his work, letters, and reports in connection with the abolition and missionary movements, the Freedmen's Bureau, and Freedman's Bank have left ample record of his life. Other references to Alvord are in Swint, *The Northern Teacher in the South*, appendix I, pp. 143–144; American Tract Society, *The Rev. J. W. Alvord's Work in the Army* (pamphlet), 1863, American Missionary Association Archives, Amistad Research Center; Richard Bryant Drake, "The American Missionary Association and the Southern Negro 1861–1888" (Ph.D. dissertation, Emory University, 1957); Gilbert H. Barnes and Dwight L. Dumond, eds., *Letters of Theodore Dwight Weld, Angelina Grimké Weld, and Sarah Grimké 1822–1844* (New York: D. Appleton-Century Co., for American Historical Association, 1934).

and made decisions on many matters concerning the Bank, yet in financial affairs he seems to have deferred to Hewitt and, after Hewitt's resignation in 1868, to the actuary and the Finance Committee. But in decisions on publicity, expansion, organization, and employment policies, especially in the early years, his influence was enormous.[38]

Selecting New York City—the nation's financial center—as their headquarters, Alvord and the executive officers opened their home office, which was a central bookkeeping concern and not an actual bank, in early May. They paid $1,200 annual rent for space beneath the American Exchange Bank at 87 Cedar Street and furnished it inexpensively. The next few weeks saw a flurry of activity: the officers printed 2,000 copies of their charter and bylaws, procured a journal and stationery, printed circulars, and ordered sets of books for their proposed agencies and passbooks for future depositors.[39]

As yet the Freedman's Bank had no working capital or deposits, and expenses mounted rapidly. To meet pressing demands, the trustees requested that members of the board each lend $100 to defray expenses. Although this was a loan, not a gift, the response was somewhat less than enthusiastic: fifteen members contributed $50 each.[40] Nevertheless, this $750 sufficed to allay temporarily the Bank's creditors.

To interest the mass of freedmen, the officers solicited the cooperation of President Lincoln in a letter dated four days before his death. "As this institution is national," they argued, "and for the benefit of those who at present are dependent on public care, we have deemed it advisable to act, so far as possible, under the auspices of the Government." They asked that Lincoln commend their company and its laudable purpose to the freedmen and to the secretaries of war and the treasury so as to facilitate their movements in occupied areas. Lincoln died before he could act on their suggestion, but in early May Secretary Alvord received a reply from President Johnson praising the benevolent objectives of the Freedman's Bank and requesting heads of government departments to furnish "such facilities in reaching the freedmen, and for the safekeeping and transmission of funds as the Company may need."[41] Accordingly, the treasury secretary and General O. O. Howard, commissioner of the Freedmen's Bureau, sent letters providing railroad passes and introductions to bank executives and military officers.[42]

Implicit in all the actions of the officers was the desire to establish a

38. See below, chs. 2, 5.
39. Journal, May 11, 1865.
40. *Ibid.*, May 16 and June 8, 1865. The money was returned to the trustees in 1866. See Journal, October 11, 1866.
41. Woodward, *Savings Banks*, pp. 53–54.
42. Journal, May 11, 1865; Woodward, *Savings Banks*, p. 54.

national institution to serve thousands of freedmen. The trustees and officers probably realized all along that they would have to open branch offices throughout the South, thus increasing enormously the problems of management. Although branch banking had been common in pre–Civil War America, it rapidly disappeared after the war, and thus the Freedman's Savings and Trust Company's branch banking system was almost unique. At its peak the Freedman's Bank was destined to have more interstate branches than its closest structural antecedent, the Second Bank of the United States.[43]

The legality of this structure troubled the trustees a good deal, for Congress had intended to charter one banking office in Washington. Among Alvord's letters appears an undated draft of an amendment to the charter. It would have permitted the corporation to "establish branch agencies in the several states where the freedmen reside."[44] No action was taken, and yet the Bank never hesitated in its southward push. In 1873 a national bank examiner summarized the thinking of the officers of the Freedman's Bank:

> The question of the establishment of "branches" does not seem to have been provided for by the charter, while the spirit of the charter, which seems to have been intended to bring about the moral elevation of the freedmen, four millions in number, would seem to imply the necessity of such an arrangement in order to reach him where he lives; and in no other way could this intention have been carried out, and such appears to have been the views of the gentlemen who founded the institution, and they number among them some of the first philanthropists and business men of our nation.[45]

Washington, Norfolk, and Richmond became the first centers for the missionary efforts of the Bank. "It was necessary," said Alvord, "that the subject be presented so simply and so cogently to the people that they would become convinced of its utility and special adaptation to their needs."[46] In early June Hewitt and Alvord visited Washington and Richmond, met with black leaders, and drew up a favorable report of the company's prospects for the trustees in New York City. Hewitt then returned to the home office to organize matters, while Alvord continued on to Norfolk.[47]

Although plans for the Norfolk, Washington, and Richmond branches had emerged simultaneously, Norfolk seems to hold the distinction of

43. For a discussion of branch banking, see Appendix B.
44. "Copy of Amendment to Savings Bank Charter," n.d., Bank Letters, BRFAL.
45. *Report of the Comptroller of the Currency*, 1873, p. 9.
46. *New Era*, March 31, 1870, p. 3; Minutes A, May 17, 1865, p. 1.
47. Journal, June 8, 1865.

opening, in June, 1865, the first branch of the Freedman's Savings and
Trust Company.[48] Norfolk was the site of General Butler's military savings bank, which the trustees all along felt would become an important
part of their new company. This occurred more precipitously than expected because the military bank ran into serious trouble. In early June,
1865, Bank officials in New York began to hear stories that Negro soldiers
in Norfolk lacked confidence in the military bank, that they withheld
their money and were being defrauded by the sharpers who hovered
around their camps.[49] Alvord hastened to Norfolk and arranged a meeting with black leaders at St. John's African Methodist Church. With the
church's pastor, the Reverend John M. Brown, presiding, all agreed
upon the desirability and necessity of establishing a branch office of
the Freedman's Bank. There agreement ended, for the Norfolk people
wanted a black cashier and brought forth as their candidate Joseph T.
Wilson, a young Norfolk-born free Negro who had been a seaman and
soldier and was later to become a historian of black soldiers in the Civil
War.[50] Although Wilson does not appear to have had formal schooling at
the college level, he was probably pushed for the cashiership because he
was a free black who, as a seaman and soldier, had had much practical
experience of life and could capably fill any position requiring honesty
and moderate business capacity. The impasse over the cashier's position
was broken on June 21, when Alvord overruled the local leaders and
appointed two white men, Jonathan Dickinson and H. C. Percy, as
cashier and assistant cashier. Soon after the selection of a cashier, Alvord received the funds (almost $8,000) of the old military savings
bank, which he transferred to the New York office.[51]

The Bank's corresponding secretary requested that Dickinson, the

48. *Report of the Comptroller of the Currency,* 1873, p. 6; Journal, September 14,
1865; Mahlon T. Hewitt to Alvord, June 28, 1865, Bank Letters, BRFAL. The transfer of the funds of the Norfolk military bank to the Freedman's Bank marks the
beginning of the first branch. *New Era,* March 31, 1870, p. 3, however, claims that
the Washington branch received the first private deposit; in this sense, it would
be the first branch.

49. Jackson to Alvord, June 5, 1865, Bank Letters, BRFAL.

50. W. T. Andrews and J. W. Cromwell, *Eulogies: In Memoriam,* ed. Tally R.
Holmes of South Carolina and Col. Joseph T. Wilson of Virginia (Washington:
Bethel Literary and Historical Society [1891]), p. 7. Wilson's career is interesting.
Before the war he moved from Norfolk to New Bedford, Mass., where he became
a seaman. He was in Chile when the war broke out; he then sailed to New Orleans
to search for his father, who had been sold in that city. Wilson served with the
74th U.S. Colored Troops and the 54th Massachusetts Colored Infantry and was
wounded at the battle of Olustee, Fla. He held minor political positions in Virginia
during Reconstruction. As a historian his best-known work is *The Black Phalanx*
(1890; reprint, New York: Arno Press and New York Times, 1968). See Sara Dun-
lap Jackson's biographical sketch of Wilson in the 1968 edition.

51. Hewitt to Alvord, June 28, 1865, Bank Letters, BRFAL.

new cashier, organize a "Committee of Colored men who are to encourage the thing among the people." Thus originated the advisory board, which became a fixture at every branch.[52] Perhaps Alvord intended the committee as a sop to those who wanted a black cashier, but this is mere conjecture. The purpose, however, was explicit: the advisory board was a booster committee created to weld the branch to the community and bring in depositors.

Bank officers established the second branch at Washington, D.C. It was a logical site: Washington was the center of efforts to aid the freedmen; its Negro population was large and increasing; and it was situated in close proximity to large numbers of Negro troops. A group of Negro businessmen gathered at the behest of Alvord and Hewitt and, after listening to their presentations, selected an advisory committee. On July 11 Alvord commissioned a Negro teacher, William J. Wilson, as cashier and charged him with making the Bank known to freedmen in the District and the surrounding areas.[53] At first the choice of Wilson seemed a good one; though he had little business experience, Wilson had been born and raised in Washington and was a well-known teacher. He had worked in the pay department of the army and in 1869 would become a trustee of Howard University. Later he would receive some publicity because of his protests against violations of the civil rights of black people.[54]

The branch struggled along for the first few months. Its office, if such it could be called, was located in the upper story of a brick house on G Street and was open only in the evenings. Cashier Wilson, who received no compensation for his work, gave the Bank what time he could spare from his full-time position in the schools. Because of the Bank's newness as well as the heritage of slavery, Wilson encountered distrust and prejudice in his first efforts to teach adult freedmen the advantages of saving. Consequently, he took his message to his pupils in the first instance of what was to become a common practice—the joint efforts of the schools and the Bank to instill principles of industry and thrift among the young freedmen. The first deposit at the Washington branch resulted from this effort. A freedman named Hill, the father of one of his students, learned of the Bank and, having just been robbed of a considerable amount, brought his remaining twenty-four dollars

---

52. Alvord to Jonathan Dickinson, June 21, 1865, *ibid.*
53. Journal, June 8, 1865; *New National Era*, December 14, 1871, p. 3.
54. Walter Dyson, *Howard University* (Washington: Graduate School of Howard University, 1941), p. 418; *Register of Officers and Agents . . . in the Service of the United States 1865* (Washington: Government Printing Office, 1865), p. 191; *Evening Star* (Washington), February 16, 1871, p. 1; *New National Era*, May 11, 1871, p. 1.

to the new institution. The second depositor was the wife of the Reverend Henry H. Garnet, the famed abolitionist, orator, army chaplain, and at this time pastor of Washington's Fifteenth Street Presbyterian Church. The third depositor was Walker Lewis, owner of a large amount of city real estate and later a Bank trustee. Both Mrs. Garnet and Lewis made deposits to show their confidence in the Bank and inspire faith in others. During the first few weeks, Wilson took the Bank's deposits with him wherever he went, and it is reported that he had little to carry.[55]

In June, 1865, Hewitt and Alvord took the initial steps toward opening the third branch at Richmond by calling a meeting of sixty to seventy "intelligent, representative" Negroes. Believing that a bank would be useful and profitable, these leaders appointed a committee of fifteen to canvass the city and environs to determine public sentiment. It was hoped that the branch might include the city of Petersburg and thus accommodate 50,000 people. If encouraged by the canvass, the committee was to report to a Mr. W. L. Coan of the American Missionary Association and organize a permanent advisory board. The results were favorable, for Richmond opened in mid-October.[56]

From New York in late June, Vice-President Hewitt made arrangements to extend the company's activities to a much larger area. Even at this early date, he wrote Alvord, he felt a growing confidence in the institution. Alive to the importance of following the Negro troops, Hewitt busied himself in seeking an honest, dedicated worker to accompany the Twenty-fifth Army Corps then being transferred to Texas. Hewitt also began to correspond with people in New Orleans and Louisville with a view to establishing branches there.[57] Eventually he was to send representatives all over the South, spreading news of the Bank.

The Norfolk, Washington, and Richmond branches established the precedent of using black personnel in leadership roles, a subject on which much will be said later. Exactly why a Negro cashier was denied at Norfolk and permitted at Washington is not known, but William J. Wilson became the first of twenty-one or more black cashiers. The idea

55. *New National Era*, December 14, 1871, p. 3.
56. Journal, June 8, 1865; Minutes A, June 13, 1865, pp. 3–6; U.S., Congress, Senate, *Report of the Select Committee to Investigate the Freedman's Savings and Trust Company*, 46th Cong., 2nd sess., 1880, Senate Report No. 440, appendix, p. 41. Although plans and initial steps for the Richmond branch originated in June, 1865, the office itself did not open until mid-October. Therefore, the Louisville branch, which opened in August, 1865, might well be considered the third branch to go into operation.
57. Hewitt to Alvord, June 28, 1865, Bank Letters, BRFAL.

of advisory committees dominated by blacks had also emerged. "The Colored Men," wrote Alvord in his report to the Agency Committee, "are to act upon the Colored population instructing them, awakening interest, encouraging deposits, etc."[58] That the Bank's officers considered black committees an absolute necessity for popularizing the branches probably accounts for their creation, since the trustees' attitudes toward black leadership in 1865 were ambivalent. At a meeting in April, several trustees desired to fill the vacant trustees' positions with Negroes, but the board declined, saying ambiguously that it was not prepared to nominate any.[59] Concerning the advisory board at Washington, Hewitt wrote: "I am not positive that our board of trustees will sanction an entire board of [Colored] men in Washington, but think they will. My wish is to try it, they can reject it if they don't approve."[60] They did not approve at that time, for three years later the Agency Committee resolved that to improve the Washington branch an advisory board of "leading colored men [should] be appointed by the trustees to act for that Branch."[61] The Agency Committee approved advisory committees at all the branches in 1867 and 1868, but these committees had functioned officially or otherwise as early as 1865 and 1866. Perhaps the trustees hesitated at institutionalizing in Washington so novel a thing as an all-black committee. Later many black advisory boards were led by white men, and throughout the Bank's history—except at the very end—the most important positions were held by whites. Nevertheless, the Negro advisory boards at Norfolk and Richmond, and the cashier and the informal committee at Washington, indicated that there would be substantial black participation in the leadership of many branches.

In looking at the Bank as it emerged in 1865 and 1866, many people probably questioned the significance of black cashiers and advisory boards. Theoretically, the autonomy of the branch bank was strictly limited: from the home office in New York, where there were at first no black officers, the Agency Committee supervised the election of local board members and approved their actions. Nevertheless, the great distances between the home office and the branches and the need for vigorous local leadership resulted eventually in greater independence. Furthermore, from the beginning, black cashiers and advisory boards played a vital role in promoting the Bank. In time, many cashiers and

58. Minutes A, June 30, 1865, p. 7. For information on the black committees at Norfolk, Richmond, and Washington, see ch. 5.
59. Journal, April 4, 1865.
60. Hewitt to Alvord, June 14, 1865, Bank Letters, BRFAL.
61. Minutes A, August 12, 1868, p. 79.

advisory board members were acknowledged as community leaders, and their very presence and example helped to encourage the growth of a middle class and the development of middle-class principles.

Four months after its incorporation the Freedman's Savings Bank was a going concern, although it no longer resembled an "ordinary savings bank." Designed to help black soldiers and freedmen save their money, the Bank was a practical philanthropy. Its cost was minimal; the burden of work would be upon the freedmen themselves, and they would not become a tax upon the government's largesse. In short, the Bank initiated a crusade against poverty, with all the benefits, moral overtones, and limitations of mid-nineteenth-century social service.

2

A Miniature Financial Empire

From its modest beginning in New York, the Freedman's Savings and Trust Company grew phenomenally, extending its business as far as Mobile and Houston. The first three branches had been exciting innovations, but by the end of 1865, when the company added seven more, branches were a commonplace matter of business. Less than two years after its founding, the Bank could count twenty-two branches in thirteen states and the District of Columbia.[1] Like the Second Bank of the United States, the Freedman's Bank reached out across the country—although, unlike the Second Bank, the Freedman's Bank would reap the harmful consequences of overextension. Knowingly or unknowingly, the trustees and officers had created a miniature financial empire, in the early years more impressive in extension than in fiscal strength.

The Freedman's Bank established branches in cities that had large concentrations of black people, such as Charleston, Baltimore, New Orleans, and Savannah, and also in smaller cities (such as Vicksburg and Houston) where it expected to receive soldiers' bounty money and back pay. The Savannah branch was a typical case. A report from that city revealed that large numbers of soldiers in the area needed the services of a bank they could trust. Moreover, a significant part of the laboring population of the city was black, and without a bank the freedmen might recklessly spend or lose their hard-earned money. Savannah Negroes needed confidence in the idea of saving, especially since some of them had deposited money before the war in white banks which had subsequently failed. For these reasons Savannah was a logical site, and a branch opened there in January, 1866.[2]

1. *Report of the Select Committee to Investigate the Freedman's Savings and Trust Company*, Senate, 1880, appendix, p. 41.
2. J. W. Alvord to Hiram Roberts, September 6, 1865; N. B. E. Bickford to Alvord, September 23, 1865, Bank Letters, BRFAL.

Baltimore was an important location because of its large antebellum free Negro community. In early 1866 the candidate for cashier, Nathaniel Noyes, a white agent of the American Missionary Association and a businessman, sounded out the Negro community about opening a branch; since leading Negroes seemed anxious to share in its benefits, Noyes organized the branch early that year. When deposits failed to materialize, he concluded that the black people lacked confidence and perseverance because they suspected that every new business venture was an attempt to swindle them—a not very surprising attitude, considering their history. Noyes set out to win their confidence through a series of public meetings, and in May he reported to Alvord that he had received deposits of more than $5,000, of which $3,000 belonged to Negro soldiers. Deposits from civilians trickled in slowly; but soldiers came forth with little hesitation, and their deposits and withdrawals stimulated the community's confidence. Over the next few months deposits increased so much that Alvord could call the successful Baltimore bank a model branch.[3]

Jacksonville, Florida, a relatively small community at the close of the Civil War, was chosen as a branch site because Negro soldiers from that area were about to receive substantial sums of back pay and bounty money. The branch opened in March, 1866, specifically to receive the money of the Twenty-first and Thirty-third United States Colored Troops (USCT). At that time the Jacksonville area had no bank of any kind, so the opportunity to do a large business (some of it with white people) could not be overlooked.[4]

New York, too, seemed to offer a substantial business potential. As the center of an important Negro community and the financial capital of the United States, New York could provide sizable deposits, and success there would boost the morale of southern freedmen.[5] In July, 1866, an all-black committee organized the branch, and John J. Zuille, a Negro community leader and political organizer who had been active in the Underground Railroad and the New York African Society for Mutual Relief, was chosen cashier.[6]

3. Nathaniel Noyes to Alvord, February 20 and 27, May 18, 1866, *ibid.*; Alvord to Noyes, January 14, 1867, Letters Sent, Book 11, Educational Division, BRFAL.

4. J. M. Hawks to Gen. Rufus Saxton, December 19, 1865; N. C. Dennett to Alvord, June 14, 1866, Bank Letters, BRFAL.

5. M. T. Hewitt to Alvord, September 12, 1866, *ibid.*

6. William Howard Day to Alvord, July 21, 1866 *ibid.*; *Charleston Daily Courier*, September 13, 1866, p. 1; Benjamin Quarles, *Black Abolitionists* (New York: Oxford University Press, 1969), pp. 171, 184; Roi Ottley and William J. Weatherby, eds., *The Negro in New York* (New York: Praeger, 1967), pp. 61, 87. It is in-

While the black laborers and artisans of New York were the primary attraction for the first northern branch, several trustees were attracted by the possibility of obtaining large deposits from white immigrant communities. For this reason the New York branch deposit books were printed in English, French, and German. After a slow start, white patronage became substantial; a bank examiner estimated that by 1874 as many as one-fourth of the New York depositors were white. Bank records confirm that they were largely of immigrant stock, but this case of whites patronizing what was generally considered a Negro bank was most unusual.[7]

Between 1866 and 1868 the Freedman's Bank considered many plans for expansion, some of which were premature and others quite unrealistic. When the Louisville branch was established, plans were begun for still another Kentucky branch. Lexington, so the argument ran, was the next most important place for the Bank's operation, for it was located in the center of a large former slave district, had a sizable population of respectable black people, and would receive soldiers' money which would otherwise be squandered on drink.[8] In Alabama the Mobile branch was so successful that inquiries were made about opening for business in Montgomery, but the Bank's investigator threw cold water on the whole idea. He doubted that the Montgomery freedmen could match more than 10 percent of the Mobile Negroes' assets.[9] A proposal for a branch at Atlanta was made by the Freedmen's Bureau's state superintendent of education in Georgia, G. L. Eberhart. Eberhart felt that Atlanta would yield larger deposits than Augusta or Savannah, for Atlanta was "on the make," and nowhere else did Negroes earn so much.

---

teresting that New York branch officials sought to honor General O. O. Howard by renaming their office the "Howard Savings Bank, Branch of the National Freedmans Savings and Trust Company." Their petition to change the title was unsuccessful. See Cashier John J. Zuille to Alvord, August 7, 1866, Bank Letters, BRFAL.

7. Hewitt to Alvord, February 1, 1866, *ibid.*; Passbook No. 6084, Caroline Doeschner, Letters Rec'd by the Commissioners and by the Comptroller of the Currency as ex officio Commissioner, 1870–1914, FS&T Co.; U.S., Congress, House, *Report of the Commissioner of the Freedman's Savings and Trust Company*, 43rd Cong., 2nd sess., 1874, House Miscellaneous Document No. 16, p. 63; New York Signature Books, FS&T Co. The decision to include French among the foreign languages in the New York deposit books is puzzling, for the French-speaking population of New York County, especially in proportion to the German, was very small. Perhaps New York's deposit book, with a different cover, was also designed for use in New Orleans, where there was a large French-speaking population, both white and black.

8. Max Woodhull to Alvord, April 6, 1866, Bank Letters, BRFAL.

9. J. Gilsley to Alvord, October 30, 1866, *ibid.*

The superintendent's motives were not purely altruistic—he hoped to be cashier of the branch.[10] Other cities considered for expansion were Little Rock, St. Louis, Macon, and Raleigh. In 1867 all of these sites were topics of wishful thinking, but by 1872 they had all entered the company's branch system.[11]

Many small cities which could not possibly support a freedman's bank requested a branch and had to be refused outright. Their requests reveal how widespread was interest in the Bank. From Winchester, Virginia, W. L. Coan, an agent for the American Missionary Association and later the cashier at Jacksonville, wrote to Alvord in January, 1866, about the interest he had created for a branch.

> I have just come from a large and interesting meeting of colored people convened for the purpose of hearing (from myself and others) statements in reference to your Bank and to consider the question of the best means and facilities for "Savings."
>
> They decided in favor of your Bank and I write at their request to ask you or Mr. Hewitt to come here *immediately* and (bringing with you a sett [*sic*] of Books and documents Copies of Charter etc) establish an agency here for this vicinity.[12]

At Staunton, Virginia, in late 1867, a Freedmen's Bureau official described the Bank to a large meeting at the Bureau school and obtained instructions to request a branch.[13] At Leavenworth, Kansas, a Bureau agent took steps to open a branch to serve the growing Negro community (about 6,000) and the large concentration of troops from Missouri, Arkansas, and Texas. Unfortunately, the failure of a local private bank, which resulted in the loss of many Negroes' savings, had soured opinion on all savings banks.[14]

Rapid expansion brought many problems which made the bank officers cautious about establishing new branches in 1867. The hasty creation of a miniature financial empire had already produced a severe organizational problem. Quite simply, how does one put into practice an integrated set of banking principles for the management and operation of twenty-odd scattered branches with limited funds and a largely

10. G. L. Eberhart to Alvord, August 3, 1867, *ibid.*

11. W. Deivuse [?] to Gen. O. O. Howard, September 3, 1867, Letters Rec'd, I, Educational Division, BRFAL; Alvord to S. L. Harris, April 29, 1867, Letters Sent, Book 12, Educational Division, BRFAL; *Report of the Select Committee*, Senate, 1880, appendix, p. 41.

12. W. L. Coan to Alvord, January 29, 1866, Bank Letters, BRFAL.

13. Thomas P. Jackson to Alvord, November 11, 1867, *ibid.*

14. John C. Douglass to F. A. Seeley, August 15, 1867; Seeley to Alvord, August 21, 1867, *ibid.*

untrained staff? Communications between the New York headquarters and the branches were poor at best; it took eleven to twelve days to receive a reply to a letter sent to New Orleans.[15] Many branches in the Deep South had almost no contact with the central office. The sole inspector could not be everywhere at once; indeed, there were some branches that he never visited.[16] Many amateurish cashiers ignored the tedious paperwork required by the central office. In 1866 Hewitt complained that only five branches regularly sent in reports.[17] The trustees and officers never did succeed in mending some of these fundamental flaws.

The personnel of the Freedman's Bank, which could hardly afford to pay a living wage, necessarily consisted of a mélange of untrained officers. Expanding rapidly and paying only $60 to $125 per month to cashiers and assistant cashiers (a salary equal at best to that of a schoolteacher), the Bank had no hope of hiring "model bankers," who would demand no less than $200 to $300 per month.[18] Most of the cashiers—drawn largely from missionaries, the Freedmen's Bureau, and the black community—had no banking experience, a fact made painfully evident in the books and records of several branches. The Washington cashier, William Wilson, continually had trouble balancing his books, and the Chattanooga cashier on one occasion frantically asked the home office for instruction in the use of the Bank's complex set of books. In January, 1867, a discrepancy of $8,000—the Bank's first loss, but unfortunately by no means its last—was discovered at the Charleston branch. While fraud was strongly suspected (but, according to available evidence, not proven), Alvord somewhat hastily concluded that the cashier had made an error and that no dishonest act was contemplated. Nevertheless, the cashier was removed. In contemplating these cases one wonders just how bad the cashier at Raleigh was, for he was deemed the most incompetent bookkeeper in any of the branches.[19] Quite understandably, Alvord collected suggestions for precautionary measures. He urged that the cashiers be bonded and that advisory boards be required to hold monthly meetings, provide transcripts of their sessions, and carefully scrutinize the cashiers' work.[20] Whether these proposals were ever put

15. Harris to Col. D. L. Eaton, February 2, 1869, *ibid.*

16. U.S., Congress, House, *Freedman's Bank*, 44th Cong., 1st sess., 1876, House Report No. 502, p. 2.

17. Hewitt to Alvord, January 20, 1866, Bank Letters, BRFAL.

18. *New South* (Jacksonville), July 22, 1874, p. 2.

19. See Appendix C for information on the backgrounds of the cashiers. White cashiers are discussed in ch. 3, black in ch. 4.

20. Alvord to Hewitt, January 25, 1867; Alvord to Hewitt, January 28, 1867, pp. 292–293, Letters Sent, Book 11, Educational Division, BRFAL; Hewitt to Alvord, January 29, 1867, Bank Letters, BRFAL.

into practice is uncertain. The branch cashiers were not the whole problem anyway—the record-keeping at the Bank's central office was also consistently poor. The original treasurer kept the books in a most irregular fashion; the actuaries who succeeded him struggled forever to balance them but were seldom successful.[21] Given severely limited funds, the newness of the institution, and the difficulties of communication—to say nothing of southern attitudes toward blacks—the Bank carried an inescapable burden of administrative, personnel, and organizational problems.

Not all freedmen in 1865 were penniless ex-slaves. Thousands had served in the Union army, and, although they were paid little, many managed to accumulate one or two hundred dollars, or even more. Between 1865 and 1868 the soldiers' money provided the Bank's first sizable deposits. Since concern for the black soldier had first stimulated interest in a Negro savings bank, it is not surprising that back pay and bounty money of Negro soldiers came to dominate the early expansion of the Freedman's Savings Bank. Bank officers made concerted efforts to be present when soldiers received money, and some of the riskiest branch expansions were connected with the pursuit of the black soldiers. It would be no exaggeration to say that the very survival of the company in its first year was due to these deposits.

All through the Reconstruction period the government paid bounty claims to Negro soldiers or their relatives, and even as late as 1880 $510,000 in unclaimed money remained outstanding.[22] In 1867 Congress placed General Howard and the Freedmen's Bureau in charge of bounties for Negro soldiers, and for a while it was hoped that all the money designated for black soldiers would be channeled through the Freedman's Bank. Alvord at first had believed that "all such monies are, by arrangement with the Bureau, to be deposited with our Freedmans Savings & Trust Company for the benefit of those to whom they may belong, to be drawn for by the disbursing officer when their claims are properly presented."[23] But this was a misapprehension. In early 1869

21. Harris to Alvord, March 27, 1867, Bank Letters, BRFAL; Alvord to Hewitt, July 16, 1867, Letters Sent, Book 12, Educational Division, BRFAL; *Freedman's Bank*, House, 1876, p. 2; *Report of the Select Committee*, Senate, 1880, p. 252; Minutes A, February 10, 1870, p. 148; Examiners Report, Raleigh, May 26, 1874, Letters Rec'd by the Commissioners, 1870–1914, FS&T Co.
22. *Peoples Advocate* (Washington), January 3, 1880, p. 1.
23. Alvord to Col. S. M. Bowman, June 24, 1865, Bank Letters, BRFAL; U.S., Congress, House, *Charges against General Howard*, 41st Cong., 2nd sess., 1870, House Report No. 121, p. 393.

Inspector Samuel L. Harris, who had been the cashier at Beaufort, lectured D. L. Eaton, the actuary, on the official bounty policy: "The funds must be by law, deposited in the U.S. Treasury whenever there is one at hand. Necessity in other cases or sufferance form the only exceptions. . . . When the soldier is paid, then only can we legitimately ask for the deposit of his funds."[24] A general order from the War Department in 1873 re-emphasized this policy.[25] But Alvord hated to relinquish his dream. In 1870 he wrote to General Howard:

> Would it not be wise to have pensions and bounties for colored soldiers, which sharpers are so apt to get from them, (even after the money is in their own hands,) placed, in some way, in the savings bank as a depository or receiver, thus affording these soldiers its friendship and some legal hindrance against their enemies?[26]

Having failed to establish the Freedman's Bank as the depository for Negro bounty funds, bank officials did the next-best thing: they arranged for their cashiers to aid or work closely with the Freedmen's Bureau agents in their city or to become local disbursing officers. In at least nine branches (Richmond, New Orleans [temporarily], Savannah, Vicksburg, Mobile, Charleston, Jacksonville, Norfolk, and Louisville) the cashiers doubled as Bureau disbursing officers.[27] At other locations the cashiers worked in unofficial capacities to see that former soldiers received their bounty—and that the Bank received as much as the soldiers could possibly spare.[28]

The activities of one individual, Anson M. Sperry, reflect the importance which bank officials attached to work among the soldiers. An army major and paymaster from Illinois, Sperry had long been interested in aiding black soldiers and had even designed a general allotment system with the allotment commissioner of Massachusetts. Upon applying to the president for a commission to permit him to establish his allotment plan, he had learned of the Freedman's Bank and had canceled his plans, for the Bank "was a better thing altogether." The trustees se-

24. Harris to Eaton, February 2, 1869, Bank Letters, BRFAL.
25. General Order No. 111, War Department, November 22, 1873, in Letters Rec'd by H. C. Percy, Cashier, Norfolk, Va., BRFAL.
26. John Alvord, *Letters from the South Relating to the Condition of the Freedmen* (Washington: Howard University Press, 1870), p. 27.
27. *Charges against General Howard*, pp. 388, 394; Bounty Register, Richmond, Va., Vol. 416, records of the Chief Disbursing Officer, BRFAL.
28. *Charges against General Howard*, pp. 388, 394; *Proceedings, Findings, and Opinion of the Court of Inquiry . . . in the Case of Brigadier General Oliver O. Howard* (Washington: Government Printing Office, 1874).

lected the energetic Sperry as their first special agent to do field work among the soldiers.[29]

Agents such as Anson Sperry were needed immediately. In September, 1865, John Alvord had learned from the paymaster general of the U.S. Army that large sums of money were due Negro soldiers in Texas.[30] In an attempt to make arrangements for the safety of the soldiers' money, he had reminded the commanding officer of the Twenty-seventh USCT that the paymaster general "commends strongly, as does General Howard of this Bureau, the *National Trust* Co. for Freedmen." Alvord requested this officer or his chaplain to collect any money the freedmen did not immediately need and to hold it until their agent, Anson Sperry, arrived.[31]

Carrying a letter of introduction from the president and the secretary of war, Sperry set out to follow the Twenty-fifth Army Corps to Texas in order to receive money for the Bank.[32] Thus began the odyssey which carried him from New York and Washington to the Rio Grande and the wilds of Texas. His close association with the Freedmen's Bureau enhanced his influence over the freedmen. The Bureau placed him on its payroll and paid his traveling expenses, while he aided in establishing a Bureau-sponsored school system.[33] In late 1865 he initiated steps for a branch bank at Houston, which opened in mid-1866. In December, 1865, the New York officials were cheered by the receipt of $7,400 from their agent, then at Galveston.[34] Sperry may even have temporarily opened a branch there, for in one letter from Alvord the secretary asked, "Is the Galveston Branch destined to flourish?"[35] Nevertheless, Sperry's business was basically transient; he followed the black soldiers wherever they went—to Galveston and Houston, Brownsville, White Plains, and to every encampment in Texas. Extant Louisville bank records contain certificates of deposit by Kentucky soldiers written from many scattered Texas locations.[36]

Standing at the paying tables, he enjoyed an enormous advantage in

29. *Report of the Select Committee*, Senate, 1880, p. 246.

30. Alvord to Maj. Gen. G. W. Brice, September 2, 1865, Bank Letters, BRFAL.

31. Alvord to Commanding Officer of 27th USCT, 25th Army Corps, n.d., *ibid.*

32. *Report of the Select Committee*, Senate, 1880, p. 246.

33. Anson Sperry to Alvord, January 29, 1867, Miscellaneous Unentered Letters Rec'd, Educational Division, BRFAL; Alvord, to Sperry, December 20, 1866, Letters Sent, Book 11, Educational Division, BRFAL. For a discussion of the cooperation between Bank and Bureau officials, see ch. 3.

34. Minutes A, September 24, 1865, p. 17; D. L. Lambert to Alvord, December 4, 1865; Hewitt to Alvord, March 16, 1866, Bank Letters, BRFAL.

35. Alvord to Sperry, December 26, 1866, p. 195, Letters Sent, Book 11, Educational Division, BRFAL.

36. Louisville Signature Book, FS&T Co.

influencing black soldiers, almost all of them ex-slaves, who had probably just received more money than they had ever possesed in their
entire lives. In March, 1866, he sent $16,000 from a Baltimore regiment
and $14,000 from a Louisville regiment.[37] Sperry and the Freedman's
Bank made it possible for Private James Martin, Company I, 117th
USCT, to transfer $149 safely to the Louisville branch and consequently
to his family.[38] Private Martin and thousands of others like him enabled Sperry to forward $120,000, a moderate fortune in those days,
to the central office and its branches before he returned in mid-1867.[39]

Despite these successes, Sperry faced serious problems in Texas. The
Houston branch was not prospering, and its expenses exceeded the
profits earned from investing the deposits. In the long run the branch
would succeed, he pleaded, "if we can sustain our present expenses."[40]
"I have no doubt of our *ultimate* success there, but the time looks far
off sometimes. Perhaps we may have to contract to the great centres
and there bide our time. This especially if we are to lose control of
affairs and be at the mercy of the civil authorities."[41]

The end was not far off. Heavy expenses at the branch, gradual withdrawals and mustering out of Negro troops, and perhaps to a certain
extent political unrest spelled the end of Sperry's usefulness in Texas.
After reimbursing the depositors at Houston and receiving the four
months' pay of the 117th USCT, he closed the branch in mid-1867 and
began his return.[42] His work, however, had benefited thousands of
black soldiers and added necessary funds to a capital-starved company.
Bank officers justly praised Sperry for his diligence and rewarded him
with further employment.

Although neither the success of Anson Sperry nor the heroic size of his
undertaking could be duplicated, various branch officials pursued the
military work on a smaller scale in all parts of the South. Alvord himself took to the field in South Carolina and obtained sizable amounts
of soldiers' money when Generals Littlefield and Bogart transferred
their soldiers' savings to the Freedman's Bank.[43] Among Alvord's letters
is the withdrawal order of one black soldier, written shortly before the
transfer. It represents one small success in his labors among the soldiers.

37. Hewitt to Alvord, March 7, 1866, Bank Letters, BRFAL.
38. Record of James Martin, No. 957, Louisville Signature Book, FS&T Co.
39. *Report of the Select Committee*, Senate, 1880, p. 246; Hewitt to Alvord,
December 28, 1866, Bank Letters, BRFAL.
40. Sperry to Hewitt, January 10, 1867, Miscellaneous Unentered Letters Rec'd,
Educational Division, BRFAL.
41. Sperry to Alvord, February 2, 1867, Bank Letters, BRFAL.
42. Alvord to Hewitt, May 12, 1867, Letters Sent, Book 12, Educational Division,
BRFAL; Sperry to Alvord, March 17, 1867, Bank Letters, BRFAL.
43. Minutes A, August 15, 1865, pp. 11–12.

Charleston July 31, 1865

I have this day given J. W. Alvord Secretary of the Freedmans Savings & Trust Company, an order on General Littlefield for the bounty money due me (545 Dolls) of which he is to hand me two hundred dollars & keep in the Bank of which he is secretary the remainder until I want it.[44]

As important as Alvord's travels in search of soldiers' deposits were his activities as corresponding secretary. He kept up a steady stream of communication concerning troop payments and the protection of soldiers' money. Do you know of any frauds against Negro soldiers? he would write the cashiers. Was the cashier acquainted with the claims agents in the city, and were they dealing fairly with Negro soldiers?[45] Learning of the imminent discharge of black troops in South Carolina, Alvord requested General R. K. Scott, assistant Bureau commissioner for South Carolina, to help save Negro troops from fraud, either through personal effort or by an advisory letter warning the inexperienced freedmen. Alvord believed that gamblers, swindlers, and others who preyed upon the naïve were sure to infest the paying tables.[46]

When news of troop payments reached Alvord (and also Vice-President Hewitt), he alerted all the cashiers in the states in which the troops were stationed, urging them to secure as much money as possible from the soldiers. Writing to the Louisville cashier, for example, Alvord expressed the hope that at the local regiment's final payment the cashier could visit the camp to accept deposits.[47] On another occasion, after receiving information from the chief disbursing officer of the army, he cautioned the New Bern cashier to watch for large amounts of bounty money, approximately $6,000, to be paid to soldiers in his vicinity. Since the money would not arrive for several days, he hoped the cashier would make adequate preparations to secure it.[48]

Alvord heard that at Norfolk, considerable sums of money were due Negro soldiers. By July, 1865, applications for discharged soldiers' back pay and bounty money, some of them from widows, were accumulating, and remittances would fall into the hands of dishonest agents unless the Bank acted.[49] General Orlando Brown urged the Bank to establish

44. Statement by Peter Overton, July 31, 1865, Bank Letters, BRFAL.

45. Alvord to C. S. Sauvinet, February 18, 1867, Letters Sent, Book 12, Educational Division, BRFAL. Similar letters were sent to at least six other cashiers, and probably to all the others as well.

46. Alvord to Gen. R. K. Scott, March 19, 1866, Bank Letters, BRFAL.

47. Hewitt to Alvord, May 1, 1866, *ibid.*; Alvord to H. H. Burkholder, July 3, 1867, Letters Sent, Book 12, Educational Division, BRFAL.

48. Alvord to A. A. Ellsworth, January 17, 1867, Book 11, *ibid.*

49. Jackson to Alvord, July 8, 1865, Bank Letters, BRFAL.

a claims agency at its office. "You must," he said, "put more energy into your institution in this state if you wish it to succeed."[50] In the fall the Norfolk cashier, H. C. Percy, reported that a Reverend Brown of the Bute Street Church had arranged matters so that the Bank could get a substantial amount of back pay.[51] When the 36th USCT was paid at Fort Monroe, Percy was on hand to accept deposits, predicting to Alvord that the Bank would be several thousand dollars "richer."[52]

By early 1867 Percy, on behalf of the Bank, had entered the bounty business in earnest. By that time many soldiers' accounts had been settled "in a heap," and treasury certificates had just begun to reach the Negro community. Percy described his operations thus:

> You know the payments are made by a Certificate payable at the Treasury in Washington. It has been the custom for the city banks and brokers to cash these at 3% *discount*, which is a little steep, and besides draws the money away from our Bank.
>
> Now I have this month received as *Cash Deposits*, issuing books thereon, nearly $2000.00 in these Certificates, which I mail to Wilson at Washington, who collects and transfers the act t [account] and I have managed to retain about three-fourths in the Bank!
>
> By paying the depositor $50.00 he is usually content until the paper is collected, and frequently he leaves the whole.[53]

Percy proposed a working arrangement with the claims agent next door, taking in certificates, issuing deposit books, and getting money for the certificates. He hoped to gain half of the bounty and back pay as permanent deposits.[54] His expectations, however, proved overly optimistic; during the next month he complained that too many payments went to soldiers residing forty miles or more from the city, and they could not see the benefit of banking their money in Norfolk.[55] Moreover, Percy had competitors in the bounty business and some of them, without presenting any proof, accused him of taking a percentage.[56] In spite of this accusation, Percy continued his work among the soldiers for several years, and at some point during this time his position was made official as Freedmen's Bureau disbursing officer.[57]

50. Gen. Orlando Brown to Alvord, July 8, 1865, *ibid.*
51. Percy to Alvord, September 15, 1865, *ibid.*
52. Percy to Alvord, November 30, 1866, *ibid.*
53. Percy to Alvord, February 20, 1867, *ibid.*
54. *Ibid.*
55. Percy to Alvord, March 14, 1867, *ibid.*
56. Alvord to Percy, March 11, 1867, Letters Sent, Book 12, Educational Division, BRFAL.
57. Capt. A. S. Flagg to Percy, May 4, 1866, Letters Rec'd by H. C. Percy, Cashier, Norfolk, Va., BRFAL.

Nathaniel Noyes at Baltimore also did a vigorous business among the soldiers. "I have just had conference with a very intelligent and influential Colored man about the Maryland Regiment about to come into City Point, and he knows ¾ of one of the Regiments, and heartily approves of your action in trying to get them to deposit with you nearly all their money until they get home at least."[58] Letters about discharge dates and troop arrivals passed hurriedly between Noyes and Alvord's office in late 1866. Alvord informed another cashier that he could not visit him because pressing affairs, the discharge of Negro troops, occupied him at Baltimore and the bank there was receiving large deposits.[59] On December 11, 1866, a general telegraphed Alvord concerning the movements of the 9th USCT; Alvord in turn notified Noyes, who prepared to meet them.[60] Two months later Noyes was working among the soon-to-be-paid 19th Regiment. "I am doing all I can with them to induce them to deposit in [the] Bank, and I think from what I can see and learn that they are intending to do so to a considerable extent."[61] A week later Noyes reported disappointing results. Claims agents had practically fought over the soldiers so that they had become confused and had kept their money. He had collected only $2,000 at the camp and $2,400 at the bank, even though Anson Sperry had proselytized these same troops in Texas.[62]

Despite these occasional disappointments, the Bank's efforts among the soldiers were generally well rewarded from 1865 through 1868, and soldiers' money provided the major share of the deposits in the first two years. Nine months after its incorporation the Bank's total deposits had reached $232,000, but of this amount approximately $180,000 had been transferred from the military banks of General Saxton at Beaufort and General Butler at Norfolk.[63] Some of this money had been withdrawn, but the majority of it remained on deposit. Between 1865 and 1867 Sperry forwarded $120,000 from soldiers in Texas. At Charleston, 209 of the first 319 depositors had been soldiers, while at Washington a regiment from Kentucky deposited $6,000 in one week.[64] At Baltimore, it will be remembered, the soldiers sustained the Bank while the civil-

58. Noyes to Alvord, March 7, 1866, Bank Letters, BRFAL.
59. Alvord to Charles Spencer, November 27, 1866, Letters Sent, Book 11, Educational Division, BRFAL.
60. Western Union telegram, Brevet Maj. Gen. E. M. Gregory to Alvord, December 11, 1866; Western Union telegram, Alvord to Noyes, December 11, 1866, Bank Letters, BRFAL.
61. Noyes to Alvord, February 9, 1867, *ibid.*
62. Noyes to Alvord, February 16, 1867, *ibid.*
63. Journal, September 14, 1865; Woodward, *Savings Banks*, appendix, p. 97.
64. Nos. 1–319, Charleston Signature Books, FS&T Co.; *South Carolina Leader* (Charleston), December 9, 1865, p. 3.

ians watched and debated.[65] Although many civilians there and elsewhere may have been quite willing and eager to deposit, in 1865 they lacked the substantial, readily available sums which the soldiers had accumulated.

The Freedman's Bank's rapid expansion and generally successful business among the soldiers between 1865 and 1867 belied its actual financial condition. Judged by the size of deposits and the yield from investments, the Bank was an insecure enterprise in its early years. For two years the officers had established branches without sufficient regard to costs. "Impressed as they were with the sense of the many benefits of savings institutions among the freedmen of the South," wrote Frederick Douglass in 1874, "they were tempted into a sort of banking missionary movement" and began branches in remote places where it was impossible for them to become speedily self-sustaining.[66] Successful savings banks in New York and Massachusetts had the expense of only one office and a small staff, but the Freedman's Bank, with less money to invest, paid the charges on over twenty offices and as many small staffs. It was only natural that, after the early proliferation of branches, expansion slowed in the latter half of 1866 and stopped altogether in 1867. By then the Freedman's Bank had many of the problems of a financial empire but few of the benefits of security, efficiency, and prestige. Because expenses exceeded income, the Bank for the first time failed to pay interest in January, 1867.[67] Officials considered closing several branches and, indeed, the whole company. After almost two years of business, the Bank was struggling for survival.

A substantial part of the crisis was a result of postwar demobilization. Soon after Appomattox Negro regiments began to be discharged; by April, 1866, there was only one regiment in Georgia, two in Alabama, and one each in South Carolina and Florida.[68] By the end of 1867 deposits in the form of pay and back pay had largely disappeared. Increasingly the military business shifted to bounty money.

The bounty money deposits, while important for the Bank, might not have been as large as a superficial observation would lead one to suspect; they alone certainly could not sustain the company. While substantial

65. See above, p. 22.
66. *Report of the Select Committee*, Senate, 1880, appendix, p. 143.
67. The Bank's income from investments was rather small. Until 1870 the Freedman's Bank invested solely in government securities, which provided only a modest return. In addition, a large sum, the available fund, was not invested but was kept on hand to meet ordinary demands.
68. *Charleston Daily News*, April 19, 1866, p. 1; Nashville *Republican Banner*, October 26, 1865, p. 1.

sums of bounty money were paid by cashiers, Bureau disbursing officers, and friends of the Bank, it is impossible to determine how much went into the Bank and remained there. Vicksburg, a branch established primarily for the reputedly heavy business with soldiers, is the only branch for which there is even an estimate. By 1870 about one-third of its deposits—$52,000 out of $147,000—had originated from bounties.[69] Some branches seem to have received very little bounty money. Almost all of the $73,000 on deposit in Mobile in March, 1867, for instance, belonged to civilians.[70]

There are a few indications that the bounty money deposits in the Bank may have been disappointingly small. On one occasion Alvord wrote to Hewitt that bounty money was being paid at the Washington branch and that the Bank was getting some.[71] He undoubtedly would have mentioned the amount had it been substantial. Cashier Charles Spencer, who served also as a clerk and disbursing officer in the Freedmen's Bureau, reported that although he and a chaplain had pushed the Bank's interests assiduously during a Richmond troop discharge, very few had made deposits.[72] Between 1869 and 1872 Spencer paid $18,200 in bounty money. An investigation of twelve recipients chosen from the list at random shows that none of them made deposits in the Bank.[73] At Savannah between June, 1871, and March, 1872, Bureau agent and cashier I. W. Brinckerhoff paid only $951.50 in bounties to four people, and none of them opened accounts at that time.[74] Additional evidence that the amount of bounty money deposited in the Bank may have been relatively small comes from the disbursing officer and Bureau agent in Louisiana, Edward C. Beman:

> I would take their money in currency, count it out to them, and explain to them the denomination of the bills, and give them a card to the Freedmen's [sic] Savings Bank, and ask them to go there and get the cashier to count their money, and they would go to the grog-shop and lose half of it. I think there were about three of them who put their money into the bank, out of the 4,321 cases that I paid. I think the cashier told me that.[75]

69. *Charges against General Howard,* p. 394.
70. *The Nationalist* (Mobile), March 21, 1867, p. 2.
71. Alvord to Hewitt, April 29, 1867, Letters Sent, Book 12, Educational Division, BRFAL.
72. Spencer to Alvord, March 10, 1867, Bank Letters, BRFAL.
73. Bounty Register, Richmond, Va., Vol. 416, records of the Chief Disbursing Officer, BRFAL.
74. Reports of Bounty Payments, B–C, *ibid.*
75. *Proceedings, Findings, and Opinion . . . Oliver O. Howard,* p. 149. Beman's account was given in 1870. In January and February, 1872, when he paid out $13,000, two of his bounty claimants opened accounts at the Bank. Forty-two-year-

Despite Beman's pessimistic assessment, the disappointment which bank cashiers experienced may more properly be attributed to the fact that discharged black soldiers, while suddenly acquiring one or two hundred dollars or more, owned nothing, had no jobs, and had heavy expenses in establishing homes and finding work. O. S. B. Wall, a Negro captain in the 104th USCT and previously an Oberlin businessman, said as much when he observed that his regiment and the 33rd, both about to be mustered out, might not fulfill his expectations, for "money down here is in such great demand for Planting purposes we may not do so well as we anticipate."[76]

Although it is impossible to estimate with any precision how much of the money deposited in the Freedman's Savings Bank can be credited to soldiers, their money must have formed the greatest part of the total deposits in 1865 and 1866. It became a progressively smaller share as troops were discharged and withdrew their savings. Bank officials often commented upon the impermanence of soldiers' deposits. A Captain James Low, who was cognizant of Bank affairs in South Carolina, wrote to Alvord that "as regards the building up of the business of the Bank upon savings of the colored people, other than soldiers, Charleston is by far the best location. The deposits of the soldiers are but ephemeral, and no solid basis for an Institution."[77] In 1866 Hewitt gave Alvord similar advice: "I have been satisfied for some time that our dependence for success was on Negro Industry, not to any large extent upon the soldiers."[78] At Louisville, Alvord wrote the next year that "the soldiers on whose money they depended, are nearly all mustered out, and they need a *grand popular demonstration* among the common people."[79]

With the dwindling of soldiers' business, the Bank had to make a painful transition to depending primarily on civilian deposits, and the

---

old Anna Johnson, who supported herself by washing, ironing, and cooking, received $219.40, the bounty of her deceased husband, and opened an account nine days later. How much she deposited is unknown. A similarly employed widow, Mary Williams, accepted $222.76 due her deceased husband and opened an account the same day. Her initial deposit is also unknown. See record of Anna Johnson, No. 4379, and Mary Williams, No. 4439, New Orleans Signature Books, FS&T Co.; Reports of Bounty Payments, B–C, records of the Chief Disbursing Officer, BRFAL.

76. Capt. O. S. B. Wall to Alvord, February 12, 1866, Miscellaneous Unentered Letters Rec'd, Educational Division, BRFAL. Wall was an early supporter of the Charleston branch, and in the 1870's he became a member of the board of trustees.

77. Capt. James Low to Alvord, September 14, 1865, Bank Letters, BRFAL.

78. Hewitt to Alvord, January 22, 1866, *ibid.*

79. Alvord to Harris, July 19, 1867, p. 422, Letters Sent, Book 12, Educational Division, BRFAL.

basic problems of a savings bank serving an ex-slave population in desperate need of capital began to appear. In spite of the officers' hopes concerning "Negro Industry," Negro civilians responded slowly. At many of the branches (so Bank officials believed, at any rate) they lacked confidence in the local agency, its officials, or the entire institution. (Considering the Bank's weaknesses and its eventual fate, this may indicate that black people were much shrewder and more thrifty than Bank officials ever imagined.) Lack of confidence seemed to be the problem at Charleston, where deposits were mainly transfers from other branches.[80] Because the people had taken no interest in their branch, Hewitt suggested that a change of cashiers might be necessary, and accordingly ordered the Bank's inspector to reorganize the branch —to identify the people with it.[81] Richmond suffered similar problems. In this instance President Hewitt decided to send Alvord "to get at the people" and see what hindered their success.[82] Perhaps Hewitt, Alvord, and the trustees were a bit unreasonable and impatient by late 1866 and were looking for easy solutions to the problems; they did not realize that it would take time to establish a new financial institution, especially one intended for an economically and socially subordinate group in a land unsettled by war and poverty.

Besides "lack of confidence," which Bank officials used as a catch-all phrase, there were plenty of substantial reasons for the Bank's slow growth. Needing jobs, homes, and land, the freedmen could at first save little. One cashier informed the officers that "the colored people are buying small pieces of land, that is to say those who have money & I do not think that we will receive many deposits before May or June, when the garden vegetables & other crops are coming in."[83]

In some places the Bank had to compete with churches for the slender savings of the Negroes. At Savannah, to take an extreme case, the Reverend W. J. Campbell, pastor of one of the largest Baptist churches in the South, encouraged his 2,500-member congregation to avoid the Bank and give all they could to the church. Actuary Eaton reported that, instead of the 5,000 depositors which this branch should have had, it could claim only 1,000; he strongly urged the advisory board to suggest ways to breach this "anti-financial Zion."[84]

To be sure, some Negroes may have misspent the first earnings they made as free men. It would seem that improvidence could be expected

---

80. Hewitt to Alvord, November 12 and December 7, 1866, Bank Letters, BRFAL.
81. Hewitt to Alvord, November 12, 1866, *ibid.*
82. Hewitt to Alvord, December 7, 1866, *ibid.*
83. Edward Woag to D. L. Lambert, January 20, 1866, *ibid.*
84. Minutes A, 1869, p. 116.

from a group so long held in slavery, for slavery provided no pay and no future—no opportunity to learn to budget income for future needs. But except for missionaries' reports of gambling and drinking, hard evidence of improvidence among black civilians is scanty. Numerous reports affirm that some black soldiers wasted their pay and bounty money, but soldiers, black or white, were notorious for spending sprees.[85] Most freedmen, thrust upon their own resources between 1862 and 1865, used their scanty means just to get by. Many had no opportunity to be improvident. The several reasons which explain why many freedmen declined to deposit do not necessarily suggest improvidence but emphasize an overriding truth—that the Freedman's Savings Bank was a poor company seeking to establish itself in a poor land among poor people who had a wealth of needs.

In 1866 a chorus of complaints lamenting the lack of deposits and the heavy expenses foretold troubles to come. From Charleston Captain O. S. B. Wall reported that interest was lively but deposits small; a month later, in February, 1866, Hewitt wrote Alvord that "Mobile opens out this morning with a Check for $2500 & Memphis with $500, this is the first from those branches."[86] Late that summer Hewitt reported that money was coming in very slowly; drafts were not large but continuous, and all in all he was quite anxious about the future.[87] Affairs at New York City were especially bad: expenses totaled $3,000 annually, while interest from the investment of that branch's deposits amounted to only $500.[88] In the fall of 1866 the branches at Huntsville, Memphis, Vicksburg, and Charleston did poorly, while in July, 1867, the Agency Committee described the branches at Wilmington, New Bern, Huntsville, Jacksonville, and Tallahassee as unproductive.[89] Although total deposits due depositors had climbed to $304,437.57 by the end of 1866, only about $200,000 of that sum was invested and earning income. The company operated with a deficit of several thousand dollars for the entire year.[90]

By late 1866 Bank officers were searching for ways of keeping the

85. *Proceedings, Findings, and Opinion . . . Oliver O. Howard*, p. 149; "The South as It Is," p. 779; *Freedmen's Bureau*, House, 1866, pp. 348–349; Wilson, *Black Phalanx*, p. 508.

86. Capt. Wall to Alvord, January 24, 1866, Hewitt to Alvord, February 20, 1866, Bank Letters, BRFAL.

87. Hewitt to Alvord, August 18, 1866, *ibid.*

88. Minutes A, January 17, 1867, p. 30.

89. *Ibid.*, July 11, 1867, p. 44; Hewitt to Alvord, September 28, 1866, Bank Letters, BRFAL.

90. Statement for December, 1866; Hewitt to Alvord, January 29, 1867, *ibid.*; Alvord to Hewitt, January 31, 1867, Letters Sent, Book 12, Educational Division, BRFAL; Journal, March 8, 1866.

Bank afloat. Because most of the trustees generally neglected the Bank, the work of financial salvage fell to Hewitt, Alvord, the actuary, and the Agency Committee.[91] In mid-July Hewitt had assessed the Bank's situation: deposits had not reached expectations, the majority of the branches were a burden, and depositors did not have the capacity to increase deposits so as to neutralize expenditures.[92] There was talk of closing the weak branches. Hewitt himself estimated that $6,000 could be saved permanently by closing Vicksburg, Memphis, Houston, and New York.[93] With the situation so critical, he urged the Agency Committee to take the following steps, which clearly reveal the Bank's strong and weak points.

1. That the Baltimore, Beaufort, Charleston, Louisville, Nashville, Mobile, Norfolk, and Washington branches be continued with no cut in expenses.
2. That Alexandria, Huntsville, and Vicksburg "are virtually closed."[94]
3. That the Augusta, Houston, Jacksonville, Tallahassee, and Savannah branches be continued until May 1, 1867, and that they be closed if interest on permanent deposits does not equal expenses.
4. That the New Bern, Wilmington, and Richmond branches be continued at present expenses [which were small] because of the convenience of paying Texas soldiers who reside in those areas.
5. That the New York branch be continued with a guarantee from the parties concerned that expenses shall not exceed $1,500.
6. That S. L. Harris be continued as financial inspector.
7. That Sperry be continued as agent in Texas, for "his operations have resulted in a Financial success to the Co."[95]

In early January, 1867, the trustees accepted these recommendations and rejected for the moment a proposal to close the Bank in its entirety. They also added Memphis to the list of those branches "virtually closed."[96] (Later in the year Houston was closed permanently.[97]) The

91. Journal, December 17, 1866.
92. Hewitt to E. A. Lambert, July 17, 1866, Bank Letters, BRFAL.
93. Hewitt to Alvord, December 14, 1866, *ibid.*
94. The wording here is disturbingly ambiguous. It most likely describes the officers' intention rather than an actual condition. In spite of their recommendation, there is no evidence that Huntsville and Vicksburg (or Memphis, which was later added to the list of "virtually closed") were ever phased out. The Alexandria branch, however, was temporarily closed. See Minutes A, January 17, 1867, p. 30.
95. Hewitt to E. A. Lambert, July 17, 1866, Bank Letters, BRFAL. The seven points summarized here are not exact quotations.
96. Journal, January 21, 1867.
97. See above, p. 29.

crisis continued, however. The day after the trustees' meeting Hewitt warned Alvord that the next meeting of the Board of Trustees would prove vital to the future of the Bank: the trustees might recommend closing the institution. "The [Agency] Committee seemed despondent as to the future of the Bank, and it was evident to [*sic*] if the Board was in sympathy with the Committee it would be closed."[98] In reply, Alvord stated that $20,000 in expenses certainly was all that the company could bear annually, but that he had not realized that the Bank had exceeded that amount by $10,000.

> The over-estimate, however, is on the ground of our faith that there would be larger income, which, had it not been for the short crops, disturbed state of the country, and what we think is the totally discouraging administration of affairs by the Executive here at Washington [*sic*].
>
> But, my dear Sir, we can back off, I think, and lighten our craft, so that it can float in such depth of water as is granted us. The question is *first what* to throw overboard.[99]

Most officials regretted these severe steps; indeed, they were repulsed by the very idea of closing branches. Although John Alvord looked for something to "throw overboard," he had strongly opposed discontinuing any branches. "Glad to know," he wrote Hewitt, "that you are pressing down on expenses. But will it not be a bad policy to stop Branches in such important places as Memphis & Vicksburg? looking like approaching failure all around."[100] To the former president, William A. Booth, Alvord argued that by closing branches they were killing the goose to get the egg. Closing the weak branches and refusing to pay a dividend (simultaneous occurrences) would have an adverse effect on all the branches: the strong branches would be hurt; withdrawals would commence; and the Negro's confidence in "us white folks," already strained, would vanish.[101] It is probably due to these very real fears that the attempt to close permanently the weaker branches succeeded only in the case of Houston.

Austerity measures had to be imposed. No new branches were established in 1867, and at all the old ones expenses, especially the cashiers' salaries, were curtailed.[102] Officials granted no raises; in the case of the Reverend S. S. Ashley, who had worked without compensation pre-

98. Hewitt to Alvord, January 22, 1867, Bank Letters, BRFAL.

99. Alvord to Hewitt, January 31, 1867, Letters Sent, Book 12, Educational Division, BRFAL; Hewitt to Alvord, January 29, 1867, Bank Letters, BRFAL.

100. Alvord to Hewitt, December 20, 1866, pp. 184–185, Letters Sent, Book 11, Educational Division, BRFAL.

101. Alvord to William A. Booth, January 29, 1867, Book 12, *ibid.*

102. Minutes A, 1867, *passim.*

viously, a salary was denied. However, Alvord did offer him a percentage of all the deposits he brought in.[103] The Bank searched for other ways to decrease expenses; it sought closer cooperation with the Freedmen's Bureau and established an expense policy for future branches.[104] For example, when the company moved into St. Louis in January, 1868, the Agency Committee declared that "their branch is expected, with the aid of the Bureau, to be able to pay its current incidental expenses *from the first*, and reimburse to the Company, at an early date, the above amount of salary."[105]

The history of the Memphis branch in 1866 and 1867 illustrates the measures taken to save a weak branch. Rumors of the branch's imminent demise forced Inspector Harris (who, as the Bank's traveling agent, felt responsible for the Memphis bank) into action. He believed that the Bank's officers should do everything possible to salvage the company's efforts in Memphis despite the disappointing beginning. While Memphis had only $3,000 in deposits, Harris believed this small amount could form the basis for useful work in the black community.[106] Before a month passed he had won Hewitt's support and had received aid from a Colonel Palmer of the Freedmen's Bureau and from the American Missionary Association's superintendent of schools in Memphis.[107] Harris cut expenses to $300 a year (which included $80 for sign painting but nothing for a cashier).

> . . . who was I to get to do the business for nothing as that amount would be absorbed by rent. The plan is to appoint a colored man Cashier and have the Bank in a well located store paying the Bookkeeper of the establishment $20 per mo. to do all the writing. The Col'd Cashier is available only because of his influence and the satisfaction his appointment might give the Col'd people. I have been steadily averse to any experiment in our work and regret that I have had to act as I have here.[108]

A black cashier was thus engaged to work gratuitously and to increase the branch's popularity. Harris added, however, that this was a temporary arrangement, for he hoped soon to provide an adequate

103. Alvord to S. S. Ashley, July 19, 1867, Letters Sent, Book 12, Educational Division, BRFAL.

104. Alvord to Harris, March 26, 1867, *ibid.*; Eaton to Col. J. R. Lewis, May 21, 1869, Letters Rec'd by the Georgia Superintendent of Education, III, Educational Division, BRFAL.

105. Minutes A, January 31, 1868, p. 59.

106. Harris to Alvord, February 12, 1867, Bank Letters, BRFAL.

107. *Ibid.*; Harris to Alvord, February 18, 1867, *ibid.*

108. Harris to Alvord, February 22, 1867, *ibid.*

salary and procure a separate banking office—and probably hire a white cashier. His efforts brought results immediately; in two days the branch received $900 and was able to send on $500, an amount equal to the entire sum sent to the central office in the previous year.[109] One month later, Alvord echoed Harris's sentiments concerning ultimate success in Memphis.[110] Events would prove both men correct.

Although the company could save most of its branches, the same cannot be said for its January, 1867, interest payment, which the officers called a dividend.[111] The Bank had suffered a $10,000 deficit for 1866, but the trustees insisted upon ordering a dividend for the first of the year.[112] At this time, however, President Hewitt discovered the $8,000 loss at the Charleston branch and canceled the trustees' order.[113] The Bank simply could not afford the dividend. "I know depositors are distrustful and lack intelligence," said Hewitt, "but I think that even they must see the loss of dividend is a small contribution on their part toward the establishment of their Bank." Hewitt reasoned that it was not bad faith to refuse to pay a dividend when the interest would have to be taken from the deposits instead of the profits.[114]

Bank agents were quick to voice their fears and to protest the Bank's latest financial cutback. Because a 2½ percent dividend had been promised so often, wrote Nathaniel Noyes from Baltimore, "I believe that the success of this Branch will be sure if the dividend is paid now, but if not I am very much afraid that our days are numbered."[115] Inspector Harris, too, felt that the shock from withholding the dividend after so many promises would create widespread demoralization and lack of

109. Harris to Alvord, February 18, 1867, *ibid.* This black cashier has not been identified; all the known cashiers of the Memphis branch were white.

110. Alvord to Harris, March 26, 1867, Letters Sent, Book 12, Educational Division, BRFAL.

111. Today we speak of banks as paying interest, not dividends. "Dividend" was commonly used in the mid-nineteenth century; Emerson Keyes uses the term in his two-volume *History of Savings Banks in the United States*. There is a very fine—but fortunately not vital—distinction between interest and dividend. According to William H. Kniffin, Jr., "*Interest* has a special, legal and technical significance. It is the 'price paid for the use of money'—an amount usually if not always fixed and determined in advance, either by law or by agreement; or as one authority puts it, 'The increase in a debt due to the lapse of time.' A *dividend* is something *divided*, and is usually indeterminate until profits are estimated and the dividend and its rate *declared*." Kniffin concludes that savings banks generally pay dividends, but that the dividend is generally called "interest." Strictly speaking, he maintains, a more exact term would be "interest-dividend." See *The Savings Bank and Its Practical Work* (New York: Bankers Publishing Co., 1918), pp. 350–351.

112. Hewitt to Alvord, January 29, 1867, Bank Letters, BRFAL.

113. Hewitt to Alvord, January 24, 1867, *ibid.*

114. Hewitt to Booth, January 30, 1867; Hewitt to Alvord, January 29, 1867, *ibid.*

115. Noyes to Alvord, February 2, 1867, *ibid.*

confidence and would destroy chances for increasing deposits.[116] Alvord similarly feared the effects of Hewitt's decision: cashiers would be discouraged, Congress would be upset (a baseless fear), and the enemies of the Negro would triumph. Moreover, the Washington branch would be especially hurt, for government clerks and teachers were just beginning to deposit there.[117]

Surprisingly, few repercussions resulted from the failure to pay the dividend; the predicted catastrophe in the form of wholesale withdrawals and loss of patronage did not materialize. Undoubtedly some depositors had forgotten about the dividends, while others decided that the struggling institution's decision was justified. The policy of cashier A. A. Ellsworth of New Bern offers a hint as to why many acquiesced in the Bank's policy. Ellsworth was not in the habit of paying any dividend except on sums of $100 or more that remained in the branch for at least a year. He believed that the dividend generally was a trifling matter; in any case, he rationalized, the depositors were usually satisfied with the principal.[118]

A few recalcitrants demanded their interest, and in a startling move the company accommodated them: it bought them off to quiet them and maintain public confidence in the Bank. The protesters received their interest, while the masses who remained silent were ignored.[119] On February 27, 1867, H. C. Percy of Norfolk wrote to Alvord: "I had paid $5.00 on a presumed dividend before I knew we were not to have one. If some charitably disposed 'Peabody' would donate us enough to pay the *few* who are a little disappointed it would be of considerable aid in sustaining the good repute of the Bank."[120] Percy did not initiate this idea, for two days earlier Alvord had written to cashier Charles Spencer to determine how many of his Richmond depositors would be disappointed by the lack of a dividend. He indicated that friends of the Bank were planning a special donation from their own pockets to meet the emergency.[121] Alvord made $50 of his own money available

116. Harris to Hewitt, February 6, 1867, *ibid.*

117. Alvord to Hewitt, January 28, 1867, pp. 292–293, Letters Sent, Book 11, Educational Division, BRFAL.

118. Ellsworth to Alvord, March 12, 1867, Bank Letters, BRFAL.

119. Why this brazen irregularity did not lead to a further loss of confidence cannot be explained, except by assuming that the Bank's duplicity went unnoticed by the general body of depositors—and this supposition is inadequate at best.

120. Percy to Alvord, February 27, 1867, Bank Letters, BRFAL. The "Peabody" of this quotation is George Peabody, a merchant, financier, and philanthropist who was best known among southern missionaries and educators for a grant of $3,500,000 for the improvement of southern education.

121. Alvord to Spencer, February 25, 1867, Letters Sent, Book 12, Educational Division, BRFAL.

to the Baltimore branch, and in early March he took pains to prod at least one other trustee into fulfilling his promise to contribute to the special dividend fund.[122]

Probably all branches received a share of the special fund donated by a number of officers, trustees, and friends of the Bank. On March 5, 1867, Percy reported that he had received $50 for the payment of a certain clamorous few, and that he would make careful use of it and report all drafts on the fund.[123] Spencer received $25: "I make this as a private donation, that the credit of the Bank may not suffer," Alvord wrote.[124] Noyes at Baltimore was grateful for Alvord's $50, for he had been critical of the decision not to pay a dividend and had given up hope of avoiding depositors' charges of broken faith. In fact, Hewitt had once told him that if he wanted to assuage his conscience on the dividend issue, he should obtain a state charter, make the Freedman's Bank in Baltimore a state institution, and then pursue his own dividend policy. Now a compromise had been reached: in cases where depositors clamored for the dividend, Noyes was to enter the interest to their credit or pay them in cash and charge this to Alvord.[125] The officials even remembered little New Bern: cashier Ellsworth received $15 to pay those whom he could not pacify.[126]

Although the Bank experienced severe financial difficulties in 1866–67, it was on the threshold of a tremendous period of growth. While it is true that the problems of organization, personnel, and excessive overhead costs—the problems of many large interstate businesses—were never entirely solved, the austerity measures enacted by the officials began to take effect by late 1867. They were soon rewarded by increasing deposits. Financial growth after 1867 complemented and completed earlier physical growth, and this in turn stimulated further expansion. Later developments saw the Bank achieve such success in its influence among black people that it emerged as one of the significant missionary forces for uplifting the black South.

122. Alvord to H. S. Hatch, March 6, 1867, *ibid.*
123. Percy to Alvord, March 5, 1867, Bank Letters, BRFAL.
124. Alvord to Spencer, February 1867, Letters Sent, Book 12, Educational Division, BRFAL.
125. Hewitt to Alvord, February 4, 1867, Bank Letters, BRFAL; Alvord to Noyes, March 4, 1867, Letters Sent, Book 12, Educational Division, BRFAL; Noyes to Alvord, February 2, 1867, Bank Letters, BRFAL.
126. Alvord to Ellsworth, March 9, 1867, Letters Sent, Book 12, Educational Division, BRFAL.

3

On Saving Men and Money:
The Bank as a Missionary Agency

"The saving man," Andrew Carnegie once said, "is par excellence the model citizen—peaceable, sober, industrious and frugal."[1] This observation could readily serve as a statement of the Bank's *raison d'être*. Its officials always believed that training in thrift could transform ignorant freedmen, beset by temptations to idleness, intemperance, and gambling, into morally upright citizens. John Alvord quite typically identified the moral, educational, and financial ideals of the Freedman's Bank as a single crusading purpose.[2] Another Bank official once described the institution as "a great aid to progress in educating and humanizing, and elevating this whole people."[3] The Bank would save men as well as money.

The belief that the Freedman's Savings and Trust Company was an institution essential for the progress of black people was central to its existence. The *New York Herald* described the Bank as an institution upon which the happiness of hundreds of thousands of freedmen depended, while the *South Carolina Leader*, a Charleston Negro paper, called it a necessity for the African race.[4] If historians later doubted that it was as essential as sympathetic contemporary accounts maintained, the trustees and officers never doubted its seminal importance and so hoped to persuade the freedmen. They mounted a quasi-religious campaign to spread the good news and help the freedmen.

The principal work of preaching was to be done by the branch cashiers, and Alvord set the tone in his advice to them: "I need not say,

---

1. Quoted in Charles Banks, *Negro Banks of Mississippi* (pamphlet [1909]), p. 128.
2. Minutes A, p. 145.
3. *Ibid.*, p. 125.
4. *South Carolina Leader* (Charleston), January 27, 1866; undated clipping from *New York Herald*, in Letters Rec'd by the Commissioners, 1870–1914, FS&T Co.

what you know so well by experience, that our work in this first period
of our history, is *missionary*,—almost religiously so. The real improvement of these people in *any* direction, depends on their individual
thrift. . . . This is a work of patience, ingenuity and toil, in private and
in public, such as the officers of no business institution were ever before
called to perform. How, then, to occupy *both* 'the counter' and pulpit—
be Cashier *and* preacher. . . ."[5]

Bank officials gave the cashiers plenty of practical advice on the tactics
of spreading the message of hope. Alvord told them to arrange frequent public meetings, organize and stimulate the monthly meetings of
the advisory committees, hire outside agents for a nominal fee to work
among the people, advertise on cards or in newspapers that circulated
among the freedmen, and establish a system of miniature savings in the
schools.[6] The financial inspector, the Reverend Samuel L. Harris, encouraged school canvasses in the branch cities and implored cashiers
to do field work. "I feel more and more the importance of this work I
am doing at the Branches and the close correspondence I have with
Cashiers. I am pressing upon our cashiers the importance of personal
labor among the people—that they may all know they have a Bank of
their own."[7]

Most of the cashiers, whatever their shortcomings in bookkeeping
and business technique, labored diligently in their communities to instruct the freedmen and increase their patronage. The Washington
cashier, William J. Wilson, increased his branch's business by personal
persuasion and by making speeches and holding meetings in the Negro
community. He designed circulars, secured the endorsement of prominent Negro leaders, and instituted a ten cent and twenty-five cent savings program for those who could not open an account with the minimum five-dollar deposit.[8] Soon Wilson could report that he had made
improvements in the Washington office and "succeeded in obtaining the
confidence and cooperation of most of the influential colored men in
Washington." He received plaudits not only for his work in Washington
but also for his efforts in Richmond, where he aided in the publicity
campaigns.[9] The assistant cashier at Norfolk likewise hoped to extend
the Bank's interests to Portsmouth, Wilmington, Hampton, and other
nearby towns. He thought he should visit Hampton weekly to collect

5. J. W. Alvord to "Sir," October 1, 1866, p. 102, Letters Sent, Book 11, Educational Division, BRFAL.

6. *Ibid.*, pp. 100–102.

7. S. L. Harris to Alvord, March 27, 1867, Bank Letters, BRFAL.

8. William J. Wilson to Alvord, August 7, 1867, *ibid.*

9. *Ibid.*; *New Era*, June 23, 1870, p. 3; Alvord to M. T. Hewitt, January 21, 1867,
pp. 259–260, Letters Sent, Book 11, Educational Division, BRFAL.

deposits. "When our circulars arrive," he predicted, "I doubt not the customers will be drawn in, for the people are already talking and inquiring about the Institution."[10]

Cashiers usually tried to arrange for local people to advertise their branches and occasionally paid those who cooperated a small honorarium. The Agency Committee reported efforts to awaken interest in the Memphis area by employing temporary traveling agents at a total cost of $150.[11] In New York the Reverend H. H. Garnet voluntarily lectured at Negro churches, telling his listeners that it was their duty to patronize the Freedman's Bank.[12] The Richmond cashier arranged for two teachers to accept the deposits of students at the First African Church and employed a black minister as an agent.[13] The pastor of the Third Street Church in Richmond suggested that there should be an agent at every church to collect deposits and receive a percentage as a commission. Impressed by this proposal, the cashier recommended it to the central office.[14]

While cashiers and local agents sought support in their own communities, officials from the principal office busied themselves on a larger scale. S. L. Harris established himself as a publicity agent. Inspecting books and checking reports by day, he lectured the freedmen at night on the values of thrift and industry. He took pains to encourage the cashiers to leave their offices and enter the field. Harris reported that at New Orleans he had "doubtless spoken to one in every twelve of the Colored people. The average in other cities is one in five. Tonight we expect an audience of 2000 persons. My address occupies about two hours and covers the history[,] safety[,] and importance of the Bank."[15] D. L. Eaton, the Bank's actuary, also made southern tours. On one occasion he called together a branch's advisory board in order to listen to reports of their work, problems, and financial situation. His meeting aroused considerable excitement and enthusiasm, and he was especially gratified by one Negro minister who vowed to speak for the Bank on his circuit. On Sunday Eaton addressed four Sunday schools, striking the theme of black economic progress.[16]

---

10. H. C. Percy to Alvord, September 16, 1865, Bank Letters, BRFAL.

11. Minutes A, October 12, 1871, p. 208.

12. William Bowen to Alvord, August 28, 1866, Bank Letters, BRFAL. Later Garnet offered to continue this work for $50 a month. The Bank's response is unknown. See Hewitt to Alvord, December 7, 1866, *ibid.*

13. Charles Spencer to Alvord, November 29, 1866, *ibid.*

14. *Ibid.* No evidence exists that this plan was put into effect.

15. Harris to Alvord, October 9, 1866, March 27, 1867, *ibid.*

16. Minutes A, June 10, 1869, pp. 110–111.

John Alvord made frequent southern tours, visiting schools and banks in his position as superintendent of schools and finances for the Freedmen's Bureau. While seldom devoting as much time to the banks as to the schools, he never neglected the company's interests. Arriving in a small Alabama or Georgia town, he would spend the day visiting the schools, churches, and the bank, and in the evening he would address a crowded meeting at the largest Negro church. There he would make some "stirring remarks" calculated to awaken interest in the schools and the Bank, and to outline the various blessings which freedom had brought.[17]

Bank officials, black leaders, and friends of the freedmen held public meetings—usually in the churches—in all the branch cities and proposed sites. At Mobile in 1867 the local cashier spoke to the congregation of the Stone Street Baptist Church about the Bank's many benefits and future plans and concluded by calling for an "expression from the Congregation to see if each one intended to open an account at once, which was agreed by acclamation." Twenty-one new depositors opened accounts the next day.[18] A similar scene unfolded at Nashville in 1868, when St. Paul's Colored Church was host to a large meeting—not, as the Nashville *Press and Times* pointedly remarked, for political purposes, but for "inculcating into the minds of the colored people the great importance of economy and money saving." The audience listened to the usual appeals to industry and to the necessity of saving to buy homes and other property.[19]

Cashier Nathaniel Noyes organized the most extensive series of public meetings at his Baltimore branch. Unsuccessful in his attempts to have General O. O. Howard, the popular commissioner of the Freedmen's Bureau, speak at the branch, Noyes settled for John W. Alvord.[20] In November, 1866, Alvord reported "another public meeting of immense enthusiasm" at Baltimore. He exhorted nearly fifteen hundred people, the majority of them men, to patronize the Bank, and he happily reported that deposits were beginning to increase.[21] Two months later Alvord reported another large meeting, this time at Baltimore's Howard Street Colored Church.[22] Noyes planned to bring his campaign to a

17. Reverend W. D. Siegfried, *A Winter in the South* (Newark: Jennings Bros., 1870), pp. 12–13; *Freedman's Bank*, House, 1876, p. 47.
18. C. A. Woodward to Alvord, March 26, 1867, Bank Letters, BRFAL.
19. Reported in *National Savings Bank*, June 1, 1868, p. 1.
20. Nathaniel Noyes to Alvord, November 23, 1866, Bank Letters, BRFAL.
21. Alvord to Hewitt, November 28, 1866, pp. 157–158, Letters Sent, Book 11, Educational Division, BRFAL.
22. Alvord to Hewitt, January 10, 1867, pp. 230–232, *ibid.*

climax with a grand meeting in mid-July, at which he intended to as-
semble delegations from the Masons, Odd Fellows, Sons of Temperance,
beneficial societies, churches, and Sunday schools to meet with Alvord,
General Gregory, himself, and, he hoped, General Howard. The purpose of this particular meeting was to persuade the Baltimore Negro
community to withdraw its funds from white banks and deposit them
in the Freedman's Bank.[23]

Noticing considerable increases in deposits after each of these gather-
ings (the Baltimore branch was probably the most successful branch
in the early years), Alvord recommended that similar meetings—"a
whole series of them"—be held at each branch, and he began to make
arrangements at Washington, Alexandria, and Richmond. His odd reaction to some problems in scheduling the Washington meetings reveals
how sacred the Bank was to him. "Were it not for the religious interest
in all the colored churches in Washington occupying their houses
of worship every evening," he complained in a gross overstatement,
the Washington bank would have the same course of meetings as
Baltimore.[24]

Bank officers supplemented the public meetings with a variety of
other materials to publicize their activities and the Bank's benefits. They
designed and published cards, circulars, and pamphlets and advertised
in Republican journals and sympathetic Democratic papers. On one
occasion they appropriated $1,500 for "judicious advertising."[25] Special
efforts were made to enlist Negro newspapers in the cause. In May,
1867, the Agency Committee resolved that the actuary should be furnished a list of newspapers published by Negroes and be instructed to
advertise in each.[26] The _South Carolina Leader_, for instance, printed
a typical advertisement announcing the hours of business and the names
of local bank leaders and declaring that "all the profits belong to the
depositors."[27] The _Louisianian_, a New Orleans Negro paper, advertised
the Bank as an "institution which gives colored men who know how to
do business the chance to be useful; it is a good school for worthy, but
inexperienced colored men to learn something of financiering; while on

23. Noyes to Alvord, March 25, 1867, Bank Letters, BRFAL.
24. Alvord to Hewitt, November 28, 1866, pp. 157–158; January 10, 1867, pp.
230–232, Letters Sent, Book 11, Educational Division, BRFAL.
25. Journal, July 8, 1869.
26. Minutes A, May 30, 1867, p. 37. The list, drawn up by Alvord, included:
Elevator (San Francisco), _Pacific Appeal_ (San Francisco), _New Orleans Tribune_,
South Carolina Leader (Charleston), _True Communicator_ (Baltimore), _Zion's
Standard and Weekly Review_ (New York), _Christian Recorder_ (Philadelphia),
People's Journal (Brooklyn), and _Colored Citizen_ (Cincinnati). See Alvord to D.
L. Eaton, June 1, 1867, Letters Sent, Book 12, Educational Division, BRFAL.
27. March 23, 1867, p. 3.

the other hand, it helps our race to lay by something for a rainy day.' "[28]

The officers entered the advertising business directly by establishing their own booster newspaper, the *National Savings Bank*, and by arranging for the publication of a history of the Bank. The latter, a somewhat gushing work by the Mobile cashier, C. A. Woodward, was entitled *Savings Banks: Their Origin, Progress and Utility, with a History of the National Savings Bank for Colored People*. It mingled some early banking history, Freedman's Bank progress reports, and extravagant praise of the Bank's character ("the most stupendous charity of the 19th century").[29] With an introduction by John Alvord and dedicated to Senator Charles Sumner, the book appeared in 1869 and was sold at several branches for thirty cents a copy.[30] The Bank's newspaper reflected a similar style and purpose; it printed homilies on saving, success stories, financial reports, and news of the branches. Distributed without charge by Bank officers, missionaries, and teachers at the branches, the journal had a circulation of 15,000 copies per month. On at least one occasion Alvord himself became a newsboy; while passing through Marietta, Georgia, "I distributed bank paper [sic] to-day from the cars which were taken by the younger freedmen who could read."[31] Because of rising costs, the trustees discontinued the paper in 1871 after three years of productive work.[32]

Every piece of Freedman's Bank literature revealed the officers' missionary zeal. Bank officials incessantly distributed, in D. L. Eaton's words, "tracts and papers . . . on temperance, frugality, economy, chastity, the virtues of thrift & savings; explaining how daily savings in small sums at interest will accumulate & the duty of men to provide for their families—and in a word giving short & simple homilies on the virtues which constitute the moral life of civilized communities."[33]

The Freedman's Bank would help bridge the chasm between slavery and freedom by encouraging ex-slaves to work. President Lincoln, it was advertised, had stated that the Bank was precisely what was

---

28. *The Louisianian* (New Orleans), May 18, 1871, p. 2. *The Louisianian* had had various titles, among them the *Weekly Louisianian* and the *Semi-Weekly Louisianian*.

29. Woodward, *Savings Banks*, p. 48; Journal, January 9, 1868, and January 21, 1869.

30. *New Era*, May 12, 1870, p. 3.

31. Alvord, *Letters from the South*, p. 28; Woodward, *Savings Banks*, p. 57.

32. Journal, December 14, 1871; *Freedman's Bank*, House, 1876, p. 16.

33. Eaton to Committee on Freedmen's Affairs, July 5, 1868, Committee on Freedmen's Affairs, National Freedman's Savings and Trust Co., Legislative Records, NA, RG 233; hereafter Committee on FA, NA, RG 233.

needed, for no country could afford to support four million paupers.[34]
Because they were now their own masters, the freedmen were told, it
was their duty to work—to provide for their own well-being and that
of their families. The Bank's paper declared, "The man who by the
plow would thrive / Himself must either hold or drive." While slavery
encouraged improvidence and irresponsibility, the Bank emphasized
thrift, the value of money, and building for the future. The *National
Savings Bank* declared that it was "each man's duty to earn all he can
honestly; to use it for the support of his family and for sending his
children to school. All after that he should put by in some safe place
where he will get interest on it."[35]

The road to wealth passed through the Freedman's Bank; the key
was steady work and patient saving. In pamphlets, deposit books, and
the *National Savings Bank* the officers recited their favorite verse:

> How doth the little busy bee
> Improve each shining hour,
> And gather honey all the day
> From every opening flower.[36]

Another of their ventures into poetry was:

> Tis little by little the bee fills her cell;
> And little by little a man sinks a well;
> Tis little by little a bird builds her nest;
> By littles a forest in verdure is drest;
> Tis little by little great volumes are made;
> By littles a mountain or levels are made;
> Tis little by little an ocean is filled;
> And little by little a city we build;
> Tis little by little an ant gets her store;
> Every little we add to a little makes more;
> Step by step we walk miles, and we sew stitch by stitch;
> Word by word we read books, cent by cent we grow rich.[37]

The buzzing beehive on the masthead of the *National Savings Bank* and
branch stationery symbolized their message.

The trustees delighted in fables; the tortoise and the hare endlessly
ran their race through the Bank's literature. Even the tritest of aphorisms and slogans never palled: "Save, Save, Save." "Save the pennies,

34. *National Savings Bank* (pamphlet), 1867, Committee on FA, NA, RG 233.
35. *Ibid.*, January 1, 1868.
36. *Ibid.*
37. *Report of the Commissioner of the Freedman's Savings and Trust Co.*, House,
1874, p. 85.

and the dollars will take care of themselves." "The ocean is made up of drops; the mountain of grains." "No good, solid wealth comes in a day."[38] "A tree grows very slowly. You cannot see it grow. Still it does grow. So with your deposits."[39]

Saving was the surest way to get a start in life, Bank literature proclaimed. "The man who earns but fifty cents a day if he spend but forty will make sure figures if slow. The man who earns five dollars a day and spends it all is on the next day the poorer man of the two, and at the end of the year the first man will have thirty dollars in hand, the other not a cent."[40] Bank officials showed with relish how a person could save a large sum by regularly banking so much per day, week, or month. Once embarked upon this line of advertising, the officers almost made a game of it. At ten cents per day, at current interest rates, a depositor could save $476.06 in ten years; at twenty-five cents per week, $169.07; at five dollars per month, $782.72; at twenty-five cents per day, $1,-190.59, and so on.[41] Some deposit books even projected the amount of savings calculated in one-half cents.[42] The *National Savings Bank* preached its dream of infinitely increasing deposits with inspirational success stories: of a black rag merchant who deposited over $1,000, the result of several years of saving; and of another Negro who kept a candy store and was able to deposit $800. Both men began with nothing, and now their interest for one year totaled nearly $100![43] In another *National Savings Bank* testimonial a hard-working shoemaker boasted, ". . . by working at my trade, [I] have saved enough to buy a farm of two hundred acres; own two mules. I rent the farm, and own the largest part of the implements. I began using the Bank in November, 1866. I have received one hundred and thirty-four dollars in interest alone."[44]

Cashiers urged their depositors to become independent farmers. The Augusta cashier, for example, advised freedmen to emulate the Yankees: buy a small piece of land and plow, hoe, and cultivate every inch of it.[45] Property-owning freedmen would raise their children to become re-

---

38. *New Era*, March 17, 1870, p. 3.

39. *National Savings Bank*, June 1, 1868, p. 2; *New Era*, May 12, 1870, p. 3.

40. Undated clipping, *New York Herald*, in Letters Rec'd by the Commissioners, 1870–1914, FS&T Co.

41. *Freedman's Savings and Trust Company* (pamphlet), 1869, p. 15.

42. Passbooks, Letters Rec'd by the Commissioners, 1870–1914, FS&T Co.

43. *National Savings Bank*, February 1, 1868, Committee on FA, NA, RG 233.

44. *National Savings Bank*, quoted in *New Era*, June 30, 1870, p. 3.

45. *National Savings Bank*, January 1, 1868, Committee on FA, NA, RG 233. Bank officials persistently used the Yankee paragon when discussing the virtues (or lack of them) of the ex-slaves. Thus a diligent shoeblack had "shown that smartness and 'cuteness' don't belong exclusively to Yankees." See *National Savings Bank* (pamphlet), 1867, Committee on FA, NA, RG 233.

spected and prosperous citizens by setting them an example of thrift.[46] The Louisville cashier asked rhetorically, "Do you want a nice little home? Do you want to be respected in the community? Do you want to be looked upon as an influential person by your acquaintances? If you do, then put all your spare earnings in the National Savings Bank."[47]

Bank literature was liberally sprinkled with stories of those who found success and happiness through buying land and homes. In one "inspirational account" a widow with three children bought a lot and was saving small amounts from her earnings as a washerwoman in order to build a house.[48] A few of the successful savers even put the hard-working shoemaker in the shade. The Beaufort cashier told of one depositor who at the close of the war owned only the clothes on his back and sixty dollars in silver hoarded through forty years of slavery. Now, the cashier reported with undisguised relish, he owned eight hundred acres of land, ran three plows, and last year hired thirteen hands.[49]

The Bank's moral teaching was also, of course, devoted to condemning sins against thrift. Bank literature warned freedmen not to use tobacco, frequent lottery dens or candy shops, wear cheap jewelry and flashy clothes, or drink liquor, for the man who did these things would remain poor.[50] Officials labeled the lottery shop the "Bank of Idleness," the whisky shop the "Bank of Misery," and the savings bank the "Bank of Happiness."[51] An 1869 pamphlet included the story of the good printer who saved his money while his fellow workers caroused during working hours. In five years he had amassed $521.86 and had not lost one day from ill health, while three out of five of his fellow workmen became drunkards and were discharged. In a storybook ending, the teetotaler purchased the business and amassed a fortune of $100,000.[52] Equally intriguing was the sad story of the mythical cigar smoker. Smoking four five-cent cigars a day, he spent twenty cents a day, or $73 in one year, or $730 in ten. Drawing interest, this money would have totaled $1,200 in ten years. "So the cigar smoker will have burnt up and blown away through his nose a nice farm of forty acres of land at

46. *National Savings and Trust Company* (pamphlet), 1867, back cover.
47. "National Savings Bank," circular, Louisville, in Index to the Deposit Ledger, Louisville, FS&T Co.
48. "Savings Bank," circular, Savannah, in letter from I. W. Brinckerhoff to Alvord, January 8, 1870, Letters Rec'd, III, Educational Division, BRFAL.
49. *New Era*, July 7, 1870, p. 3.
50. Undated clipping, *New York Herald*, in Letters Rec'd by the Commissioners, 1870–1914, FS&T Co.
51. Martin Abbott, *The Freedmen's Bureau in South Carolina, 1865–1872* (Chapel Hill: University of North Carolina Press, 1967), p. 111.
52. *Freedman's Savings and Trust Company* (pamphlet), 1869, p. 12.

Government price, a yoke of oxen, two mules, a nice cottage, and a neat, substantial barn."[53]

The evils of gambling deeply troubled the Bank. One advertisement warned that those who gambled would probably lose and become miserably poor. The Savannah cashier believed that Negroes in that city spent a good deal on lottery tickets, and those who so wasted their money were usually the ones whose families needed it most.[54] Probably Bank officials fought demon rum and gambling as much because they were evils to be stamped out as because they wasted money. Bank officials, and of course the teachers and missionaries who often voluntarily aided the Bank, came from backgrounds steeped in the early nineteenth-century reform tradition. They were reformers ready to fight the traditional vices at the drop of a hat (or rather, at the pop of a cork).[55]

Alvord and most of the cashiers were active temperance men. "Whisky," said the Tallahassee cashier, "is a subject above my comprehension—the thought of it is appalling to me." "It brings to my mind every species of degredation [sic], wretchedness, and sin."[56] The Savannah cashier, who was also a Bureau teacher, wrote a pamphlet on the subject, *A Warning to Freedmen against Intoxicating Drinks*. He described in detail the consequences of yielding to temptation: the ruin of worldly prospects, a tendency toward pauperism, enfeeblement of the mind, and destruction of body and soul. The cashier concluded with the words to a popular temperance song:

> Oh, bright is the wine, the ruby wine,
>   That sparkles in the cup;
> But dim are the eyes, the bloodshot eyes
>   Of him who quaffs it up.
>   (Chorus)
> Then shun the cup, the death-fraught cup
>   That dooms the soul to hell,
> And drink the draught, the cooling draught
>   That comes from the crystal well.[57]

53. *National Savings Bank*, June 1, 1868, p. 2.

54. *Ibid.*, February 1, 1868, Committee on FA, NA, RG 233; U.S., Congress, House, *Freedmen's Affairs in Kentucky and Tennessee*, 40th Cong., 2nd sess., 1868, House Executive Document No. 329, p. 13.

55. See the following chapter.

56. *New Era*, March 17, 1870, p. 3; Woodward to Alvord, January 22, 1868, Miscellaneous Unentered Letters Rec'd, Educational Division, BRFAL.

57. I. W. Brinckerhoff, *A Warning to Freedmen against Intoxicating Drinks*, pp. 6–10, 16, Committee on FA, NA, RG 233.

The Reverend George Whipple, a Bank trustee and the American Missionary Society's corresponding secretary, was once shocked to discover that a Norfolk cashier was not pledged to temperance and even took a drink now and then. Norfolk soon had a new cashier.[58]

Just as the righteous man found security from worldly temptation in sober conduct, so his savings were secure from the world's threats in the Freedman's Bank. Much Bank advertising stressed this issue of safety. The Bank's paper told of one depositor who opened an account with $200 and an apology for not saving more, but a friend had recently filched $25. Asked if he regarded such a man as a friend, the depositor replied that the man would have taken all of his money had he not been a friend. The moral was that freedmen should put their money in the Savings Bank, where their friends could not get at it.[59] Fear of loss or theft, the *National Savings Bank* attempted to show, could have far-reaching consequences. For example, many husbands and wives could not attend church together because someone had to remain at home to guard their money.[60] And the man who was guarding his money had many worries: "The wind blows the boughs of the tree against the window at night, and the good man of the house lies awake all night because he thinks somebody is breaking in to get his money."[61] Cashiers urged depositors to take advantage of the Bank's fireproof vaults and emphasized the foolishness of keeping money at home where it could be stolen or destroyed by fire. Who ever heard of the loss of money at the Freedman's Bank, they asked.

Advertisements declared that "no matter what happens to the Bank, it will pay back the money; for no amount that can be lost, burned up, or stolen at any of these Banks can in the least affect the depositor's money." Rarely did advertisements omit statistics of increasing deposits and lists of the important branch cities, while almost every pamphlet included paragraphs on the company's progress. The symbols on the Bank's stationery—the wide-open eye and the vault—suggested watchfulness and security,[62] while the literature promised, "all profits go to the depositors, or to the educational purposes for the freedmen and their descendants."[63]

58. Reverend George Whipple to Alvord, July 19, 1867, Miscellaneous Unentered Letters Rec'd, Educational Division, BRFAL.

59. *New Era*, July 28, 1870, p. 1; *National Savings Bank*, February 1, 1868, Committee on FA, NA, RG 233.

60. *National Savings Bank*, February 1, 1868, Committee on FA, NA, RG 233.

61. *Ibid.*

62. Pamphlets and circulars of the Freedman's Bank in Library of Congress; see also Bank stationery found in FS&T Co.

63. *National Savings and Trust Company* (pamphlet), 1867; *New Era*, September 1, 1870, p. 3.

Every depositor received his own deposit book, which summarized the safety features of the Bank, mingling excerpts from pamphlets, the charter, and the bylaws. The books were, to be sure, records of deposits and withdrawals, but in addition they made excellent individualized advertising pamphlets. On the covers of one set of deposit books stood President Lincoln, holding in one hand the broken shackles of slavery and resting the other upon the "Freedman's Safe." The imposing vault was guarded by an eagle and a large mastiff. In the background were a United States flag, a warship, and the inscriptions, "The Freedman's Savings and Trust Company" and "Lincoln and Freedom"; pictures of Howard, Grant, Sherman, Stanton, and Farragut surrounded the entire scene.[64] The symbols of freedom had become the symbols of bank safety.

Newspaper advertisements and circulars relied strongly upon the names of Bureau officials (especially Howard) and Union generals (Grant and Sherman) as examples of integrity and security. Usually advertisements featured the names of leaders of the local advisory boards as well.[65] Most common was the egregious use of Abraham Lincoln's name. Said one 1867 pamphlet:

> Abraham Lincoln's Gift
> to the
> Colored People
> His Signature to the Bill one of the last acts of his life
>
> He gave *Emancipation*, and then this Savings Bank.
> Your *freedom* and *prosperity* were in his heart united.[66]

The name of Jay Cooke, the famous Civil War financier, appeared frequently in Bank advertisements, although he had no connection with the Bank and was associated with it only tangentially because his brother and business partner, Henry D. Cooke, became chairman of the Finance Committee in mid-1867.[67] That the Cookes had no connection with the Bank before 1867 did not prevent the *Semi-Weekly Louisianian* from praising their roles in its establishment.[68] Later Bank officials used the Civil War fame of Jay Cooke specifically to bolster confidence in the Bank's investment policy and generally to highlight the Bank's sound financial standing.

64. See, for example, passbooks, esp. No. 720, John Johnson, Mobile, Ala., Letters Rec'd by the Commissioners, 1870–1914, FS&T Co.
65. See, for example, *Vicksburg Weekly Republican*, October 3, 1869, p. 3; *Alabama State Journal* (Montgomery), June 19, 1870, p. 3.
66. *National Savings Bank*, February 1, 1868, Committee on FA, NA, RG 233.
67. *Alabama State Journal*, June 19, 1870, p. 3.
68. October 26, 1871, p. 2.

In many ways the propaganda stretched the truth to the breaking point by implicating the government in Bank affairs. The officers pointed frequently to the complete safety of the Bank's investments in government securities. "Unless utter destruction sweep the nation out of existence," the bonds would be good.[69] "It is safe. It can not fail, for it is founded on the United States Government. No money loaned to individuals. There is no speculation, and consequently no risk in this Bank. Economy and good faith cardinal features in its management."[70] Frequently the Bank hinted that the government sponsored it and guaranteed its business. What other conclusion were the freedmen to draw from the claim that the government had "made this bank perfectly safe"?[71] The *Semi-Weekly Louisianian* declared that "there is no possibility of loss, for the reason that the government of the United States is responsible for every dollar deposited." "Every security is assured to depositors by the guarantee of the National Government."[72] The covers of many deposit books implied government sponsorship; a typical New York branch book displayed on its cover,

> Chartered by the United States
> Freedman's Savings & Trust Company
> (a National Savings Bank)

There followed a replica of the seal of the United States, with an eagle clutching in its claws an olive branch and arrows and holding in its beak a banner inscribed with E Pluribus Unum.[73] Frequently the Freedman's Bank was called the "National Savings Bank" or the "National Freedman's Savings and Trust Company." The New York City Directory of 1869–70 even listed the Freedman's Bank under "national" rather than "savings" banks. Small wonder that most freedmen never knew that the only power Congress had over the Bank was the right to inspect the books if it wished—which it didn't. Many people, black and white, came to believe that the Freedman's Savings and Trust Company was a government institution similar to the Freedmen's Bureau.

In general, Freedman's Bank literature, with all its edifying homilies, aphorisms, and stories, was characteristic of its day, and in many ways

69. *The Charter and By-Laws of the Freedman's Savings and Trust Company* (pamphlet), 1872, p. 7.

70. "National Savings Bank," circular, Louisville, in Index to the Deposit Ledger, Louisville, FS&T Co.

71. Advertisement in Passbook No. 901, James Brown, Tallahassee, Fla., Letters Rec'd by the Commissioners, 1870–1914, FS&T Co.

72. December 29, 1870, p. 2; June 1, 1871, p. 2.

73. See cover of New York passbooks, Letters Rec'd by the Commissioners, 1870–1914, FS&T Co.

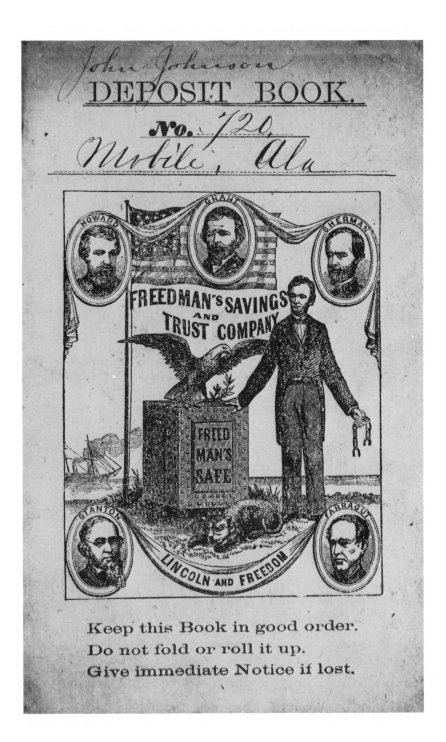

John Johnson

DEPOSIT BOOK.

No. *720.*

Mobile, Ala.

HOWARD GRANT SHERMAN

FREEDMAN'S SAVINGS AND TRUST COMPANY

FRIED MAN'S SAFE

STANTON FARRAGUT

LINCOLN AND FREEDOM

Keep this Book in good order.
Do not fold or roll it up.
Give immediate Notice if lost.

No. **5861** *C.*

Thomas Roe ✗

Susan H. Roe

CHARTERED BY THE
UNITED STATES.

Freedman's Savings & Trust Company

(A NATIONAL SAVINGS BANK.)

185 BLEECKER STREET,
NEW YORK.

BANK HOURS.

Daily, Sundays and Holidays excepted, from 9 o'clock A. M. to 4 o'clock P. M., and on Monday and Saturday nights, from 5 to 8 o'clock P. M.

it markedly resembled the moralizing literature directed at poor white laborers. The Bank's literature was most certainly not cynical. The officials had absolute faith in the Bank's mission; they truly believed a man could become rich by saving small amounts, and that the Bank would enable freedmen to become morally respectable citizens. Years later Frederick Douglass reflected, perhaps in disillusion, on the purposes and methods of the officials:

> Their aim was now to instill into the minds of the untutored Africans lessons of sobriety, wisdom, and economy, and to show them how to rise in the world. Like snowflakes in winter, the circulars, tracts and other papers were, by this benevolent institution, scattered among the sable millions, and they were told to "look" to the Freedmen's Bank and "live." [74]

The results of this educational campaign are to be seen in the phenomenal increase of black people's deposits between 1868 and 1873.

If the tone of the Bank's advertising reflected the general spirit of the age, the actual operations of the Bank reflected its specific role in the complex of institutions which set out to protect and uplift the freedmen in the Reconstruction South. From the beginning the officers called upon missionary and freedmen's aid associations for help. [75] The teachers, religious workers, Freedmen's Bureau officials, and Bank officers who went South to work among the freedmen perceived that they had similar programs and common goals. Together they formed a white mission to the former slaves.

Alvord and other officials took care to select cashiers who could carry out the grand missionary purpose. The cashiers' business acumen, diligence, honesty, and, most significantly, rapport with the people would determine the success of the Bank. Officially their duties were restricted: cashiers received deposits and withdrawals, recorded all financial transactions in the bank ledgers and depositors' passbooks, forwarded all sums to Washington (except a small working capital), and provided the central office with business statements. [76] But as chief officers of a financial institution in the black community, cashiers could not be confined to the banking office or the business day. They would have to go

74. Frederick Douglass, *Life and Times of Frederick Douglass* (Hartford: Park Publishing Co., 1881), p. 409.

75. Eaton to Col. J. R. Lewis, May 21, 1869, Letters Rec'd by Georgia Superintendent of Education, III, Educational Division, BRFAL; Minutes A, 1869, p. 125; "Freedman's Savings and Trust Company," circular, April 12, 1866, AMA Archives, Amistad Research Center.

76. Minutes A, June 13, 1865, p. 4.

into the community to stimulate business and encourage people to deposit their money; they would have to occupy Alvord's counter and pulpit. Consequently the responsibilities of a banker (which were more aptly those of a bookkeeper) were subordinated to those of a preacher and publicity agent.[77] It was not of primary importance that many cashiers had relatively little business experience. Indeed, some were new to the business of bookkeeping, although it is untrue, as critics later charged, that some were unlettered.[78] The aim of Alvord and other Bank officials was to arrange matters so completely that any honest man of moderate business capacity could soon learn the routine.[79] Humanitarianism, a desire to work among the freedmen, honesty, diligence, piety, and morality (as defined by nineteenth-century reformers) came to be higher criteria than business training in selecting the cashiers. Thus it was reassuring when a bank employee would ask Alvord to "remember in prayer those of us away from home and friends."[80] If one's heart were right, how could he do wrong?

In piety, morality, and honesty, if not in business capacity, the cashiers had to be practically above reproach. A bank, said Anson Sperry, was to some extent like a woman's virtue: one allegation against it and all is lost.[81] This the cashier at Wilmington woefully learned. A member of "the mission family," the cashier suddenly found his financial condition and moral character questioned because of his attentions to young ladies, the name of an American Missionary Association teacher being raised specifically.[82]

It was extremely important to the Bank's missionary purpose that its closest associates in the black communities be recognized humanitarians. Applicants for cashier had especially impressive credentials if they were ministers, the assumption of course being that ministers were usually honest and moral men. Furthermore, the work of the clergyman, preaching Christian ethics and morality, and the work of the cashier, teaching hard work, self-discipline, abstention, and thrift, coincided; the Protestant ethic was fundamental to both. Thus it was that ministers occupied the office of cashier for various periods at Alexandria,

77. Alvord to "Sir," October 1, 1866, Letters Sent, Book 11, Educational Division, BRFAL.

78. *Freedman's Bank*, House, 1876, p. 2; Hewitt to Alvord, September 16, 1865, Bank Letters, BRFAL.

79. Alvord to Harris, September 15, 1866, Letters Sent, Book 11, Educational Division, BRFAL.

80. Harris to Alvord, November 1, 1867, Bank Letters, BRFAL.

81. *Report of the Select Committee*, Senate, 1880, p. 249.

82. Alvord to Whipple, August 13, 1869, AMA.

Atlanta, Chattanooga, Jacksonville, Macon, New Bern, Savannah, Vicksburg, and Wilmington.[83]

Cashiers often were teachers, and even when engaged full time at the Bank they aided the educational work and kept informed of school affairs—a connection which proved extremely useful in teaching principles of thrift. Cashiers were teachers, principals, or superintendents of schools in at least twelve branch cities.[84] At Augusta, where the cashier, Charles H. Prince, was deeply involved in school affairs and was for a while state superintendent of education, the Bank easily worked through the schools.[85] S. L. Harris's statement that "I am having the schools here thoroughly canvassed in the interest of the Bank, and the children are depositing" seems to summarize the general situation at many branches.[86] The Bank's affinity for educational work was symbolized by the large number of its officers and trustees who served on the board of trustees of Howard University, the newly created Negro college founded by Bureau officials and Congregational Church members.[87]

Seeking dedicated individuals to serve in the cause of racial uplift, Alvord and his associates relied heavily upon northern missionaries. At least forty-six of the approximately sixty-eight cashiers who served during the Bank's entire history were white men, almost all from the North.[88] With the possible exception of the two at Louisville and Baltimore, there is no evidence that any cashier was ever a native white Southerner. The white men who became cashiers came South as ministers, Bureau or AMA teachers, Bureau agents, missionaries in religious or educational work, Sabbath school aides, Republican politicians, or army officers or chaplains. As such, it was assumed that they could provide the missionary leadership and the necessary outside counterforce to white southern hostility and intransigence.

83. See Appendix C.
84. Noyes to Alvord, January 15, 1866; Harris to Hewitt, February 6, 1867, Bank Letters, BRFAL; William J. Wilson to Whipple, October 25, 1865, AMA; Minutes A, June 10, 1869, p. 113; S. S. Ashley to Alvord, March 13, 1867, Letters Rec'd, I, Educational Division, BRFAL. The branch cities were Atlanta, Augusta, Baltimore, Chattanooga, Columbus (Miss.), Lexington (Ky.), Little Rock, Montgomery, Norfolk, Shreveport, Washington, and Wilmington. See Appendix C.
85. Minutes A, July 9, 1868, p. 71; Harris to Hewitt, February 6, 1867, Bank Letters, BRFAL; *Biographical Directory of the American Congress, 1774–1961*, p. 1483. After a few years in the Bank's service, Charles H. Prince resigned and entered politics, winning a seat in Congress as a Republican.
86. Harris to Alvord, November 1, 1867, Bank Letters, BRFAL.
87. Dyson, *Howard University*, ch. 1.
88. For brief descriptions of the individual cashiers, see Appendix C. The black cashiers are discussed in ch. 4.

While the Bank welcomed support from all those who labored in their cause, it established the closest possible ties with the two greatest organizations in the field, the Freedmen's Bureau and the American Missionary Association. The AMA, the Bureau, and the Bank—the weakest member of this missionary triad—worked together throughout the South. Indeed, in the course of time it became difficult for Southerners to distinguish between them, for their personnel and finances interlocked at all levels.

The origin of the Bank's connection with the American Missionary Association extends all the way back to the Lane Rebellion in 1833 and the founding of Oberlin College, when antislavery Lane Rebels George Whipple and John Alvord became fellow theological students and close friends. Whipple and Alvord graduated from Oberlin Theological Seminary in 1836 and labored together for the next three decades in the antislavery cause. Whipple, a Congregational minister like Alvord and until 1846 an Oberlin professor of mathematics, was serving as the AMA's corresponding secretary when he helped to found and organize the Freedman's Bank. He was a Bank trustee throughout its existence.[89] The AMA, founded in 1846 by three midwestern antislavery societies, was thickly populated with Oberlin graduates, many of them friends of Whipple and Alvord. According to Robert S. Fletcher, "Oberlin was a dominating factor in the society; up to 1860 over nine-tenths of all its workers were former Oberlin students, and both its able executive secretaries, George Whipple and Michael Strieby, came from Oberlin."[90] The AMA rose to be the strongest missionary association in the post-bellum South; certainly it was foremost in educating the freedmen, a fact which gave the Bank excellent leverage through its AMA connections. Although associated with the Congregational Church, the AMA was more successful in tapping the funds of Northern evangelical Christians of different denominations than any other freedmen's aid group. When the Freedmen's Bureau was created in 1865, it was natural for the AMA to become interested in the new government agency.

General O. O. Howard made the acquaintance of Alvord while marching through Georgia with General Sherman in 1864. The Christian General Howard and Alvord, the secretary of the American Tract Society, became close friends, and it was probably Alvord who introduced

89. Oberlin College, *Alumni Register: Graduates and Former Students, Teaching and Administrative Staff,* 1833–1960; Drake, "American Missionary Association," pp. 66, 40–55 *passim.*

90. Drake, "American Missionary Association," pp. 3–4; Robert Samuel Fletcher, *A History of Oberlin College from Its Foundation through the Civil War* (Oberlin: Oberlin College, 1943), I, 259.

Whipple to Howard. Alvord and Whipple, ordained ministers in Howard's Congregational Church and zealous apostles of evangelicalism and anti-slavery, commended themselves to Howard's sense of missionary zeal. The three formed an intimate friendship.[91] Howard appointed Alvord superintendent of schools and finances for the Freedmen's Bureau; the latter thereupon turned for support to Oberlin graduates and his AMA friends. Frequently Alvord and Whipple suggested missionaries and Oberlin graduates as workers for Howard's Bureau. John Mercer Langston, Negro lawyer and graduate of Oberlin's Collegiate and Theological departments, became general inspector of Bureau schools. Later he was an important Bank trustee. John H. Cook, another Oberlin Negro graduate, was chief clerk of the Bureau between 1867 and 1872, and Captain O. S. B. Wall, a Negro businessman from Oberlin, was appointed employment agent of the Bureau. Later he too would be a trustee of the Freedman's Bank. The AMA workers in the South became Howard's eyes and ears, keeping him informed of the activities of his own Bureau agents. Oberlin College itself benefited from this connection with the Bureau. "Howard, Alvord and Langston were naturally partial to Oberlin men and women and to the Oberlin-affiliated American Missionary Association. Bureau funds to the extent of nearly a quarter-of-a-million were turned over to the Association for the extension of its educational program. Money was even allocated to Oberlin to help build college buildings, because it trained so many white and Negro teachers for the South. In 1868, nearly a quarter (532) of all the teachers under Alvord's supervision (2,300) were supplied by the Oberlin-dominated AMA."[92] Howard became a faithful member of the executive committee of the AMA and extended financial aid to the association. Indeed, the Bureau aid given to the AMA seems to have been larger than that extended to any other freedmen's aid society. In obtaining government funds through the Bureau for educational work in the South, the AMA played down its denominational character, although this connection hardly seems to have bothered the Congregational Howard.[93]

Alvord tied the Freedman's Bank and the AMA together as closely as possible on the local level. In many branches this was easily accomplished by appointing AMA personnel to Bank cashierships. At least nine cashiers were AMA teachers, principals, or superintendents, while another nine worked for the AMA in other capacities. The Bank always showed a very decided preference for AMA ministers and teachers as

91. Drake, "American Missionary Association," pp. 26, 36, 37, 40–43.
92. *Ibid.*, p. 70; Fletcher, *History of Oberlin College*, II, 913–914.
93. Drake, "American Missionary Association," pp. 40–43, 59, 63.

cashiers and used every means to work its way into the schools. The Beaufort cashier, for instance, encouraged the AMA to continue its schools in his area and offered to serve as superintendent of education without compensation. He also offered to open his home to the teachers until they could become settled permanently. The cashiers and assistant cashiers at Memphis were frequently involved with the AMA schools, ordering books and on occasion recommending teachers.[94] Cashier Edwin Beecher of Montgomery wrote the AMA informing it of his regrets on the conclusion of its educational work in his city. He argued indirectly for a continuation of its work, for the AMA was the only means of educating Negroes in Montgomery. The Southern teachers, he believed, would shortchange the freedmen.[95] Finally, the close association between the AMA and the Bank was financial as well as administrative and organizational. The AMA used the Freedman's Bank to handle its fiscal affairs at Norfolk, Jacksonville, Wilmington, Nashville, Chattanooga, Memphis, Savannah, and Atlanta.[96]

The activities of H. C. Percy and John G. Hamilton, Bank cashiers and superintendents of schools, illuminate the close connection between the AMA and the Bank in two branch cities, Norfolk and Lexington. The New England–raised Percy supervised the schools in his AMA position in Norfolk and Portsmouth and became deeply involved with their mundane problems of supply, repairs, construction, and financing.[97] As if the official duties of the Bank and schools were not enough, he took on many other time-consuming tasks. "I presume I need not *tell you*" he wrote to the corresponding secretary of the AMA, "that the 'man in charge' at a Mission House where *fourteen ladies* reside, if he has nothing else to do, will find plenty of business for his stray minutes. (or, at least, *they* will!)"[98] In the following year he had charge of a large Sabbath school and was assisting with a mission school. He also somehow found time to take part in a battle against the dramshops.[99]

Percy received $100 per month for his community services, one-third from the Bank and the remainder from the AMA, but the combined pay was hardly sufficient to support one man. Percy viewed his salary as

94. Nelson R. Scovel to the Rev. E. P. Smith, March 5, 1868, and October 20, 1869; Charles J. Smith to E. M. Cravath, May 23, 1872; A. M. Sperry to Whipple, May 26, 1868, AMA.

95. Edwin Beecher to "Dear Sir," August 19, 1871, *ibid.*

96. Drake, "American Missionary Association," p. 68.

97. Percy to the Rev. E. P. Smith, October 26, 1866; Percy to William E. Whiting, September 22 and 29, 1866; Percy to Whipple, November 6, 1866, AMA.

98. Percy to Whipple, November 6, 1866, *ibid.*

99. Percy to Whipple, November 29, 1867, *ibid.*

"a low price for the service rendered. No man,—save as he might work for love of the cause—would agree to fill my place for less than $125. per month. But I *do* love the cause—hence my terms."[100] There is some evidence that Percy, quite untrained in accounting, mixed up the finances of the schools and the Bank. He wrote:

> Have received $58.00 from other sources, this month, and spent nearly $800.00 which I advanced from Cash of our "Savings Bank." This being not the "regular" way of doing business, I have paid this loan from S.B. [Savings Bank] by depositing a Draft "No. 8" for $700.00 on your [AMA] Treasury. I will have all right again in about a month.[101]

The Bank's Lexington cashier, John G. Hamilton, was a young Oberlin graduate who had journeyed South at the end of the war as an AMA missionary teacher. Ostracized by the white community, he worked diligently among Negroes and was largely responsible for the Northern contributions which financed the new schoolhouse in Lexington.[102] For Hamilton the work of the Bank was at first largely secondary, for, as he put it, the schools had become "the apple of my eye."[103] He attended to Bank matters after school hours, employing an assistant to manage the daily business. "Occasionally I am called to the Bank to meet emergencies and I do not want the school interests to suffer."[104]

Hamilton soon had to readjust his priorities, for the Bank needed more attention. Once the school was organized, he devoted himself to the Bank and paid the school only occasional or emergency visits. He found this arrangement rather unsatisfactory and began to think that dividing his attention between the two "must work injury to *one* if not *both*." But the chairman of the Lexington advisory board held the opposite view; he believed that the work of the schools and the Bank was a unit, and he advised Hamilton not to sever his connection with the schools for that would be harmful to the Bank.[105] Hamilton eventually concluded that he "ought to hold carefully every position of usefulness and influence and cause them to benefit each other," and so he shouldered the double burden until 1874.[106] The Bank's identification with the AMA was extremely important to its fortunes, though it grossly overworked men like Percy and Hamilton.

The Bank's connections with the Freedmen's Bureau were just as

100. Percy to the Rev. Samuel Hunt, October 3, 1866, *ibid.*
101. Percy to Whiting, November 13, 1866, *ibid.*
102. *Report of the Commissioners*, 1874, p. 71.
103. John G. Hamilton to Cravath, December 5, 1871, AMA.
104. Hamilton to Cravath, November 14, 1870, *ibid.*
105. Hamilton to Cravath, December 18, 1871, *ibid.*
106. Hamilton to Cravath, April 23, 1874, *ibid.*

intimate as those with the American Missionary Association. Eventually the Bureau came to provide free advertising, travel expenses, advisory personnel, and vital savings in expenses, and sometimes Bureau workers became cashiers. Between 1867 and 1869 the Bank and the Bureau worked so closely together that freedmen quite naturally assumed that the Bank was part of the Bureau or, at the very least, a government institution similar to the Bureau.

At the highest levels several Bank officials held Bureau positions. John W. Alvord, with his dual positions in the Bank and the Bureau, provided the most important link between the two organizations; by 1867 several other Bureau officials—General George Balloch, the chief disbursing officer; General Eliphalet Whittlesey, the Bureau's Adjutant General; and Colonel A. P. Ketchum, an aide to the commissioner—were also serving as Bank trustees.[107] General O. O. Howard himself was closely associated with the Bank. He was intimately acquainted with high officials in both organizations and had been coaxed to accept the positions of trustee and vice-president of the Bank. He had declined because of his many burdensome duties, although sentiment and interest—as in the case of his brother, Charles, who sat on the Bank's Agency Committee—tempted him to accept.[108] Later, in 1870, he may have been a trustee for a month, and in 1872 he was elected to that position once again but refused to serve. In 1871, although having no official connections with the Bank, he was sufficiently close to its administrative affairs to urge a friend to become a trustee of "our National Freedman's Saving and Trust Company."[109]

Because of Howard's enormous prestige among the masses of freedmen, it was of great consequence that he looked on the Bank with favor. The deposit books repeated his famous statement, "I consider the Freedmen's Savings and Trust Company to be greatly needed by the Colored People, and have welcomed it as an auxiliary to the Freedmen's Bureau."[110] His preaching of the virtues of thrift and saving to the freedmen was extremely useful in the Bank's advertising. Howard also commended the Bank to his officers in all the southern states.[111]

107. Alvord to Harris, May 19, 1867, Letters Sent, Book 12, Educational Division, BRFAL.

108. *Ibid.*; Journal, September 14, 1865.

109. Howard to R. P. Buck, October 14, 1871, O. O. Howard Papers, Bowdoin College Library; *Charges against General Howard*, p. 393; John A. Carpenter, *Sword and Olive Branch: Oliver Otis Howard* (Pittsburgh: University of Pittsburgh Press, 1964), p. 189.

110. Pamphlets concerning Freedman's Savings and Trust Company (1867, 1869, 1872) in Library of Congress.

111. *New Era*, March 31, 1870, p. 3.

In spite of Howard's endorsements, Bank officials were disappointed with the Bureau in 1865 and 1866, for they were seeking substantial financial aid and close cooperation between the two organizations. Bureau aid was more apparent than real because the Bureau itself was hard pressed for funds. Apart from Howard's gestures and the fact that the Bureau paid the expenses of the Washington branch, Bank officials thought they got little real cooperation from the Bureau in the first years.

This was not exactly true, since in at least one branch city, and probably in others, mutual cooperation had existed from the beginning. At Vicksburg things got off to a most promising start. The cashier wrote,

> Col. Thomas [assistant commissioner in Mississippi] is Chairman of the Advisory Committee, to whom all reports are made and by whom all accounts and statements are examined and approved. The bank receipts which I used in its business were printed (in blank) by Col. Thomas' order, in his office, and bear the imprint of the Bureau, and the Bureau furnishes $750.00 a month for the contingent expenses of the bank, by order of the Assistant Commissioner. From this it is easy to see that the two institutions are distinct, but NOT separate; and Col. Thomas is the virtual President of the Mississippi Branch of the "National Freedmen's Saving [sic] and Trust Company.
>
> I opened the business of the bank while an officer of the Bureau, and under Col. Thomas' direction and in his office.[112]

But in the absence of policy guidance from Bureau and Bank headquarters, local relationships of this sort could easily turn sour, as was certainly the case at Vicksburg. Bank President Hewitt charged that the Vicksburg branch was being ruined by antagonism between Bureau and Bank personnel, and by early 1867 he was denying that General Howard had given any significant aid to the Bank. Howard, he wrote, "could have done us a great service, but he had not 'Confidence' as Mr. A. [Alvord] stated. That is a thing of growth."[113]

This quarrel between the Bank and the Bureau resulted in a crisis of confidence and reduced deposits, both of which thoroughly frightened Bank officials. The trouble at Vicksburg forced Hewitt to clarify the Bank's policy toward the Bureau. He appealed to Colonel Samuel Thomas, the offending assistant commissioner of Mississippi, for aid, counsel, and cooperation from the Freedmen's Bureau as from all benev-

---

112. Undated Vicksburg newspaper clipping, found in letter from Col. S. Thomas to Alvord, February 13, 1866, Bank Letters, BRFAL.

113. Alvord to Hewitt, October 5, 1866, Letters Sent, Book 11, Educational Division, BRFAL; Hewitt to W. A. Booth, January 30, 1867, Bank Letters, BRFAL.

olent friends of the Negro.[114] Hewitt regretted the difficulties and affirmed that "we are confident in the perfect safety of deposits and trust you will inspire the negro with that fact, and the importance to him of saving his money."[115] Shortly thereafter Hewitt laid down the rule that Bank agents were not to quarrel with the Bureau.[116] The Bank managed to iron out its differences with the Mississippi Bureau, and by March, 1867, harmonious relations had been restored. When the Vicksburg branch threatened to collapse in the Bank's 1867 crisis, General Gillem, assistant commissioner of the Bureau in Mississippi, urged that the branch be kept open. He feared that if it closed "the people—though each one may get all he is entitled to—will lose confidence in our stability and would never hereafter deposit should we again open the Branch." General Gillem promised to support the Vicksburg branch.[117]

It was fortunate that these harmonious relations had been restored, since with the general crisis and need for retrenchment in 1867 the Bank officials were able to turn to the Bureau for support. Bank officials, rather than approaching the Bureau with accounts of impending catastrophe, recounted their glowing hopes for the institution, and succeeded in convincing General Howard that their company stood on the threshold of prosperity and needed only encouragement and a rise in the level of deposits to bring success.[118] When the commissioner attended a trustees' meeting in New York in early 1867, officials worked out a semi-formal plan of organization. From the Bureau's Washington headquarters to branch cities all over the South, Bank and Bureau officers would work closely together. To realize the promise of Bureau support, Bank officials took a momentous step: they transferred the home office from New York to Washington so that they could share offices and personnel in the nation's capital. In April Alvord informed the financial inspector about this new arrangement.

> They changed the ByLaws, & bring the Principal Office here [to Washington] placing the Bank, for the time being, under the special auspices of the Bureau. This, I think accords with your judgment. Such aid will be rendered by Gen'l Howard as will relieve us very soon of the present embarrassment. The bounty moneys . . . will be passed over to the Claimants on 'their order' as held by our Cashiers, to a great ex-

114. Hewitt to Thomas, February 26, 1866, Bank Letters, BRFAL; *National Encyclopedia of American Biography*, XXV, 31.
115. Hewitt to Thomas, February 26, 1866, Bank Letters, BRFAL.
116. Hewitt to Alvord, July 28, 1866, *ibid.*
117. Harris to Alvord, March 6, 1867, *ibid.*
118. Alvord to Booth, February 12 and April 20, 1867, Letters Sent, Book 12, Educational Division, BRFAL.

tent; and thus we hope, by right influence, to obtain a larger amount of deposits.[119]

"The Bureau," said Alvord in early 1867, "will favor our Bank in this business all it can—but how much this will be cannot be told, until we have some practical experience."[120] As the Bank and the Bureau put their agreement into practice, they drew closely together, assuming a similar appearance. "Here at Hd Qrs.," wrote Alvord, "we look very much like one concern—a number of Bureau Officers occupying the back room of our Bank, though, as before said, we are really only in fraternity as institutions."[121]

Thus in early 1867 Howard committed the Bureau to aid the Bank in return for the help of the Bank's cashiers in identifying and paying Negro bounty claimants in southern cities.[122] The Bank was only too happy to accommodate. The Bank and the Bureau saw reciprocal advantages in close association, and of course both were interested in uplifting the ex-slaves.

After the merger Bureau officers in all areas of the South helped in extending the influence of their "auxiliary institution." For example, in Memphis a Colonel Palmer arranged meetings between the Bank's inspector and the local people.[123] Bureau agents felt that "It is for the interest of the colored men that these banks should be protected and promoted."[124] In 1868 Major General Nelson A. Miles, assistant commissioner in North Carolina, was the prime mover in the formation of the Raleigh branch. He suggested the possibility of establishing a branch in that city, drew up a tentative list of local trustees, which included W. W. Holden, governor of North Carolina, and when the Bank was established issued an order recommending it to the freedmen of his state.[125] Another Bureau official, General William P. Carlin, attempted to bring a branch to Knoxville because, as he believed, it was essential to save the freedmen's bounty money and induce the local population to deposit its money until needed for purchasing homes.[126]

Bureau officials especially paid tribute to the Bank's educational and

119. Alvord to Harris, April 19, 1867, *ibid.*
120. Alvord to Hewitt, March 30, 1867, *ibid.*
121. Alvord to Harris, May 19, 1867, *ibid.*
122. *Ibid.*; March 26, 1867, *ibid.*; Alvord to Hewitt, April 4, 1867, *ibid.*
123. Harris to Alvord, February 12, 1867, Bank Letters, BRFAL.
124. H. C. Corson to Howard, February 17, 1870, Letters Rec'd, III, Educational Division, BRFAL.
125. Minutes A, January 9, 1868, p. 57; July 9, 1868, p. 75.
126. Report on Knoxville, Superintendent of Education Burt to Gen. William P. Carlin, May 8, 1867, Letters Sent by the Tennessee Superintendent of Education, XXXVI, Educational Division, BRFAL.

moral work. Their statements provided good advertising copy. The *National Savings Bank* featured General Wager Swayne's endorsement of the Bank.

> No matter how small the week's earnings may be, it is not very hard to lay by part of it, though but a little. To do this is to provide a support in case of accident or sickness, to be able to do something for a friend in need, and to avoid useless and expensive habits. The Freedman's Savings and Trust Company offers to colored persons the best and safest opportunity I know to do this, and I recommend it warmly.[127]

William Colby, the first cashier of the Little Rock branch and Bureau superintendent of education for Arkansas, praised the Bank's newspaper as the type of reading needed by the freedmen. "Habits of temperate living and systematic saving," he said, "are of primary importance to all classes and ages of colored people."[128] The superintendent of education for Virginia, R. M. Manly, reported to Howard that temperance and the savings bank "are made an important staple in all educational addresses by myself and my assistants. Education, temperance and economy are subjects vitally connected in the present and future of the freedmen."[129] Bureau agents encouraged the Bank's program of juvenile finance (as did the AMA) by teaching economy and thrift in their schools.[130] One superintendent of education described the results of the Bureau's and the Bank's cooperation: "The three savings banks in my district are known and patronized by many of the pupils in our schools. The little paper issued by the company is circulated extensively among them. In spite of the many extravagances in which these children are indulged, very many of them are learning to save their money; a most important element of a good education."[131]

The financial aid given by the Bureau was perhaps as significant as official endorsements, personal encouragement, and free advertising. Immediately after the plans for cooperation had been formulated,

127. *National Savings Bank*, June 1, 1868, p. 2.

128. William Colby to Alvord, November 12, 1868, Letters Sent by the Arkansas Superintendent of Education, Educational Division, BRFAL.

129. R. M. Manly, Report to Howard, January 1, 1870, Letters Sent by the Virginia Superintendent of Education, LIV, Educational Division, BRFAL.

130. Woodward to Alvord, April 9, 1867, Bank Letters, BRFAL; John W. Alvord, *Ninth Semi-Annual Report on Schools for Freedmen*, January 1, 1870: *Semi-Annual Reports on Schools and Finances for Freedmen, 1866–70* (Washington: Government Printing Office, 1866–70), p. 65. Hereafter reports in this series will be designated by author, title, and date.

131. Alvord, *Eighth Semi-Annual Report on Schools for Freedmen*, July 1, 1869, p. 17.

Howard provided the Washington branch with a much better office and had it furnished in style.[132] Besides furnishing this office and several others, the Bureau paid the rent of numerous branches, including those at Tallahassee, Jacksonville, Washington, Norfolk, Vicksburg, Beaufort, and Charleston.[133] At Wilmington and Richmond the Bank and the Bureau shared the same office, with the latter organization paying the bill.[134] The Bureau also paid the traveling expenses of the several cashiers who had received appointments as bounty agents.[135] This financial aid reduced the Bank's expenses enormously. For example, the operating costs of one particular branch amounted to $750, but the Bureau allocated to it the sum of $800 for the numerous duties it performed.[136] According to one estimate, the Bureau paid one-third of the Bank's expense in some years.[137]

The intimate association between the Bank and the Bureau is exemplified by Bank cashiers who also served as Bureau disbursing officers. The combined offices were mutually beneficial: the Bank influenced Negroes who received large sums of bounty money, while the Bureau obtained a reliable, honest agent to locate and pay people to whom government money was due. All this was achieved quite cheaply, for the cashiers received no money (unless in the form of rent supplements) for their Bureau work—it being rightly assumed that the Bank eagerly sought a connection with the bounty business. And those cashiers who were not disbursing agents received information concerning bounty payments that enabled them to help the cause by answering questions and directing the freedmen to the Bureau's agents.[138]

So beneficial was the relationship that the Bank's Agency Committee resolved in May, 1869, to make the merger complete by arranging "a plan of joint offices and expenses at every Branch where this can properly be done."[139] By this time, however, the Bureau was beginning to be phased out, and its aid was declining. The efforts of these two organiza-

---

132. Alvord to Booth, April 20, 1867, Letters Sent, Book 12, Educational Division, BRFAL.
133. *Charges against General Howard*, pp. 217, 289, 388, 486; George R. Bentley, *A History of the Freedmen's Bureau* (Philadelphia: University of Pennsylvania Press, 1955), pp. 146–147.
134. *National Savings Bank*, June 1, 1868, p. 2.
135. Alvord to A. A. Ellsworth, September 26, 1867, Letters Sent, Book 13, Educational Division, BRFAL; Alvord to Harris, March 26, 1867, Book 12, *ibid.*
136. Eaton to Whipple, March 18, 1869, AMA.
137. *Charges against General Howard*, pp. 389–390.
138. Willard Saxton to cashiers, October 2, 1866, pp. 76–98, Letters Sent, Book 11, Educational Division, BRFAL; *Charges against General Howard*, p. 394.
139. Minutes A, May 13, 1869, p. 108.

tions had redounded to each other's benefit—and, in the 1860's at least, to that of the freedmen. Without reciprocity neither the Bank nor the Bureau could have accomplished as much as each did.

In theory and law the Bank, the Bureau, and the American Missionary Association were separate organizations, but in practice their personnel and activities in behalf of the freedmen frequently blended. Cooperation seemed quite normal, for, as Richard Drake has written, "in that empire of four million souls governed by the puritan magistrate, Oliver Otis Howard, it was natural that puritan ministers such as Whipple and Alvord should share in its rule, even as in colonial Massachusetts."[140] At Washington the interlocking officials of the Freedmen's Bureau, the Freedman's Bank, and Howard University reflected a pattern which extended all over the South: counterparts of George W. Balloch, a Bank finance committee member, chief disbursing officer of the Freedmen's Bureau, treasurer of Howard University, superintendent of the First Congregational Sunday school in Washington, and friend of AMA workers in the South, could be found in a number of branch cities. A historian of the Bureau has concluded that the Bank and the Bureau "worked so closely together and their personnel were so much intermingled that the Bank almost appeared to be a branch of the Bureau."[141] Small wonder, then, that most freedmen arrived at a similar conclusion. This belief—encouraged on occasion by the cashiers—stimulated deposits, for it gave an authenticity and a security which no private institution could claim.

Basically, Bank officials felt confident that the mission community provided the humanitarian zeal to carry out their redemptive efforts. Later Bank officials and black depositors would be dismayed or outraged at the opportunism, incompetency, or dishonesty of some missionaries in the South, cashiers among them. But even at their best, the qualities of the missionaries—honesty, humanitarianism, and a desire to work among the freedmen—cannot necessarily be equated with egalitarian attitudes. On the issue of equality, Bank officials, like many of the abolitionists and missionaries, remained somewhat ambivalent.[142]

Bank officials spoke with egalitarian rhetoric, although sometimes their actions and comments displayed paternalistic attitudes. Bank policy

---

140. Drake, "American Missionary Association," p. 75.

141. Bentley, *History of the Freedmen's Bureau*, p. 146.

142. Willie Lee Rose, *Rehearsal for Reconstruction* (Indianapolis: Bobbs-Merrill, 1964), pp. 123, 158–159, 220–223 and *passim*. Several other historians have presented similar viewpoints in the 1960's. See, for example, William H. Pease and Jane H. Pease, "Antislavery Ambivalence: Immediatism, Expedience, Race," *American Quarterly*, XVII (Winter, 1965), 682–695; and Leon F. Litwack, *North of Slavery* (Chicago: University of Chicago Press, 1961), ch. 7.

required that no teacher or pastor could be a member of an advisory committee while his church or school proscribed people because of race, and two Bank officers, D. L. Eaton and Anson Sperry, clearly favored extending civil rights to the freedmen.[143] But condescension appeared not infrequently. John Alvord declared in an official report that "the trustees of this institution have from the first made many sacrifices in its behalf, discharging their responsibilities under the charter with great fidelity. Of this the freedmen should not be forgetful."[144] The entire publicity campaign to a certain extent was predicated upon the idea that freedmen would be slow to realize their own self-interest and would have to be taught patiently the simple, elementary lessons of thrift. A circular intended for the freedmen would, they erroneously believed, "of course" be referred "for advice to those more intelligent whom they have been accustomed to trust."[145] Other statements were not so subtly condescending. The Memphis cashier declared that "the fickel [*sic*] mindedness of the Colored people makes it impossible for me to remit to you yet the small sum I have as yet on deposit."[146] And President Hewitt, perhaps in a moment of anger or frustration, referred to Washington's black leaders as the "Big Niggers of Washington."[147] Perhaps these words did not sound unusual to Alvord, for in a letter written years earlier to the abolitionist leader Theodore Dwight Weld he offered a classic example of antislavery ambivalence. Referring to the presence of a black girl among white classmates, he wrote: "Cant tell how it will go. Should not be surprized if some of the white parents should smell her very bad, tho I could not perceive the girls on either side were at all aware of her niggerly odour." Yet a few lines later he affirmed that he "would dedicate his life" for the "salvation of the African race."[148]

143. *Rules and Regulations for Advisory Committees, Depositors, Field Agents, and Actuary of Freedman's Savings and Trust Company*, Committee on FA, NA, RG 233; Sperry to "Smith," August 20, 1874, p. 166, A. M. Sperry, Letters Sent, Official Correspondence of the Commissioners, FS&T Co.; Woodward, *Savings Banks*, p. 57. Reference to "A. M. Sperry, Letters Sent" indicates an unmarked volume of his letters found in the official correspondence of the commissioners in the Freedman's Savings and Trust Company's records in the National Archives. Sperry was not a commissioner. Hereafter these letters will be cited as Sperry Letters, Official Correspondence.

144. Alvord, *Tenth Semi-Annual Report on Schools for Freedmen*, July 1, 1870, p. 55.

145. Brevet Col. W. H. Sidell to Gen. O. O. Howard, December 26, 1865, Bank Letters, BRFAL.

146. A. L. Rankin to Alvord, January 15, 1866, *ibid.*

147. Hewitt to Alvord, March 13, 1866, *ibid.*

148. Barnes and Dumond, *Letters of Theodore Dwight Weld . . . 1822–1844*, II, 697.

Insights into the racial attitudes of the missionary mind are found in the dealings of Cashier H. C. Percy with John Wesley Cromwell, a Negro applicant for a teaching position. Cromwell was a teacher of considerable experience, well liked by all who knew him and popular in the Negro community; later he became a distinguished national leader and writer.[149] To Percy, Cromwell was a man of ordinary intelligence who lacked proper religious orientation. "Though professing a change of heart, he is not a member of any church."[150] In all other aspects, Percy reported, he would prove a valuable asset to the association, for he was a better teacher than most colored men they had interviewed and he intended to devote his life to the elevation of his race. He was not, however, suitable to be a superintendent or to have charge of a mission family. "I do not think, in the present state of society here, it is policy to have '*very dark*, colored persons' living in our families, as it exposes our ladies to much needless gossip both on the street and in the papers. I think Mr. C. will do well in his school, and can find board in a respectable col'd family." Cromwell, Percy suggested, could be serviceable for a lady's household; he could do the marketing and run errands to Norfolk.[151]

The occasional tendency to express reservations about equality or even opinions of low esteem for blacks, yet at the same time to believe in progress, is part of the racial ambivalence of people associated with the Bank. But if cashiers and Bank officers sometimes found Negroes lacking, they nevertheless believed generally in their capacity for development, which was the fundamental tenet of the Bank's policy. The cashiers universally believed that freedmen would learn to patronize the Bank. D. L. Eaton, the Bank's actuary, concluded that the agents "have entered upon their toil in full faith that time & effort & patience will prove the educated colored person to be like other educated people —many of them frugal, thrifty, careful, temperate, provident—as they have proved themselves already loyal citizens."[152] The Mobile cashier recognized that while slavery had degraded many Negroes (he referred to one class of former slaves as the debris of slavery), numerous evidences of manhood had survived. And all the freedmen were rapidly

149. Percy to Hunt, September 12, 1866, AMA. Later John Cromwell wrote a number of historical works, among them *The Negro in American History* (1914). A biographical sketch of Cromwell is in Reverend William J. Simmons, *Men of Mark: Eminent, Progressive and Rising* (Cleveland: George M. Rewell & Co., 1887).

150. Percy to Hunt, September 12, 1866, AMA.

151. Percy to Hunt, September 24, 1866, *ibid.*

152. Eaton to Committee on Freedmen's Affairs, July 5, 1868, Committee on FA, NA, RG 233.

moving toward a better condition.[153] Perhaps the Alexandria cashier's opinion is typical: "The freed people have a lesson to learn about saving in which I believe and hope they will prove proficient."[154]

The Bank's identification with the Bureau, the AMA, and other missionary and freedmen's aid groups was not without its drawbacks, for it could and did bring an avalanche of criticism. White Southerners resented the Bank as part of the northern effort to reconstruct southern society. Frederick Douglass ascribed a prominent place in the Bank's difficulties to "this feeling of caste, this race malignity."[155] John Alvord discovered strong prejudices against the freedmen during his southern travels and, appreciating how money conferred power and prestige, was not surprised by the attempts which were made to hinder the former "mudsill's" prosperity.[156] He related how Georgians had started rumors about the Macon cashier and thus caused fear among the depositors and a small run on that branch.[157] Reports concerning opposition became almost routine. In Mobile hostility toward the Bank increased as newspapers mounted a steady attack. This campaign of vilification, so Hewitt reported, affected draymen, porters, and others dependent upon white people.[158] "Every man who hates equality before the law hates the Bank," warned the *Mobile Watchman*, a newspaper sympathetic to Radical Reconstruction.[159] At Jacksonville a particularly harmful situation developed because the Bank's financial inspector had inadvertently forgotten to forward money promised to Negro soldiers. When they called for it and went away empty-handed, the Bank's enemies made the most of their opportunity; "The ex-slaveholders take advantage of this, and try to induce the freedmen to have nothing to do with any of the Banks."[160] At Vicksburg the cashier reported strong opposition, for many Southerners considered the Bank simply a new way to swindle the freedmen.[161] At Shreveport—where the cashier declared that Harriet Beecher Stowe was right in making the Red River Valley the mythical home of the Legrees—local people opposed the Savings Bank with intense bitterness.[162]

153. Woodward, *Savings Banks*, p. 60 and *passim*.
154. Charles Whittlesey to Hewitt, November 2, 1866, Bank Letters, BRFAL.
155. *Report of the Select Committee*, Senate, 1880, app., p. 43.
156. Alvord to the Hon. Henry Wilson, January 19, 1866, Papers of the Committee on Finance concerning Senate Bill 84, Legislative Records, NA, RG 233.
157. Minutes A, August 12, 1869, p. 129.
158. Hewitt to Alvord, October 2, 1866, Bank Letters, BRFAL.
159. Quoted in *Weekly Louisianian*, June 6, 1874, p. 3.
160. N. C. Dennett to Alvord, April 16, 1866, Bank Letters, BRFAL.
161. Thomas to Alvord, February 10, 1866, *ibid*.
162. *New National Era*, January 12, 1871, p. 1.

Conditions at certain branches led to specifically local opposition. The location of the Louisville branch—next to a Democratic newspaper's office—resulted in trouble during political campaigns, while at Nashville white people denounced the crowds of poor depositors that entered their upper-class neighborhood in order to patronize the Bank.[163]

Certainly the Bank's personnel policies did nothing to mitigate its alien status in the South. The Bank's technical purpose may have been financial, but no freedman or white Southerner could fail to perceive that in purpose and personnel it was indistinguishable from the rest of the northern reformist forces of Reconstruction. Southerners charged that these freedmen's aid groups did not really have the freedmen's best interests at heart and that only the people of the South could understand and care for their black brethren. According to Colonel Samuel Thomas at Vicksburg, the Bank met strong opposition because of the universal sentiment that freedmen should deposit where white men did and learn to do business with southern whites.[164] The branch banks were alien and hostile agencies; they were "but a part of the machinery by which poor negroes are plundered and made subservient to the political and selfish designs of those who, clothed with authority, are sent down among them for that purpose, under the pretext of affording protection and sympathy."[165] A man would be a fool, a Southerner warned a Negro, to let a group of "thieving Yankees have his hard-earned money."[166] The southern spirit is seen in an incident in Augusta in which several prominent white southern businessmen dissociated themselves from the advisory board after a short period of attendance.[167] Community prejudice in this instance dictated that no true Southerner could support a Negro bank backed by Republicans. All sons of the South should help to disabuse those ex-slaves who had been beguiled by the "false teachings, false promises and mischievous instigations of villainous carpet-bag and scalawag emissaries."[168]

Although opposition to the Bank extended throughout southern society, the state of the existing evidence makes impossible an assessment of the level and quality of hostility among the different classes and sectors. It would be tempting to speculate on the basis of very scattered data that the wealthy Southerners were a bit more disposed to tolerate the Bank than were small farmers, laborers, and poorer whites (as a group the least secure in southern society); but to attempt any such

163. Alvord, *Letters from the South*, p. 31; Minutes A, June 10, 1869, p. 124.
164. Thomas to Alvord, February 10, 1866, Bank Letters, BRFAL.
165. *Charges against General Howard*, p. 51.
166. Woodward, *Savings Banks*, p. 81.
167. *New National Era*, May 21, 1874, p. 2.
168. *Charleston Daily Courier*, August 31, 1868, p. 1.

general conclusion would be rash. It does seem, however, that two small segments of southern society—former loyalists and moderate newspaper editors—did proffer support for the Bank, albeit at times lukewarmly. Some southern whites, seeing that the Bank was intended to instruct freedmen in the principles of economy and thrift, found little to object to in the Bank's program. They perceived no threat to their status from a rising black population. Native Southerners of loyalist principles predominated in the southern "pro-Bank" group, but they may have even been joined by a few ex-Confederates of the planter class. Such native Southerners realized that a Negro bank was not a radical institution. It was designed to produce a stable, industrious, laboring population—middle class in sentiment, but nevertheless a working class. Southerners of the planter class would object to the Bank only insofar as the people who held positions in it were politically active, and only insofar as the Bank succeeded in creating independent farmers. But if the Bank could help solve the problem of securing a steady labor force, much would be forgiven.

Bank officials frequently claimed to have a good deal of white southern support, but their testimony is questionable. They were intent upon proving that the Bank was not a controversial institution and, while they frequently spoke of white support, they were less frequently specific about the names of their supporters. John Alvord declared that "men at the South, who as yet scarcely patronize free schools, speak well of these banks." Raleigh cashier G. W. Brodie stated in the *New Era* that "many white citizens who have been watching the operation of the Branch, have told me that they believe these Banks, created to benefit the colored people, are one of the best means that could have been inaugurated to elevate them."[169] North Carolina's Unionist Governor W. W. Holden "and other of the best citizens and most prominent men of the State and Colonel John Deweese, member of Congress elect, have used their influence in establishing it [the Raleigh branch] and are still lending their aid in its behalf."[170] In 1869 actuary D. L. Eaton reported that Mr. Hollingsworth, a wealthy cotton broker, "and other leading white men joined earnestly in commending our work in this city" of Macon.[171] A William P. Goodall, cashier of the city bank and a southern man who discussed banking affairs with Alvord, was probably one of these men to whom Eaton referred.[172] Eaton also claimed that at

169. *New Era*, July 7, 1870, p. 3; Alvord, *Ninth Semi-Annual Report on Schools for Freedmen*, January 1, 1870, p. 65.

170. Brevet Maj. Gen. Nelson A. Miles to Howard, September 13, 1867, Letters Rec'd, I, Educational Division, BRFAL; *National Savings Bank*, June 1, 1868, p. 1.

171. Minutes A, June 10, 1869, p. 119.

172. Alvord, *Letters from the South*, p. 19.

Wilmington "the wealthiest and most intelligent" whites are heartily for the Bank.[173] At New Orleans one Rufus Waples, a leading loyalist and integrationist in politics, chaired the local advisory board, as did Judge Bland Ballard, also an integrationist, in Louisville.[174] From Alvord in Atlanta came reports that "some of the influential white men (old residents) are upon the advisory committee."[175] It became an established policy at many branches to have one or two wealthy white native loyalists on the boards—especially if they happened to be businessmen. Some southern bankers and businessmen (how many it is impossible to say) welcomed the branch banks: A. G. Sanford, president of the First National Bank of Nashville, encouraged Alvord to extend the Bank's influence into the bounty business; the president of the Georgia National Bank, John Rice, became a member of the Atlanta advisory board; and Judge John P. King, president of the Georgia Railroad from 1841 to 1878, gave Alvord, who was inspecting schools and banks, free passes over his road.[176] According to Alvord, even a few members of the planter class gave silent assent if not support; for "the old-time slaveholder, even, is willing that the negro should save his money."[177] Yet overall, the few important and prestigious white men associated with the Bank in the South were mostly Unionist in background and thus not generally representative of upper-class Southerners.

At the Jacksonville and Beaufort branches a peculiarly local situation obtained, for numerous city merchants not only welcomed the Negro bank but actually flocked to its counter. Of course, its being for several years the only banking facility in these towns probably effected its sudden popularity.[178] Elsewhere there were always some deposits from white citizens.

Along with the small group of southern Unionists, certain southern newspapers also expressed support for the Bank. They carried the Bank's advertisements, acknowledged its growth and accomplishments, and in general offered the kind of moderate backing which anticipates the position of New South advocates on racial matters a few years later. In short, they welcomed elementary economic progress for any southern

173. Minutes A, June 10, 1869, p. 113.

174. *Ibid.*, p. 121.

175. Alvord, *Letters from the South*, p. 22.

176. A. G. Sanford to Alvord, January 20, 1866, Bank Letters, BRFAL; Minutes A, December 8, 1870, p. 183, and February 10, 1870, p. 145; Richard E. Prince, *Steam Locomotives and History: Georgia Railroad and West Point Route* (Green River, Wyo.; By the Author, 1962), p. 6.

177. Minutes A, February 10, 1870, p. 144.

178. Alvord to Harris, March 4, 1867, p. 105, Letters Sent, Book 12, Educational Division, BRFAL; Col. Low to Alvord, April 8, 1867, Bank Letters, BRFAL; *New National Era*, October 27, 1870, p. 3; Minutes A, June 10, 1869, p. 117.

people if, of course, it did not conflict with the interests of the ruling economic groups.[179] The *Charleston Daily Courier*, for example, observed that the Bank's "object is a most laudable one, offering to the freedmen the opportunity of investing their savings."[180] Similar reflections on the Bank's value appeared from time to time in the *Daily Courier* over the next few years, and when it merged with the *Charleston Daily News* to form the Democratic *News and Courier* in 1873, reports about the Bank continued to be favorable. In a lengthy front-page article in 1873, the *News and Courier* praised the work of the Negro bank: "The importance of this institution to the colored people is due to the fact that it enjoys to a remarkable degree their confidence, inspired by the attention and trouble which its officers bestowed upon even the most humble depositor, and the sedulous care with which the disposition to save money is in all cases fostered and encouraged."[181]

For a while the *Savannah Morning News* and the Louisville *Courier-Journal* pursued a similar policy.[182] On at least one occasion the *Savannah Morning News* very forthrightly acknowledged its admiration for blacks who used the Bank:

> We publish with pleasure and gratification, anything that points to the financial progress of the honest and laboring portion of our colored population, and we are pleased to see in the monthly record, the National Savings Bank, issued in Washington city, the continued successful condition of the branch of the institution of Savannah. The result shows a healthy improvement in the investments of that class of our population, and indicated that instead of spending their earnings foolishly, they are endeavoring to provide for themselves and their families, comfortable homes.[183]

In spite of the changes which the Bank's presence suggested and even helped to bring about, revolutionary change was not at all contemplated by southern newspapers when they supported the Bank. Rather, they hoped to encourage the development of an institution which would insure a steady, hard-working, loyally subordinate labor force. This attitude is seen in a *Daily Courier* article about a Negro

179. For a good discussion of the racial attitudes of New South advocates, see Paul Gaston, *The New South Creed* (New York: Alfred A. Knopf, 1970), pp. 117–150.

180. December 14, 1866, p. 2.

181. *Charleston Daily Courier*, January 11, 1868, p. 4, and March 23, 1868, p. 2; Charleston *News and Courier*, August 1, 1873, p. 1.

182. For favorable comments, see *Savannah Morning News*, April 13, 1870, p. 3; Louisville *Courier-Journal*, June 28, 1874, p. 3.

183. June 13, 1871, p. 3; quoted in U.S., Works Projects Administration, *Annals of Savannah, 1850–1937*, XXII.

who shipped the first bale of cotton from Galveston, Texas. The title summarizes its thesis: "What a Freedman Can Do through Honesty and Industry, and Keeping Aloof from Loyal Leagues." Negroes would find success in attending to their legitimate business, raising cotton, instead of frequenting the cities to engage in torchlight processions in order to place unscrupulous carpetbaggers in office.[184] The lesson of the Charleston papers was that as long as the Negro bank eschewed politics—and as long as political passions remained relatively low—it would find favor among some Southerners concerned about a stable work force.

Unfortunately, in many areas of the South even this limited support was short lived; the extreme political partisanship of the Reconstruction era aroused all the latent hostility against black people and this black bank. Although the Bank had remained out of politics, it was in southern eyes associated with northern and Republican efforts to alter their way of life. The ties to the mission community in this respect had deleterious consequences. Most of the press diminished the Bank's influence and prestige by ignoring it, but some indulged in bitter diatribes and ridicule. For example, in 1868 the *Daily News and Herald* (Savannah) lampooned black soldiers who supposedly had invested their pay in watermelons. All of their business ventures, the paper stated, were "failures as soon as some sneaking carpet-baggers, who managed the business made his [*sic*] grab."[185] In 1872, an election year, attacks on the Bank by Democratic papers increased sharply; and after July, 1874, southern Democratic papers were unanimous in their denunciation, for the Bank's failure proved what Southerners had been saying all along about who the black man's real friends were.

184. August 13, 1868, p. 2.
185. September 24, 1868, p. 3; quoted in W.P.A., *Annals of Savannah, 1850–1937*, XIX.

4

Up from Slavery:
The Bank in the Black Community

Amos McFall, Lot Proctor, Joseph M. Gibbs, Maria Washington, and Hannah Clifton were among the depositors of the Savannah branch of the Freedman's Savings and Trust Company.[1] Born and raised in Georgetown, South Carolina, Amos McFall worked as a carpenter in Savannah to support his wife and three children. By 1874 he had deposited at least $140 in the Bank. Lot Proctor, an illiterate, fifty-seven-year-old black railroad worker born and raised in Claffin, South Carolina, saved $109, a sizable sum which could serve as security for his wife and child in case of his death. Six-year-old Joe Gibbs attended school, and one can imagine how he must have saved to become the proud possessor of a bank book and $2.85. The widow Maria Washington came to Savannah from Beaufort and found work as a cook in the Savannah poorhouse, accumulating in the Bank the sum of $43; a thirty-eight-year-old widow, Hannah Clifton, engaged in planting at White Bluff and was able to deposit $6.00.

Why did Amos McFall, Maria Washington, and the others place their hard-earned money in the Savannah branch? Was banking there personally convenient? Were they attracted by promises of interest on their savings? Or were they demonstrating in the most positive way possible their support of an institution that was seeking to help their race? Did they save because social pressure encouraged thrift; or was it to buy a home or a few acres of land, or to provide against illness? No one can say exactly what these particular depositors had in mind, but surely the thousands of Lot Proctors and Hannah Cliftons who answered the call of the Bank's leaders—the white and the black cashiers, the Negro advisory boards, and the Negro ministers—believed in

1. Savannah Signature Books, Nos. 5448, 6066, 6611, 10,482, and 13,667, FS&T Co.

the Bank and in its beneficent purposes. No matter what the depositor's private reasons may have been, the freedmen as a group must have come to believe, like most Americans, that industry and thrift were sure ways to advancement. After all, the Freedman's Savings and Trust Company, with its black employees and new banking offices, provided visible evidence of the successful transition from slavery to freedom.

Deposits rose in 1867, and by mid-1868 the officers were full of optimism once again. In a cheerful mood, the Agency Committee reported in July, 1868 that "all the Branches of our Bank . . . appear now in a prosperous condition, some of them being very successful and the future prospects of the entire institution are full of promise."[2]

Future prospects were buoyed up by the freedmen's demand for new branches; as a result, the Bank began to plan for expansion as it had before the lean years of 1866 and 1867. By January, 1868, a number of Negro communities had applied for branches. The actuary and other officers made preliminary arrangements to open branches in Selma, Alabama; Charlottesville, Virginia; Charlotte and Salisbury, North Carolina; and Andersonville and Macon, Georgia, provided that expenses would not exceed income.[3] Of this group, Macon alone received a branch. The Bank's officers were encouraged by earnest applications from the spokesmen of black communities in Lexington, West Virginia; St. Louis; Raleigh; and Martinsburg, West Virginia, the last three of which received branches. Only one new branch, at Chattanooga, was opened in 1869, but in 1870 and 1871 the Bank achieved very rapid expansion. In these two years the Bank opened ten more branches, covering an area from Philadelphia to Shreveport.[4] Atlanta was welcomed into the branch system because, as one official said, "a large amount of capital and colored population is centering in this young city."[5] Little Rock finally received its branch, three years after the Arkansas superintendent of education had requested one "as soon as possible."[6] The new branches and the many applications from towns and cities all over the South reflected the widespread interest in the Freedman's Bank.

The decision to open a branch at Lexington, Kentucky, illuminates the officers' criteria for selecting branch cities and suggests why some were bypassed. A report by Alvord indicated that Lexington offered many advantages as a branch city. Negroes and several wealthy whites

2. Minutes A, July 9, 1868, p. 76; November 12, 1868, p. 87; February 11, 1869, p. 99.
3. *Ibid.*, April 9, 1868, p. 65; and July 9, 1868, p. 71.
4. *Report of the Select Committee*, Senate, 1880, appendix, p. 41.
5. Minutes A, February 10, 1870, p. 147.
6. *Ibid.*, July 11, 1867, p. 41; *Report of the Commissioners*, 1874, p. 85.

had shown great interest, and the 12,000 Negroes of the city generally were prosperous—according to Alvord, the most prosperous of any freedmen in the South. They were the city's cartmen, carriage drivers, and mechanics. Many owned their homes, he reported, and as a group paid taxes on real estate valued at $250,000. This industrious Negro community, he implied, would be supported by the local Republican newspapers and Republican organization, and together they could establish a branch. But expenses had to be limited. "Could you," Alvord wrote the future cashier, "have [a] meeting of friends of the Bank, and, on looking over the whole subject, resolve that a freedmen's Bank at Lexington could *start, and sustain its own expenses for the first year or two*?"[7]

In 1870 and 1871 Bank officers studied applications and carried on correspondence with such places as Galveston and Sherman, Texas; New Madrid, Missouri; Columbus and Albany, Georgia; Columbia, South Carolina; Jackson, Mississippi; Harrisburg, Pennsylvania, and Cincinnati.[8] The latter site was given special consideration; for, as the committee recorded in its minutes, "the report of the President respecting a Branch at Cincinnati, is favorable, and the actuary is instructed to continue correspondence with a view to establishing a branch at that point."[9] All of these applications were turned down because the Agency Committee felt that the proposed branches could not pay their expenses.

Unfortunately, the authors of the numerous applications for branches are unknown. The applications might represent the desire of only one or two individuals, or of a significant part of the black community in a particular town. One wonders, then, whether to infer from this evidence that petit bourgeois values of thrift and industry already had a significant foothold in the black community. Although slavery may have hindered the development of middle-class values, these values were not nonexistent.[10] In some cities blacks heartily welcomed the Bank, and local groups sometimes put it into operation. Probably Alvord and other white officials, conditioned by the abolitionists' views on the horrors of slavery, underestimated evidence of bourgeois values already

7. Minutes A, February 10, 1870, p. 149; J. W. Alvord to John G. Hamilton, February 26, 1870, p. 276, Letters Sent, Book 15, Educational Division, BRFAL.

8. Minutes A, February 10, 1870, p. 150; May 12, 1870, p. 160; August 11, 1870, p. 173.

9. *Ibid.*, November 9, 1871, p. 211.

10. Recently historians Charles B. Dew, Robert William Fogel, and Stanley L. Engerman have suggested this interpretation. See Dew, "Disciplining Slave Ironworkers in the Antebellum South: Coercion, Conciliation, and Accommodation," *American Historical Review*, LXXIX (April, 1974); and Fogel and Engerman, *Time on the Cross* (Boston: Little, Brown, 1974).

present. The slave who buried his money in the ground at night was obviously thrifty; hence Bank officials were not planting the seeds of thrift and industry in fallow soil. Certainly if the Bank had to persuade freedmen not to hoard their money—as the literature concerning safety stressed—then here one has an admission that the thrift ethos was already present. Conclusions on this matter are necessarily tentative, yet it does seem that Bank officials, seeking to instill concepts of thrift and industry, may have merely reinforced a tradition already present.

The establishment of branches far and wide was not an unmixed blessing to the managers of a new and insecure institution. "The wide extent and spread of our machinery is fearful," said John Alvord on one occasion.[11] By late 1870 he doubted the wisdom of creating more branches (and expenses), for hardly one-tenth of the people in the branch cities had begun to patronize the Bank.[12] Alvord's ideas were reflected in a new policy: in 1870 and 1871 Bank officers tried to balance physical expansion through a concerted emphasis on financial expansion by increasing business in the old locations.

The demand for new branches and the increasing size of the company's deposits, especially after 1869, demonstrated the Bank's rising popularity among the freedmen. Many Negroes, slaves a few months previously, began to make deposits and save. To have a bank account no matter how small became the thing to do. "Go in any forenoon," observed the Scottish journalist Robert Somers at Charleston in 1870 or 1871, "and the office is found full of negroes depositing little sums of money, drawing little sums, or remitting to distant parts of the country where they have relatives to support or debts to discharge."[13] From 1869 to 1874 tens of thousands placed their small deposits in the Bank's vaults and made the Freedman's Savings Bank a financial success.

The Bank recorded each depositor's description in a signature book as a means of identifying him should he lose his deposit book. From these descriptions it is possible to extract some provisional ideas about the types of people who deposited in the Freedman's Bank. Whether there was such a thing as a "typical" depositor is debatable, for the depositors varied from branch to branch and changed in character within a single branch over the years. Thus the depositors of the New York branch, which was situated in a metropolis having thousands of poor immigrants, differed greatly from those in Huntsville, Alabama. And the

11. Minutes A, February 10, 1870, p. 154.
12. *Ibid.*, December 8, 1870, p. 187.
13. Robert Somers, *The Southern States since the War, 1870–71* (New York: Macmillan, 1871), p. 54.

depositors of the Huntsville branch, which was situated in an agricultural region, were more likely to be farmers or engaged in some aspect of cotton-raising than were those of Richmond, where the tobacco industry and iron foundries attracted large numbers of freedmen. Nor can it be assumed that Huntsville's Negro community, or even Louisville's, approximated the wealth and social development of Charleston's. New Orleans was always out of step with the other branches—fully 25 percent of the depositors were white, and a large French-speaking free Negro group, whose influence was represented by C. S. Sauvinet, the cashier, was another unique factor. S. L. Harris mentioned somewhat cryptically the existence of rival cliques (creoles vs. freedmen?), and D. L. Eaton spoke of the need for harmony between mulattoes and blacks at the New Orleans branch.[14] Many branches (such as at Louisville, Memphis, Beaufort, and Charleston) originated to handle soldiers' money, but by the early 1870's these branches were community institutions drawing depositors from the Negro population at large instead of from Negro soldiers.

The vast differences in the Louisville branch between 1867 and 1872–73 illustrate how the composition of a branch could change over a short period of time. (See Tables 1 and 2.) In 1866 and 1867 black soldiers, most of whom did not reside in Louisville, made up 90 and 80 percent, respectively, of the new depositors. From May, 1872, through April, 1873, 95 percent of the new depositors lived in Louisville; although information for a soldier-civilian breakdown is lacking, the soldiers' influence was certainly much diminished, since 44 percent of the new depositors were women. In fact, probably none of the new depositors had seen military service, for surely this fact would have been recorded for purposes of identification. Between 1866–67 and 1872–73, white depositors increased from zero to 11 percent; the growth in the percentage of depositors who could write their signatures is just as notable, from 6 percent to 19 percent. Occupations in 1866–67 were seldom listed, because the men were or recently had been soldiers, but in 1872–73 the list of occupations ranged from artisans (7 percent), to laborers (19 percent), to a large class of cooks, washers, domestics, waiters, porters, butlers, and stewards (32 percent).

Surveys of the Charleston, Louisville, Richmond, Vicksburg, Augusta, Shreveport, and Huntsville depositors for periods of at least one

14. Minutes A, 1869, pp. 121–122; Examiner's Report of the New Orleans branch, Letters Rec'd by the Commissioners, 1870–1914, FS&T Co.; S. L. Harris to Alvord, March 27, 1867, Bank Letters, BRFAL; C. S. Sauvinet to Alvord, February 12, 1870, Letters Rec'd III, box 4, Educational Division, BRFAL.

TABLE 1. Description of Every Tenth Louisville Depositor, 1866 and 1867

Total descriptions of new depositors: 122
    1866:   71
    1867:   51

Characteristics		Number	Percent
Sex			
1866:	Male	69	97
	Female	2	3
1867:	Male	45	88
	Female	6	12
Ability to write name			
1866:	Signature	4	6
	Weak signature	4	6
	Signed with an "X"	33	46
	Unknown	30	42
1867:	Signature	4	8
	Weak signature	1	2
	Signed with an "X"	34	67
	Unknown	12	23
Race			
1866:	Negro	71	100
	Caucasian	0	0
	Unknown	0	0
1867:	Negro	51	100
	Caucasian	0	0
	Unknown	0	0
Residence			
1866:	Louisville	12	17
	Non-Louisville	52	73
	Unknown	7	10
1867:	Louisville	19	37
	Non-Louisville	28	55
	Unknown	4	8
Status at birth			
1866:	Slave	54	76
	Freeborn	0	0
	Unknown	17	24
1867	Slave	26	51
	Freeborn	1	2
	Unknown	24	47

TABLE 1. (*cont.*)

Characteristics		Number	Percent
Military experience			
1866:	Soldiers	64	90
	Non-soldiers	2	3
	Unknown	5	7
1867:	Soldiers	41	80
	Non-soldiers	6	12
	Unknown	4	8
Occupation (only 32 were listed)			
1866	Farmers	21	
and	Laborers	3	
1867:	Servants	3	
	Waiters	1	
	Teamsters	2	
	Boatmen	1	
	Ministers	1	
*Amount of Opening Deposit in Dollars**			
1866:	0–50	5	
	51–100	9	
	101–150	3	
	151–200	1	
	201–250	1	
	251+	0	
1867:	0–50	0	
	51–100	3	
	101–150	3	
	151–200	3	
	201–250	0	
	251+	2	

* For 1866, 19 of the 71 new accounts had the opening deposit listed. Of these 19, 18 were opened by men who had definitely been soldiers. The average amount deposited was $94.00.

For 1867, 11 of the 51 new accounts had the opening deposit listed. Of these 11, all were opened by soldiers. The average amount deposited was $199.00.

TABLE 2. Description of Every Tenth Louisville Depositor, May, 1872–April, 1873

Total descriptions of new accounts: 112
    33 were transfers or provided no information
    79 provided substantial information
     6 of the above were societies

73 total descriptions of new depositors

Characteristics	Number	Percent
Sex		
Male	40	55
Female	32	44
Unknown	1	1
Ability to write name		
Signature	14	19
Weak signature	13	18
Signed with an "X"	39	53
Unknown	7	10
Race		
Negro	62	85
Caucasian	8	11
Unknown	3	4
Residence		
Louisville	69	95
Non-Louisville	3	4
Unknown	1	1
Age		
1–10	5	6.9
11–15	7	9.6
16–19	6	8.2
20–29	28	38.4
30–39	14	19.2
40–49	4	5.5
50–59	4	5.5
60–69	1	1.4
70+	1	1.4
Unknown	3	4.1
Occupation		
Professional (doctors, lawyers, teachers, etc.) and white collar (clerks, proprietors, etc.)	5	7
Artisans	5	7
Farmers	2	3
Cooks, washers, domestics	23	31
Waiters, porters, butlers, steward class	8	11
Laborers (unskilled)	14	19
School children	5	7
Unemployed	2	3
Unknown	9	12

year in the 1870's, plus the impressions of contemporary observers, make possible several generalizations about depositors.[15] (See Tables 1–8.) By the 1870's the branches drew depositors from the entire black community, but young males, the group most important in the labor force, predominated. The percentage of men among the new depositors reached highs of 82 percent in Huntsville for the periods 1869–70 and 1872–73, and 80 percent in Richmond. Generally the depositors were relatively young. At Louisville and Augusta, for example, 86 and 82 percent of those whose ages were listed were under forty, while at Richmond the percentage under forty was 77.[16] At these seven branches the largest single age group was that from twenty to twenty-nine. Overall, the number of white depositors was small—except at New York and New Orleans, where one-fourth of the depositors were white, and at Beaufort and Jacksonville, where the number of white businessmen was sizeable.[17] Only one white person was discovered in the Richmond survey and none at Shreveport, yet Louisville had a notable 11 percent and Vicksburg 17 percent. In 1873 Charleston had only 200 white depositors out of 5,500, while in 1870 Norfolk counted only 30 out of 1,204.[18] Most white depositors were immigrants or members of the mission community; for example, only one of the white depositors in the Vicksburg survey was a native Southerner. Contemporaries always spoke of the depositors as freedmen or ex-slaves, but some free blacks became depositors. Unfortunately, the signature books do not provide sufficient information to determine how many.[19]

15. Freedman's Bank records in the National Archives contain incomplete Signature Books for 29 of the 37 branches. The number of branches and accounts is overwhelming; therefore, this survey is limited to seven branches and to certain years in which the branches were growing and bringing in new depositors. Except for Augusta and Vicksburg, each survey includes every tenth depositor whose account number ends in zero. Because there were so many omissions or transfers in the Augusta and Vicksburg records, I selected the next complete description when the tenth account provided no information. Thus my surveys for these branches contain descriptions for somewhat more than one-tenth of all the new depositors.

The seven branches selected for the survey and the reasons for singling them out are as follows: Charleston was selected because of its large, highly organized Negro community; Louisville and Richmond because they were branches of considerable size, generally successful, and perhaps as representative as any; and Huntsville and Shreveport because they had small, rather poor black communities. Two other Deep South cities, Vicksburg and Augusta, were added because they were of intermediate size and would provide proper balance.

16. Louisville figures discussed here and below are from the 1872–73 survey.

17. *New York Herald*, April 28, 1874, p. 5; *Report of the Commissioners*, 1874, p. 74; Examiner's Report of the New Orleans branch, Letters Rec'd by the Commissioners, 1870–1914, FS&T Co.

18. *New Era*, February 3, 1870, p. 3; Charleston *News and Courier*, August 1, 1873, p. 1.

19. One wonders if many free Negroes declined to deposit in the Bank because

TABLE 3. Description of Every Tenth Charleston Depositor, July, 1870–June, 1871

Total descriptions of new accounts: 298
    92 were transfers or provided no information
    206 provided susbtantial information
    19 of the above were societies or associations

187 total descriptions of new depositors

Characteristics	Number	Percent
Sex		
Male	126	67
Female	61	33
Ability to write name		
Signature	63	34
Weak signature	19	10
Signed with an "X"	97	52
Unknown	8	4
Race		
Negro	162	87
Caucasian	10	5
Unknown	15	8
Residence		
Charleston	135	72
Non-Charleston	42	23
Unknown	10	5
Age		
1–10	11	6
11–15	15	8
16–19	11	6
20–29	60	32
30–39	27	14
40–49	23	12
50–59	17	9
60–69	4	2
70–79	1	1
Unknown	18	10
Occupation		
Professional and white collar	9	5
Artisans (includes 12 carpenters)	30	16
Farmers (farming for others, 9; farming for selves, 12)	21	11
Cooks, washers, domestics (may include one or two cooks who worked for city restaurants and who, therefore, should be added to artisan class)	31	17
Waiters, butlers, porters, steward class	17	9
Laborers (unskilled)	39	21
School children	12	6
Unknown	28	15

TABLE 4. Description of Every Tenth Richmond Depositor, July, 1870–June, 1871

Total descriptions of new accounts: 159
    14 were transfers or provided no information
   145 provided substantial information
   17 of the above were societies and/or associations

128 total descriptions of new depositors

Characteristics	Number	Percent
Sex		
Male	102	80
Female	26	20
Ability to write name		
Signature	29	23
Weak signature	15	12
Signed with an "X"	71	55
Unknown	13	10
Race		
Negro	111	87
Caucasian	1	0.5
Unknown	16	12.5
Residence		
Richmond	110	86
Non-Richmond	15	12
Unknown	3	2
Age		
1–10	9	7.0
11–15	14	10.9
16–19	8	6.3
20–29	40	31.3
30–39	23	18.0
40–49	15	11.7
50–59	8	6.3
60–69	4	3.1
70+	0	0
Unknown	7	5.5
Occupation		
Professional and white collar	4	3.1
Artisans	15	11.7
Farmers	0	0
Cooks, washers, domestics	9	7.0
Waiters, butlers, porters, steward class	11	8.6
Laborers (unskilled)	56	43.8
School children	6	4.7
Unemployed	2	1.6
Unknown	25	19.5

TABLE 5. Description of Every Tenth Huntsville Depositor (Beginning with No. 30 on October 2, 1867, and going through December, 1870; and May, 1872, to May, 1873)

Total descriptions of new accounts: 105
  9 were transfers or contained no information

96 total descriptions of new depositors:
  1867–68: 18 depositors; 1869–70: 53 depositors; 1872–73: 25 depositors

Characteristics	Number			Total	Percent
	1867–68	1869–70	1872–73		
Sex					
Male	18	46	18	82	85
Female	0	7	7	14	15
Ability to write name					
Signature	2	11	4	17	18
Weak signature	4	1	4	9	9
Signed with an "X"	11	36	17	64	67
Unknown	1	5	0	6	6
Race					
Negro	17	50	21	88	92
Caucasian	1	2	3	6	6
Unknown	0	1	1	2	2
Residence					
Huntsville	5	25	16	46	48
Non-Huntsville	12	26	9	47	49
Unknown	1	2	0	3	3
Age					
1–10	0	1	1	2	2
11–15	0	1	3	4	4
16–19	0	3	2	5	5
20–29	4	18	6	28	29
30–39	6	10	4	20	21
40–49	1	8	5	14	15
50–59	2	8	3	13	14
60–69	0	1	0	1	1
70+	0	1	1	2	2
Unknown	5	2	0	7	7
Military experience					
Soldiers	10	18	0	28	29
Non-soldiers	0	7	10	17	18
Unknown	8	28	15	51	53
Occupation					
Professional and white collar				6	6.3
Artisans				14	14.6
Farmers				40	41.7
Cooks, washers, domestics				8	8.3
Waiters, butlers, porters, steward class				7	7.3
Laborers				8	8.3
Housewives				1	1.0
School children				4	4.2
Miscellaneous				2	2.1
Unknown				6	6.3

TABLE 6. Description of Every Tenth Shreveport Depositor, February 16, 1871–
February 17, 1873

Total descriptions of new accounts: 79
  4 were transfers or societies

75 total descriptions of new depositors

Characteristics	Number	Percent
Sex		
Male	53	71
Female	20	27
Unknown	2	2
Ability to write name		
Signature	7	9
Weak signature	1	2
Signed with an "X"	64	85
Unknown	3	4
Race		
Negro	73	97.3
Caucasian	0	0
Unknown	2	2.7
Residence		
Shreveport	37	49
Non-Shreveport	33	44
Unknown	5	7
Age		
1–10	5	6.7
11–15	2	2.7
16–19	5	6.7
20–29	26	34.7
30–39	17	22.7
40–49	11	14.7
50–59	6	8.0
60–69	1	1.3
70+	0	0
Unknown	2	2.7
Occupation		
Professional and white collar	5	6.3
Artisans	4	5.3
Farmers	22	29.3
Cooks, washers, domestics	4	5.3
Waiters, butlers, porters, steward class	3	4.0
Laborers (unskilled)	21	28.0
Housewives	2	2.7
Unemployed	0	0
Employed, but no further information	1	1.3
School children	3	4.0
Unknown	10	13.3

A majority of the depositors (ranging from a low of 52 percent in the Charleston survey to a high of 85 percent for Shreveport) could not write their names.[20] (It seems probable, since many signatures were practically illegible, that the percentage of illiterate depositors was even greater.) Charleston, not surprisingly, had more depositors who could write their names than any of the other branches: 34 percent, as opposed to 23 percent each at the next-highest branches, Richmond and Vicksburg.

Occupationally the bulk of the depositors were unskilled laborers, servants of one kind or another, or farm workers. At many branches waiters, porters, and domestics formed a large portion of the depositors. The percentage of laborers, cooks, washers, domestics, waiters, butlers, porters, and stewards reached 61 percent, 60 percent, and 47 percent, respectively, at Richmond, Louisville, and Charleston, but was significantly lower at the other four branches: Huntsville, 24 percent; Shreveport, 37 percent; Vicksburg, 32 percent; and Augusta, 30 percent. Farm workers made up a large proportion of the depositors at Huntsville (42 percent), Shreveport (29 percent), and Vicksburg (24 percent). In the Richmond survey no farmers were found, while in Louisville 3 percent of the depositors were engaged in farming, and 11 percent in Charleston and Augusta. Although the number of artisans was small, they often formed the backbone of the Negro community and played a vital role in the city's economy. At Charleston, for example, Negro carpenters, barbers, and other artisans were economically and socially more important than their numbers suggest. Sixteen percent of the Charleston depositors surveyed were artisans, and no doubt their support of the Bank bolstered the confidence of many potential depositors. In Richmond the number of tobacco workers and skilled iron foundry workers (placed in the artisan class) is noteworthy.

In 1868 Mobile cashier C. A. Woodward, who was vigorously advertising his branch's growth, counted 843 Negro male depositors, 411 female depositors, 342 children and youth, 13 soldiers, 57 societies and associations, and 22 whites, for a total of 1,688 depositors. Fourteen

---

it connoted slave status. Little information exists to throw light on this question. We know that free Negroes became cashiers and sat on the advisory boards, and that a few wealthy free blacks opened accounts at the Bank. On the other hand, a Bureau official has written that free Negroes "have objected to co-operation with the freedmen's savings bank, simply on account of its name, and from them the work in which the bureau is engaged had received no sort of aid or countenance." See Alvord, *Seventh Semi-Annual Report on Schools for Freedmen*, January 1, 1869, p. 50.

20. Cashier Woodward estimated that 65 percent of Mobile depositors signed with their mark. See *The Nationalist*, May 23, 1867, p. 2.

TABLE 7. Description of at Least Every Tenth Augusta Depositor, 1871

140 total descriptions of new depositors

Characteristics	Number	Percent
Sex		
Male	93	66
Female	47	34
Uknown	0	0
Ability to write name		
Signature	26	19
Weak signature	7	5
Signed with an "X"	105	75
Unknown	2	1
Race		
Negro	122	87
Caucasian	5	4
Unknown	13	9
Residence		
Augusta	100	71
Non-Augusta	38	27
Unknown	2	2
Age		
1–10	21	15.0
11–15	22	15.7
16–19	9	6.4
20–29	35	25.0
30–39	25	17.9
40–49	12	8.6
50–59	7	5.0
60–69	5	3.6
70 +	1	.7
Unknown	3	2.1
Occupation		
Professional and white collar	4	3
Artisans	21	15
Farmers	16	11
Cooks, washers, domestics	27	19
Waiters, butlers, porters, steward class	6	4
Laborers	10	7
Housewives	4	3
School children	32	23
Infants	1	0.7
Soldiers	1	0.7
Unemployed	1	0.7
Employed, but no further information	7	5
Unknown	10	7

TABLE 8. Description of at Least Every Tenth Vicksburg Depositor, 1871

137 total descriptions of new depositors

Characteristics	Number	Percent
Sex		
Male	84	61
Female	51	37
Unknown	2	1
Ability to write name		
Signature	31	23
Weak signature	5	4
Signed with an "X"	76	55
Unknown	25	18
Race		
Negro	112	82
Caucasian	23	17
Unknown	2	1
Residence		
Vicksburg	87	64
Non-Vicksburg	48	35
Unknown	2	1
Age		
1–10	2	1
11–15	3	2
16–19	9	7
20–29	47	34
30–39	40	29
40–49	16	12
50–59	5	4
60–69	4	3
70+	0	0
Unknown	11	8
Occupation		
Professional and white collar	15	11
Artisans	16	12
Farmers	33	24
Cooks, washers, domestics	18	13
Waiters, butlers, porters, steward class	3	2
Laborers	23	17
Housewives	14	10
School children	1	0.7
Unknown	14	10

months earlier Mobile had had 516 depositors; their occupations, as listed by Woodward, are in Table 9.[21] The majority worked at low-

TABLE 9. Occupations of Persons for Whom Accounts Were Opened in the Mobile Bank, January 1, 1866–April 15, 1867

Agents	1	Cotton samplers	2	Saddlers	Unknown
Attorneys	2	Cotton weighers	5	Seamstresses	17
Bakers	3	Domestics	28	Sextons	2
Barbers	12	Draymen	24	Shoemakers	2
Blacksmiths	1	Gardeners	5	Shopkeepers	4
Boatmen	16	Grocers	14	Slaters	1
Bootblacks	1	Hairdressers	3	Stewards	2
Butchers	2	Janitors	4	Stonecutters	1
Carpenters	21	Laborers	63	Tailors	5
Cartmen	5	Machinists	1	Teachers	4
Clergymen	1	Masons	12	Tinners	3
Clerks	1	Millers	1	Undertakers	2
Coachmen	6	Nurses	2	Varnishers	1
Compositors	2	Ostlers	2	Washers	26
Cooks	29	Oystermen	2		
Coopers	2	Painters	2	Societies	13
Cotton markers	6	Porters	4	No occupation	122
Cotton pressmen	3	Printers	1	(married women, minors, etc.)	
				Soldiers	11

paying, low-status jobs, but a significant minority were carpenters, boatmen, barbers, and other artisans. The occupational range of Mobile depositors is impressive.

Every branch tried to encourage schoolchildren to deposit. Bank agents and teachers, in making regular school canvasses, preached the value of work and thrift. According to Alvord, saving in the Freedman's Bank "would be the beginning of their manhood."[22] On one occasion S. L. Harris reported with delight the addition of several children's accounts, each ranging from five to twenty-five cents.[23] Scores of schoolchildren, who earned money penny by penny, appear in the pages of the signature books. The Augusta branch was so popular with schoolchildren that almost one-quarter of the depositors surveyed were in that category.

The Bank's business grew rapidly after 1870. The number of open accounts rose from 23,000 in that year to 61,000 by 1874. In 1873, when

21. *Ibid.*, June 25, 1868, p. 2; April 18, 1867, p. 2.
22. Alvord to Harris, November 5, 1867, p. 140, Letters Sent, Book 13, Educational Division, BRFAL.
23. Harris to Alvord, November 1, 1867, Bank Letters, BRFAL.

the *News and Courier* remarked on the crowds of freedmen gathered at the Bank's counter every day, the Charleston branch counted 5,000 active depositors.[24] The Washington branch proudly claimed over 3,000 in 1874.[25] Norfolk had 1,200 depositors in 1870 and 2,577 by 1874, while Richmond's depositors increased in these years from 1,200 to 3,850.[26] By 1874 thirteen of the thirty-three branches had over 2,000 depositors apiece.

The figure of 61,000 open accounts for the entire institution as of July, 1874, does not include those depositors who had previously closed their accounts, and thus the total number of depositors for the whole period was much larger. Between 1865 and 1870 approximately 20,000 depositors had opened and then closed their accounts. If one adds in an estimate of those who opened and then closed their accounts in the years 1870–74, the number of freedmen who used the Bank at some point in its nine-year history was probably well over 100,000.[27]

Some cashiers tried to estimate the percentage of the local population who made deposits. In spite of unusually heavy withdrawals at Savannah in 1870, the *New National Era* described the branch as increasing in the esteem and confidence of the people. The 325 new depositors in the previous three months reflected the branch's continuing growth. The cashier claimed that if Savannah had a Negro population of 10,000, then the Bank's 1,900 depositors constituted nearly one-fifth of the Negro community. (The 1870 census actually reported 13,067, and this was possibly an undercount.) One-fifth, perhaps even one-tenth, "speaks well for the intelligence, industry, and economy of the colored people."[28]

The Macon and Mobile cashiers attempted similar assessments. Although the Macon cashier felt that the freedmen could do much better in supporting the local branch, he showed that of a total population of over 4,000, some 707 Negroes had opened accounts.[29] This was approximately 17 percent of the community; even if the cashier had not controlled for those depositors living outside the census district, these figures suggest widespread participation. At Mobile, where the cashier

24. *News and Courier*, August 1, 1873, p. 1; Alvord, *Ninth Semi-Annual Report on Schools for Freedmen*, January 1, 1870, pp. 66–67; *Report of the Select Committee*, Senate, 1880, appendix, p. 22.

25. *New National Era*, December 14, 1871, p. 3; *Report of the Select Committee*, Senate, 1880, appendix, p. 22.

26. *New Era*, February 3, 1870, p. 3; *Report of the Commissioners*, 1874, p. 64; Monthly Report, July, 1870, National Freedman's Savings and Trust Co., AMA.

27. *Report of the Select Committee*, Senate, 1880, appendix, p. 22; Alvord, *Ninth Semi-Annual Report on Schools for Freedmen*, January 1, 1870, pp. 66–67.

28. *New National Era*, September 29, 1870, p. 3.

29. *Ibid.*, October 29, 1870, p. 3.

put the Negro population at 16,000 in 1868, every tenth person was a depositor.[30] Granted that errors occurred in these statistics, the cashiers' general impressions indicate extensive community support, from 10 to 20 percent of the local population. Additionally, thousands of freedmen who did not have accounts at the Bank became familiar with the Bank's objectives and activities through their churches and societies.

The Bank's daily business included the depositing and the withdrawals of many small sums. At Richmond the average daily business varied from $100 to $500 in small sums, while at Baltimore, a larger branch, a day's total varied between $500 and $2,000.[31] Cashier Wilson maintained that the Washington branch handled $6,000 to $20,000 daily.[32] The Nashville *Daily Press and Times* reported that the $34,000 at that city's branch comprised "the savings of a large number of poor colored people, who are determined to lay up something against a rainy day."[33] Whether or not they saved for a rainy day, large numbers of depositors removed their money soon after placing it in the Bank's care. According to the actuary, D. L. Eaton, the average deposit remained in the Bank only four months. (Eaton may have exaggerated, since total bank deposits steadily increased.) At one or two branches the evidence suggests that withdrawals and deposits fluctuated with the planting season and the harvest.[34]

Most of the savings accounts in what was truly a people's bank were small. The Vicksburg branch, with large amounts of bounty money raising the average account to $110, and the New Orleans branch, where 33 large deposits (amounting to $62,132.43) distorted average figures, must be regarded as exceptions.[35] Mobile and Charleston are more typical. At the former, no account exceeded $2,000, while at the latter, the average per depositor was $60.[36] At Baltimore the average total deposit in 1870 was $61; in smaller cities such as Augusta and Montgomery it was $40 and $55, respectively.[37] When the Bank failed in 1874, after withstanding three runs which resulted in the withdrawal of many sub-

30. *The Nationalist*, June 25, 1868, p. 2
31. *Report of the Commissioners*, 1874, pp. 63, 64; *The Nationalist*, January 10, 1867, p. 1.
32. *New National Era*, December 14, 1871, p. 3.
33. Alrutheus Ambush Taylor, *The Negro in Tennessee, 1865–1880* (Washington: Associated Publishers, 1941), p. 163.
34. *Charges against General Howard*, p. 394; Minutes A, pp. 86, 111.
35. *New Era*, March 24, 1870, p. 3; Examiner's Report of the New Orleans branch, Letters Rec'd by the Commissioners, 1870–1914, FS&T Co.
36. *Report of the Commissioners*, 1874, p. 78; Somers, *Southern States since the War*, p. 55.
37. Monthly Report, July 1870, National Freedman's Savings and Trust Co., AMA.

stantial accounts, the amount owed to each depositor averaged about $48.[38] Of course, many deposits amounted to practically nothing. The Bank encouraged the poor by accepting deposits as low as five cents, hoping that if people began to save they would progress from small to respectable balances. Evidently many saved money by the penny, nickel, or dime, for in July, 1874, there were 890 depositors at one branch whose accounts averaged only ninety-two cents.[39]

It must be remembered that, in terms of 1870 purchasing power, these small sums were by no means inconsequential. Sixty dollars in 1870 would buy several acres of land or three head of cattle or ten hogs. To a farm laborer it might represent one-third of a year's income, for in 1869 the average wage for a farm laborer was $15.50 a month, board not included.[40]

Often the size of a savings account had little relationship to its significance for a person's morale; to many of the poor, the idea of saving toward a better life was more meaningful than the actual size of their savings. A bank account symbolized freedom and advancement, "getting on" in the world. Louisa Anderson, a thirty-five-year-old ex-slave and widow with three children, managed somehow to save $16 from her meager earnings as a servant. Oscar Gibbs, an illiterate teamster who guessed his age as between thirty and forty, had to provide for a family of nine; yet he too had a bank account, although it contained only $4.50.[41] For Louisa Anderson and Oscar Gibbs, the Bank represented self-respect and dignity. For others, such as Frank Martin, a seventy-seven-year-old barber who could neither read nor write, the Bank provided a safe depository for his $96, which could be the basis for increasing his business and for actually accomplishing what others could only dream about.[42]

"Each Saturday," the *National Savings Bank* urged the freedmen, "let them put in the bank all they have been able to save during the week—

38. This figure is derived by dividing the total amount of deposits owed: $2,963,990.11 (*Report of the Select Committee*, Senate, 1880, appendix, p. 2), by the total number of depositors as of July, 1874: 61,000 (U.S., Congress, House, Committee on Banking and Currency, *Hearings in January, 1910, on House Bill 8776 to Reimburse Depositors of the Freedman's Savings and Trust Company*, p. 1).

39. U.S., Congress, House, Committee on Banking and Currency, *Freedman's Savings and Trust Company*, 43rd Cong., 2nd sess., 1875, House Report No. 58, p. 2. Originally, minimum deposits had been set at one dollar.

40. *Statistical History of the United States from Colonial Times to the Present* (Stamford, Conn.: Fairfield Publishers, 1965), pp. 281, 290. On the inexpensiveness of land during the Reconstruction period, see Joel Williamson, *After Slavery* (Chapel Hill: University of North Carolina Press, 1965), pp. 154–156.

41. Richmond Signature Book, Nos. 1946 and 2012, FS&T Co.

42. Richmond Signature Book, No. 2459, FS&T Co.

be it more or less, and they will be surprised soon, at the way it will accumulate."[43] Surprising indeed was the way money accumulated. Small deposits added up to large sums, and people began to take notice of the growing size of the Freedman's Savings and Trust Company. In October, 1870, when the company's deposits totaled $2,066,000, the Washington *Evening Star* predicted that deposits would probably reach $2,500,000 by March. When the prediction proved to be accurate, the paper called the Bank "truly an unparalleled success, all things considered."[44] The mayor of Savannah was surprised to learn that the local Negro bank in 1870 held over $80,000, and this soon grew to $100,000.[45] Progress, at least according to the *New Era*, embraced almost every aspect of the company's recent history. During June, 1870, the Richmond branch gained $4,000 from 129 new accounts, bringing total deposits to $81,591.31 in approximately 1,200 accounts. The *New Era* noted how tobacco mechanics saved part of their earnings every week to protect them during the annual layoffs.[46] During the year ending March 1, 1872, the Richmond branch gained 925 new accounts and $45,991.31, bringing total deposits to $130,984.30 in 2,687 accounts.[47] Charleston's growth was also impressive; the increase of its deposits from $18,000 in December, 1866, to $350,000 in August, 1873, pushed Charleston to the front rank among branch cities.[48] While dealing in sums considerably smaller than Charleston's, the Huntsville branch reported similar progress. The bank's $381.11 in 1867 increased to $3,631.02 by May, 1870, causing the cashier to gloat that his branch was the strongest and most popular bank in the United States. It was, said the cashier, quite evident that Negroes were practicing economy and thrift.[49]

Very little information exists to suggest the origin of the freedmen's money. Usually the signature books did not list the first amount deposited, and when they did they usually omitted its source. For example, a Washington school janitress, a former slave and widow with three children, opened an account with $287, a large sum indeed![50] Had she, like many other slaves, saved small amounts during her years of servitude, or had she saved this money from her meager earnings in freedom? Was this her husband's money? Perhaps he had been an artisan

43. June 1, 1868, pp. 1–2.
44. October 14, 1870, p. 4; April 21, 1871, p. 4.
45. Alvord, *Letters from the South*, p. 14.
46. July 28, 1870, p. 1.
47. Richmond *Daily Enquirer*, April 11, 1872, p. 3.
48. *News and Courier*, August 1, 1873, p. 1.
49. *New Era*, July 28, 1870, p. 1.
50. Washington Signature Book, No. 1031, FS&T Co.

or a soldier, and this was his back pay and/or bounty money. The history of the Bank contains numerous stories of Negroes who struggled against overwhelming obstacles to save sizable amounts. Said a reporter for the *New York Tribune*:

> I know of one colored washerwoman, who has a family to support, that has in one of these banks over $260 in gold and silver. I know an old black man—all his life a slave—who deposited at one time, soon after the branch was established, $380 in gold and silver. He said he earned it while a slave by working at night by the light of a pine-torch, after he had done all the overseer demanded of him. I could give scores of instances of the same character—showing conclusively the fallacy of the oft-repeated assertion that negroes are unable to take care of themselves—that their normal condition is slavery.[51]

But large deposits, no matter how accumulated, were the exception rather than the rule; when accounting for the millions of dollars placed in the Bank's vaults, one must turn to more typical depositors. Signature book descriptions show that most of the depositors, with the important exception of schoolchildren, were employed; the small yet continuous deposits seem to have been saved from their wages. As the number of depositors rose from 23,000 in 1870 to 61,000 or more in 1874, deposits increased accordingly. In a sense, then, the founders' faith had been rewarded: work and thrift had created the many small deposits of thousands of freedmen.

From a few thousand dollars in 1865, the Bank entered the million-dollar bracket before the end of the decade. The greatest increases occurred after 1869, as the following figures show:

For year ending March 1	Balance due depositors	Increase
1866	$ 199,283.42	$ 199,283.42
1867	366,338.33	167,054.91
1868	638,299.00	271,960.67
1869	1,073,465.31	435,166.31
1870	1,657,006.75	583,341.44
1871	2,455,836.11	798,829.36
1872	3,684,739.97	1,227,927.67

By June, 1873, the total amounts deposited and withdrawn were $49,629,354.25 and $45,600,684.82, respectively, leaving a balance due

51. January 31, 1867, p. 2.

of $4,028,669.43, which was the approximate amount needed for the Bank to meet all of its expenses.[52]

The Bank's growth and popularity were stimulated by an increasing number of Negro officers. When the first branches were established in 1865, Negroes received positions as advisory board members and, at Washington and Nashville, as cashiers.[53] The number of Negro cashiers steadily increased until, by 1874, they formed a majority of all the cashiers. The position of cashier was especially important: he was the Bank's top official in the local area, and he was responsible for everything pertaining to his branch. Hence the cashier held a prestigious position in the black community. Negroes also held lesser positions, of course, as assistant cashiers, clerks, messengers, and janitors; according to Alvord, they eventually comprised a majority of the company's employees. This fact was most evident at the Washington branch, where at one time all the employees in the front office were black.[54] Several of them—such as Christian Fleetwood, who was awarded a Congressional Medal of Honor, and R. W. Thomkins and George D. Johnson, who were noted for their leadership in the fight against racial discrimination—were important figures in Washington's black community.[55]

Even in the early years when almost all the trustees and most of the cashiers were white men, some officials felt that since the Bank was a Negro bank it should have black officers. Anson Sperry testified in 1880 that "the trustees always felt bound to give the preference to colored employes. We had able young colored men, but they were not bankers, to begin with, and they had to learn the business. We were gradually getting around us a corps of able young men; but they all came in as apprentices in the work."[56] The trustees claimed they added to the number of Negro cashiers whenever they found capable applicants. "Other things being equal," said Sperry, "we always gave the preference

52. *Report of the Select Committee*, Senate, 1880, appendix, p. 41; Financial Statement for the Month of June, 1873, Letters Rec'd by the Commissioners, 1870–1914, FS&T Co. It is impossible to estimate what proportion of total deposits was owed to whites. The amount due whites was quite substantial at New Orleans and New York, and perhaps great at Beaufort and Jacksonville. Elsewhere it was small. One estimate, too conservative perhaps, placed the amount due whites at 5 percent of the total. See "Five Years of Freedmen's Education as Seen in the Bureau Reports," *Freedmen's Record*, V, 7 (January, 1871), 91.

53. See above, ch. 1.

54. *Freedman's Bank*, House, 1876, pp. 50–51.

55. Christian Fleetwood Papers, Library of Congress; *Evening Star*, February 16, 1871, p. 1; James H. Whyte, *The Uncivil War: Washington during the Reconstruction, 1865–1878* (New York: Twayne Publishers, 1958), p. 244.

56. *Report of the Select Committee*, Senate, 1880, p. 250.

to colored men in filling these places, as was only right and just."[57]

Even apart from right and justice, the employment of Negroes was good business. Negro cashiers, clerks, and members of the advisory boards proved more effective than whites in reaching the freedmen and winning their allegiance. It was found that "Colored men on the Committee are best" because they more easily established rapport with the people—a critical element for increasing deposits.[58] A Negro advisory committee at Richmond was responsible for opening the company's third branch.[59] At Atlanta in early 1874 the trustees installed a Negro cashier because the white cashier had lost the depositors' confidence. Although not opposed to white depositors, several prominent Negroes complained that this cashier had been making overtures to obtain business with white people while neglecting the black community.[60] At Memphis Inspector Harris wanted to appoint a Negro cashier because it would satisfy the local people.[61] Vice-President Hewitt agreed, concluding that the presence of a white cashier would not instill confidence. "He is a white man getting up a Bank for the Negro [and] not the Negro getting up a Bank for himself and selecting white men to cooperate with him."[62] The Savannah cashier likewise recognized the desire for Negro leaders when he led in the reorganization of the advisory committee, "dropping off the rebs and making it essentially a Col'd Com [Colored Committee] and now deposits are coming in. We may look for success here."[63]

Whenever the trustees were slow to see the advantages of employing Negroes, they were soon prodded by local leaders. The freedmen forced the issue of Negro cashiers; they exerted constant pressure to have the branches put under their control.[64] Negroes wanted positions of leadership in their institution, not simply jobs as janitors, messengers, or even clerks. On one occasion the leader of a Negro cooperative association in Charleston, A. L. Stevens, demanded that Alvord tell him why, during a period of almost five years, no Negro had been appointed to a

57. *Ibid.*, p. 262.
58. Alvord to Harris, September 15, 1866, p. 51, Letters Sent, Book 11, Educational Division, BRFAL.
59. See above, ch. 1.
60. *Report of the Select Committee*, Senate, 1880, pp. 260–261.
61. Harris to Alvord, February 22, 1867, Bank Letters, BRFAL.
62. M. T. Hewitt to Alvord, January 24, 1866, *ibid.*
63. Harris to Alvord, January 31, 1867, *ibid.* It is not known to whom "rebs" refers. Perhaps the "rebs" whom the depositors distrusted were ex-Confederates who sympathized with the aims of the Bank, but not necessarily with the cause of genuine social and economic advancement for black people.
64. *Report of the Select Committee*, Senate, 1880, p. 261.

position of prestige in the Charleston branch.[65] Alvord's answer did not satisfy Stevens, who replied:

> I think I know for a fact that there is a Colored man Employed in The Branch Bank of This City as a waiter cleaning the spittoons and brushing out and shutting up the place . . . I did not ask for that to be told me. I simply want to know why it is that a Colored man of ability cannot or could not be employed as Cashier or any other position. A position . . . I mean of elevation not the drawer of water. As I stated that Colored men were Cashiers and Clerks of the Banks in other Cities I did not mean position of that menialness as referred to me in your Letter.

The Charleston branch eventually employed a Negro as assistant cashier.[66] There was also pressure for a Negro cashier at Tallahassee. Bank inspector Anson Sperry turned down one Negro applicant in the belief that he was only interested in the position because his political fortunes had declined. When the demand persisted, Sperry appealed to the actuary to send him "the Colored man *you* can trust."[67]

At the Norfolk branch a continuing controversy over the employment of Negroes versus whites dated all the way back to the selection of white cashiers in 1865. In 1867 Isaac S. Mullen, secretary of the advisory board, tried to persuade General Howard that deposits would increase if the Bank hired black clerks. "I have not the least doubt," he wrote, "that if a man having influence among my color should be employed in the Bank at Norfolk, that the Bank would be greatly benefited."[68] That Mullen himself wanted a paying position with the Norfolk branch helps explain the vigor of his argument. Mullen, whose background and qualifications must have resembled those of thousands of freedmen, readily admitted that he was unsure of his competency for a Bank position, but he declared he could learn. Having served three years in the navy, he had recently been defeated for a position as receiver in the yards and docks because, so he claimed, he was a Negro and a Republican. At the time of his appeal to Howard, he worked in the navy yard as a laborer.[69] Who, then, Mullen implied, would employ Negroes on terms of equality if not their own institutions? Negroes needed the oppor-

65. A. L. Stevens to Alvord, December 13, 1869, Bank Letters, BRFAL.

66. *Ibid.*; *Freedman's Bank*, House, 1876, p. 51.

67. A. M. Sperry to George W. Stickney, November 12, 1872, in Minutes of the Building Committee, FS&T Co.

68. Isaac S. Mullen to Maj. Gen. O. O. Howard, September 4, 1867, Letters Rec'd, I, Educational Division, BRFAL. From the context of this letter it is clear that Mullen's words, "a man having influence among my color," refer to a black man.

69. *Ibid.*

tunity for jobs of honor, profit, and trust and the chance to confound prejudice against freedmen. Mullen's arguments for Negro leadership weighed heavily upon the Norfolk advisory committee, as is indicated in a letter written by Inspector Harris eight days after Mullen's: "At first it seemed as though it would be impossible to hold a quorum of our Committee—so dissatisfied were they—at not being consulted in the matter of the Cashier. Now, however, we are getting over the trouble and moving along slowly."[70]

The demands for black cashiers caused problems, since some candidates were hardly prepared for their new duties. Although deficient training was a problem with white cashiers as well, they could easily be replaced when their incompetence became evident. Yet when this was the case with a black cashier, community pride became an obstacle. William J. Wilson of the Washington branch is a case in point. Alvord felt that he should have been removed because of repeated errors in bookkeeping, and steps were taken which resulted in 1874 in his demotion to traveling agent.

> We did it [said Alvord] as carefully as we could. He was a colored man of good standing, a pure African, but we thought he was not quite the man for the place when he could be persuaded to do such things, and we made efforts to put him in a different position. . . . The colored men seemed to think that they ought to be employed, and we wanted to employ them so far as could be, and it became a very delicate matter when one got in to set him aside. We had great trial on that subject.[71]

Looking back after the Bank's failure, Sperry remarked, "The race and color question . . . interfered, but that is a matter which I do not want to touch upon; . . . it kept incompetent men in those places."[72]

The financial troubles of inexperienced cashiers properly belong to the story of the Bank's difficulties in 1873 and 1874. But the advantages of employing black cashiers, all things considered, outweighed the disadvantages. Even the troublesome Wilson was popular in his community; while his superiors might have considered him financially inept, the people most likely believed him to be a financial wizard. The *New National Era* once compared him favorably with the famous banker W. W. Corcoran, depicting Wilson as one of the country's future financial giants.[73] In addition to the community's trust, Wilson brought dedication to his work among the freedmen. By training and inclination he was

---

70. Harris to Alvord, September 12, 1867, Bank Letters, BRFAL.
71. *Freedman's Bank*, House, 1876, p. 49; Journal, January 10, 1874.
72. *Freedman's Bank*, House, 1876, p. 7.
73. December 28, 1871, p. 1.

a teacher; the Bank duties at first were secondary and provided no pay. But Wilson had come to Washington "to work—work in the cause of my people to the best of my ability & ask in return but to live,—not to get great gain."[74] He also participated in local activities to win civil rights for Negroes.[75]

Blacks were cashiers in such important cities as Louisville, New Orleans, St. Louis, New York, Philadelphia, and Nashville and in such lesser ones as Natchez, New Bern, Alexandria, Macon, Raleigh, Shreveport, Huntsville, and Lynchburg. In 1874, when the Bank failed, seventeen blacks were cashiers in the thirty-three branches then open. All in all, at least twenty-one blacks were cashiers for various lengths of time, although their service tended to concentrate late in the Bank's history.[76] At least fourteen of the twenty-one cashiers were men of some prominence in their communities, and there is no reason to doubt that the remaining seven, of whom little is known, were men of local note. The five cashiers identified as Southerners were free before the war (including William J. Wilson, born and raised in Washington), and there is no evidence that any other cashier was freed by the war. Because the cashier served as a symbol of progress and middle-class success, Bank officials would be unlikely to hire someone closely associated with slave status. At least seven of these cashiers were Northerners. While the shortcomings of several Negro cashiers attracted much attention, most of them probably performed their duties adequately.[77] John Alvord concluded that "quite a number of these men were excellent writers and thoroughly accurate clerks, while some were not. We had some very fine colored cashiers at the branches, men who were perfectly competent, and we had also some fine fellows in the principal office."[78]

Black cashiers were selected from an elite to serve as examples of

74. William J. Wilson to the Rev. George Whipple, December 23, 1865, AMA.
75. *Evening Star*, February 16, 1871, p. 1.
76. *Freedman's Bank*, House, 1876, pp. 50, 51; *Report of the Commissioners*, 1874, pp. 61–83 *passim*. See Appendix C. The black cashiers are:

Willis Brent, St. Louis	C. S. Sauvinet, New Orleans
G. W. Brodie, Raleigh	Thomas N. M. Sellers, Macon
W. F. Bronaugh, Lynchburg	John A. Smythe, Wilmington
John J. Cary, Nashville	William Steward, New Bern
Fields Cook, Alexandria	T. G. Stewart, Macon
J. M. Hawksworth, Natchez	William Stewart, Tallahassee
C. S. Johnson, Atlanta	H. H. Webb, Baltimore
Horace Morris, Louisville	William Whipper, Philadelphia
Samuel Peters, Shreveport	William J. Wilson, Washington
J. W. Purnell, Shreveport	John J. Zuille, New York
Lafayette Robinson, Huntsville	

77. For further information on this point, see ch. 5.
78. *Freedman's Bank*, House, 1876, p. 50.

black achievement. The cashier at Alexandria, Virginia, was Fields Cook, a minister and delegate to the Republican state convention of 1867; T. G. Stewart, pastor of a large Negro church, held the top post at Macon. The New Orleans cashier, C. S. Sauvinet, was a light-colored, French-speaking Catholic who was known to his community as an "accomplished and urbane gentleman" and a dedicated parent who sent his son to Howard University. Sauvinet made news when he brought suit against a saloonkeeper who refused to serve him because of his race. Nevertheless, the reports on the New Orleans cashier were not entirely favorable. Sauvinet, wrote Harris, was "a Catholic and this works against us with the Freedmen" (but of course helped with the large Creole group). Also, complained Harris, being a Southerner, he lacked Yankee energy and was involved in political dissension, which injured the Bank. Consequently, Harris wished to remove him and appoint "an active, Christian Northerner," thus implying a nice distinction between Christians and Catholics. In spite of Harris, Sauvinet remained with the Bank until 1870 or 1871, when he won an election for sheriff; by then the branch was doing well, though perhaps not as well as some officers wished.[79]

The Huntsville cashier, Lafayette Robinson, was a freeborn black who became involved in politics, serving as a member of the Republican state executive committee and as a delegate to the Alabama constitutional convention. Samuel Peters, Shreveport's cashier, was a Northerner who was described by the *Semi-Weekly Louisianian* as "eminently qualified" and possessing the respect and confidence of the community. In 1872 acting Governor P. B. S. Pinchback appointed him divisional superintendent of education for the fourth congressional district. J. W. Purnell, formerly the bookkeeper at Philadelphia, took over Peters's duties. Willis Brent, a free Negro whitewasher who had lived in St. Louis at least as early as 1860 and probably earlier, became cashier of Missouri's only branch bank. At Tallahassee in 1871, William Stewart, who was much involved in the school affairs of the AMA, took over. John A. Smythe, a former teacher and a clerk in the Freedmen's Bureau, the Interior Department, and the Bank's central office, became the Wilmington cashier in 1873. He brought with him a law school education and great practical experience. Later he entered North Carolina politics and worked for the government in Washington, and was appointed minister resident and consul general to Liberia. Eventually he

79. Minutes A, 1869, pp. 121–122; Examiner's Report of the New Orleans branch, Letters Rec'd by the Commissioners, 1870–1914, FS&T Co.; Harris to Alvord, March 27, 1867, Bank Letters, BRFAL; Sauvinet to Alvord, February 12, 1870, Letters Rec'd, III, box 4, Educational Division, BRFAL.

reentered private life and enjoyed a fine legal career in the nation's capital.[80]

Two of the Bank's leading black cashiers were John J. Cary and Horace Morris. Cary served on Fisk University's board of trustees in addition to presiding over the Bank's activities in Nashville. Although the Freedman's Bank examiner expressed certain reservations about his business capacity, Cary was esteemed by Nashville bankers and also by blacks, who appointed him chairman of the celebration honoring the ratification of the Fifteenth Amendment. Described as quiet and clever, Cary had spent years in Canada before the war among the fugitive-slave communities.[81] Like the Raleigh cashier, G. W. Brodie, he had received his early schooling from John Alvord in Cincinnati in the 1830's. The fact that Cary had persevered and was now a man of culture and influence caused Alvord to write to General Howard, rejoicing, "We do not, General, labor in vain. As years pass on, and you become as gray in the beard as I am, thousands of prominent colored men will take you by the hand—as did these boys of mine—and thank you for having been their early benefactor."[82]

Horace Morris, listed among Louisville's "leading colored men" according to the *Courier-Journal*, was one of the Bank's most successful cashiers.[83] Educated and raised in Ohio, Morris gained recognition as a prominent Mason and member of the Underground Railroad. Before his employment as cashier, he had been a steward on the Ohio River, and after the war he became the secretary of the Louisville advisory board on colored schools. When the Bank closed, Morris moved to Washington, where he held minor governmental positions in the Treasury Department and the Marine Hospital.[84] Few doubted Morris's ability. Alvord considered him an accomplished accountant, "his books and entire premises in perfect order."[85] The bank examiner, too, was pleased with the Louisville cashier: "He is intelligent, a good penman, and correct accountant."[86] That Morris excelled not only in bookkeeping

80. *Freedman's Bank*, House, 1876, pp. 50, 51; *Report of the Commissioners, 1874*, pp. 61–83 *passim*; St. Louis City Directory, 1860; *The Louisianian*, April 2, 1871, p. 2; April 27, 1871, p. 2; March 21, 1872, p. 2; Peter Kolchin, *First Freedom* (Westport, Conn.: Greenwood Press, 1972), pp. 158, 165; Alrutheus Ambush Taylor, *The Negro in the Reconstruction of Virginia* (Washington: Association for the Study of Negro Life and History, 1926), p. 188; Simmons, *Men of Mark*, pp. 872–877; Letters of William Stewart, AMA.

81. *Report of the Commissioners, 1874*, p. 81.

82. Alvord, *Letters from the South*, p. 34.

83. June 28, 1874, p. 3.

84. H. C. Weeden, *Weeden's History of the Colored People of Louisville* (Louisville: By the Author, 1897), p. 42.

85. Alvord, *Letters from the South*, p. 34.

86. *Report of the Commissioners, 1874*, p. 70.

and financial matters but also in popularity is shown by the increase in depositors. In 1868, when he assumed the cashiership, there were 709 depositors; by June, 1874, the Louisville branch could count almost 3,000.[87]

The Bank's two northern branches, New York and Philadelphia, were directed by Negroes of recognized leadership ability. The New York cashier, John J. Zuille, was an abolitionist of Underground Railroad fame and an organizer and later historian of the New York African Society for Mutual Relief.[88] William Whipper of Philadelphia was probably the wealthiest cashier. The son of a maid and her white employer, Whipper eventually inherited his father's business and became a successful lumber and coal merchant. In the process he established close ties with black businessmen. Always active in racial affairs, he organized a Negro abolitionist group, the American Moral Reform Society, and became a supporter of black educational efforts and the black press. Although not considered a radical by his contemporaries, he was an advocate of integration.[89]

Thus among all of the identifiable cashiers one finds qualities and achievements that set them apart as influential and successful men within their communities. Certainly all had achieved middle-class status.

While many branches did not have a Negro cashier, they all had Negroes on the advisory boards. Ranging in size from five to thirty-six members, the boards were largely composed of black men who were leaders or potential leaders in their communities.[90] At first glance, these boards appear mainly as window dressing, being simply, as their name implies, advisory.[91] One bank examiner exclaimed that the board at Wilmington, North Carolina, had nothing to do, since that branch made no loans and forwarded all sums directly to Washington.[92] The Agency Committee at Washington controlled (at least theoretically) all of the actions of the advisory boards. It reviewed and then elected those nominated to the local boards and, in some cases, requested that certain individuals—a Union general, for one example—be placed on the board.[93] In 1867 the Agency Committee declared that no action by an advisory

87. *Courier-Journal*, June 28, 1874, p. 3.
88. Ottley and Weatherby, eds., *The Negro in New York*, pp. 61, 87.
89. Louis C. Jones, "A Leader Ahead of His Times," *American Heritage*, XIV, 4 (June, 1963), 59, 83.
90. *Report of the Commissioners*, 1874, p. 64.
91. *Charges against General Howard*, p. 403.
92. *Report of the Commissioners*, 1874, p. 73.
93. Alvord to N. R. Scovel, September 10, 1867, p. 10, Letters Sent, Book 13, Educational Division, BRFAL.

board was final until approved by the trustees.[94] Thus the Augusta advisory board even had to request permission to change the time of its monthly meetings.[95]

Nevertheless, the advisory boards performed a vital function: they supplied the link between the powers at the central office and their representative, the cashier, and the local community. The boards stimulated grass-roots support. In June, 1865, the Agency Committee officially declared that the advisory boards were "to act upon the Colored population instructing them, awakening interest, encouraging deposits, etc."[96]

Whether or not deposits grew often depended upon the work of the advisory board as well as the cashier, especially if the latter was a white man from outside the local community. On a tour of the branches in 1870, President Alvord considered it very important to speak with the local boards, and he reported with satisfaction that they had resolved upon increased efforts to raise deposits through public meetings and private canvassing.[97] When the actuary, D. L. Eaton, visited Norfolk in 1869, he called a board meeting; though it was noon and the committeemen had to leave their work, thirteen members out of thirty-three arrived to discuss ways of encouraging people to save.[98] It will be remembered that the Richmond branch owed its very existence to an advisory board that had canvassed the area, sampling opinion and urging support for a freedmen's bank.[99]

For a time in 1865 some officials contemplated having the local board members collect deposits. But M. T. Hewitt, then vice-president, disagreed with this view: "Colored Agents going among the negroes to get deposits, while they would not in fact be our Agents nor make us legally responsible for the funds until they were passed on our books, still if a loss should occur the depositors might assume that they were acting as our Agents and make us much trouble; that mode of obtaining deposits is looked upon as dangerous."[100] Consequently, the boards were restricted to influencing people and publicizing the Bank. "You did a very wise thing," Captain O. S. B. Wall at Charleston confided to Alvord, "when you created this large (col'd) Committee as it inspires confidence. They each one takes a pride in influencing persons to de-

94. Minutes A, September 11, 1867, p. 49.
95. Minutes B, September 12, 1872, p. 18.
96. Minutes A, June 30, 1865, p. 7.
97. *Ibid.*, December 8, 1870, p. 186.
98. *Ibid.*, June 10, 1869, pp. 100, 111.
99. *Ibid.*, June 13, 1865, p. 3.
100. *Ibid.*, p. 5.

posit." Wall reported how one Charleston member had sent in a man who deposited $200.[101]

Some advisory boards assumed a good deal of responsibility in their branches. "They have," declared a bank examiner at Richmond, "what is called an advisory board of colored men of the better class, to whom all questions of interest are submitted, and these men evidently take a deep interest in the welfare of the institution."[102] Some boards became involved with everything with which the Bank was concerned, including the temperance cause. Advisory boards supplied information to the Agency Committee, and they frequently conducted the negotiations for renting or purchasing the banking office or building; some also became involved in the selection and payment of their cashiers.[103] The St. Louis board, for example, recommended an increase in the cashier's salary and the employment of a bookkeeper.[104] In practice the Agency Committee seems frequently to have delegated to the advisory boards the authority to set the cashiers' salaries and bonds.[105] At Montgomery, where two cashiers struggled for the top position in a mix-up over resignations, the Agency Committee requested the advisory board to select the proper cashier.[106] The Baltimore board took similar action without requesting approval from the home office; when the cashier resigned in June, 1867, the local board, styling itself the "Board of Trustees of the Freedman's Savings Bank at Baltimore," met and unanimously elected a successor.[107]

Many advisory boards were rarely successful in fulfilling their duty to examine the financial transactions of the branches. Each board was ordered to select a subcommittee, the attending committee, to certify each month that the cash and accounts were correct. The "Rules and Regulations for Advisory Committees" specified that the attending committee was to be a watchdog, checking and examining all business matters.[108] Having a monthly rotating membership of three, each subcommittee was to include at least one member qualified to handle detailed financial records. Extant papers in the Freedman's Savings and Trust Company's files do not provide many clues about the activities

101. O. S. B. Wall to Alvord, January 1, 1866, Bank Letters, BRFAL.

102. *Report of the Commissioners*, 1874, p. 64.

103. Minutes A, December 8, 1870, p. 183; Nathaniel Noyes to Hewitt, December 31, 1866, Bank Letters, BRFAL.

104. Minutes A, November 9, 1871, p. 210.

105. N. C. Dennett to Alvord, April 16, 1866, Bank Letters, BRFAL.

106. Minutes A, November 12, 1868, p. 88.

107. Alvord to Samuel Townsend, June 25, 1867, Letters Sent, Book 12, Educational Division, BRFAL; Townsend to Alvord, June 28, 1867, Bank Letters, BRFAL.

108. "Rules and Regulations for Advisory Committees," pp. 7–8, Committee on FA, NA, RG 233.

of the attending committees; but in view of the discrepancies and faulty bookkeeping discovered in 1873 and 1874, the subcommittees at some branches must have been negligent or incompetent. In May, 1873, the Agency Committee had to create a new committee, the auditing committee, to assume the duties of branch examinations. The local attending committee, it noted, "has proved a failure."[109]

Some advisory boards were active, influential, and effective, while others provided very indifferent service. The Atlanta advisory board seems to have taken little interest in examining the cashier's activities; consequently, from mid-1872 through 1873 Phillip Cory, the cashier, was able to use the freedmen's money recklessly and illegally. The boards at Charleston and Macon, where there were strong, well-managed branches, were cited for their effectiveness.[110] A concerned, active, and popular advisory board was often essential to the success of the branch. To a certain extent Hewitt implied this when he compared the sagging fortunes of the Memphis branch with the success of the Nashville branch, which flourished partly because of the initiative of a strong, all-black advisory board.[111]

One of the best and most influential advisory boards was at Louisville. In January, 1866, the board, composed of seventeen Negroes and seven whites, met in full session to recommend the resignation of the cashier because of his inability or unwillingness to devote his full time to the Bank's work.[112] In October the committee met to nominate a new cashier.[113] There is little information on the board's activities during the next few years, but in 1870 President Alvord reported that he had met the very intelligent committee at the Bank, and that it had resolved to make renewed efforts to encourage depositors throughout the city and state.[114] In these years the board was reduced to fifteen members (all but three of them Negroes) for greater efficiency.[115] The Louisville *Courier-Journal* in 1874 wrote that the Freedman's Bank in Louisville

109. *Ibid.*; Minutes B, May 7, 1873, p. 52.

110. Minutes A, February 10, 1870, p. 144; *Report of the Commissioners*, 1874, p. 75; E. N. Broyles to the Commissioners, October 30, 1876, Letters Rec'd by the Commissioners, 1870–1914, FS&T Co.

111. Hewitt to Alvord, January 24, 1866, Bank Letters, BRFAL. This was the Memphis situation in January, 1866. It is not known who the advisory board members were then, but by 1868 the Memphis advisory board certainly included a number of influential white and black citizens. See Table 10. Although it is unknown whether the members in 1868 actually performed their duties, the Memphis branch was in a much better financial position than in 1866. Perhaps the influential board members had something to do with the improved financial outlook.

112. Minutes A, January 11, 1866, p. 20.

113. *Ibid.*, October 10, 1866, p. 28.

114. Alvord, *Letters from the South*, p. 34.

115. *Report of the Commissioners*, 1874, p. 69.

had accomplished a good deal under the leadership of the advisory board and its chairman, the Honorable Bland Ballard, president of the Kentucky National Bank.[116] When the Louisville branch was examined in 1874, all its financial affairs were in order.[117]

Who were the members of the advisory boards? Unfortunately, there is a paucity of information concerning these local leaders, some of whom were prominent for only a brief period. We may, however, approach an answer by sketching the backgrounds of some board members for some branches. For instance, a little information exists (in some cases only the name, race, and signature) for eighteen of the thirty-three pre-1870 Memphis board members (see Table 10) and for twelve of the twenty-five members at Washington and Huntsville (see Table 11).

Negro members of the advisory boards were selected for their leadership potential or community standing, and of course election to the board in turn conferred additional prestige. They were not ex-fieldhands. Some members received national attention as political leaders during the Reconstruction period; others achieved status because of their wealth or their skills as artisans. The ability to write in a community that was overwhelmingly illiterate placed certain members well above the masses. Most committeemen could read and write, and some had received formal education. A few were wealthy, but most were men of moderate means holding positions as artisans or professionals, especially as ministers, in the black community. Eight of the eighteen Memphis members were clergymen. The occupations of the Washington members, as listed by the Agency Committee, included six ministers, two government messengers, one hotelkeeper, one claims agent, one army captain, one merchant, and one drayman.[118] Many of the board members had been born free, and a considerable number showed evidence of white parentage.

Although Negroes always formed a substantial majority on the advisory boards, white influence on some was marked. Usually two or three whites sat on each board, although some boards were all black, such as Nashville's and probably Augusta's.[119] Sometimes these few whites, often teachers or Bureau agents, held the top positions. Judge Bland Ballard headed the Louisville committee, and Governor W. W. Holden for a short time headed the one in Raleigh; Colonel George D. Robinson, Bureau superintendent of the Mobile district, and Colonel

116. June 28, 1874, p. 3.
117. *Report of the Commissioners,* 1874, p. 69.
118. Minutes A, November 12, 1868, p. 89.
119. *New National Era,* May 21, 1874, p. 2.

G. E. Yearrington, a Freedmen's Bureau judge, temporarily held the top positions at Mobile.[120] At some branches the whites probably provided the needed financial counsel for inexperienced freedmen.

Most committees contained one or two Negro members who were known statewide or nationally. South Carolina political leaders Richard H. Cain and Francis L. Cardozo were the chairman and secretary, respectively, of the Charleston advisory board.[121] In a letter of introduction to Alvord, James Low, formerly Charleston's board chairman, described the Reverend Cain as "thoroughly acquainted with the Condition, prospects and necessities of the Colored people of this state, able to give you much information with regard to matters in which interested, and a gentleman whose views and opinions are entitled to consideration."[122] This important minister and politician was a valuable committee member. Alabama politician and later Congressman James T. Rapier sat on the Montgomery board, while the Reverend T. W. Stringer, whom the historian Vernon Lane Wharton described as the most powerful leader in Mississippi until 1869, held the top position at the Vicksburg branch.[123] Wherever Stringer went in the state, "churches, lodges, benevolent societies, and political machines sprang up and flourished."[124] Robert Smalls, J. J. Wright, and Major M. R. Delany, South Carolina political leaders, held seats on the Beaufort committee.[125]

The fact that several Negro politicians of prominence held positions on the advisory boards does not mean that most members were politicians or even politically involved. Actually, three large groups emerged: politicians, ministers, and businessmen. The Nashville committee, which was all black, had many well-known community and state leaders. One member, Nelson Walker, a barber and a wealthy Memphis civil rights leader, was a delegate to the state convention of Colored Citizens of Tennessee and held a seat on the board of commissioners to supervise Negro migration. Another member, Henry Harding, owned property estimated to be worth more than $10,000 and was president of the Colored Agricultural and Mechanical Association, a Negro cooperative organized in 1870 to advance the interests of Negroes, especially by

120. Minutes A, August 15, 1865, pp. 11, 283; *The Nationalist*, December 28, 1865, p. 2.

121. *South Carolina Leader*, March 23, 1867, p. 3.

122. James P. Low to Alvord, May 13, 1868, Bank Letters, BRFAL.

123. Minutes B, June 13, 1872, p. 10; Vernon Lane Wharton, *The Negro in Mississippi, 1865–1890* (Chapel Hill: University of North Carolina Press, 1947), pp. 148–149.

124. Wharton, *Negro in Mississippi*, p. 149.

125. Minutes A, p. 227; Alrutheus Ambush Taylor, *The Negro in South Carolina during Reconstruction* (Washington: Association for the Study of Negro Life and History, 1924), pp. 328, 338, 341.

Table 10. Descriptions of Eighteen Members of the Memphis Advisory Board (*ca.* 1868)

Name	Complexion	Age	Birthplace	Residence	Occupation	Signature	Remarks
Africa Bailey #40	black	52	Southhampton Co., Va.	Memphis (Fort Pickering)	minister, Baptist Church	Africa Bailey [weak]	—
Clement Byrd Baker #226	light	28	Memphis	Memphis	physician & druggist	Clement Byrd Baker	
Joseph H. Barnum #140	white	—	Ashtabula Co., Ohio	Memphis	AMA Principal of Schools	Joseph H. Barnum	
Thomas Bradshaw #212	[Negro]	—	—	—	barber	—	
Rev. William Brinkley #1371	—	—	—	Memphis	[probably a minister]	William Brinkley	
Rev. Morris Henderson #7	dark	—	Amelia Co., Va.	Memphis	clergyman	Morris Henderson [weak]	former slave in Shelby Co., Tenn.
Rufus H. McCain #277	yellow	25	McNair Co., Tenn.	Memphis	draying	Rufus H. McCain	formerly a soldier & treasurer of the A.M.E. Church in Memphis
W. W. Mallery #342	—	—	Canada	Memphis	clergyman, Second Congregational Church	W. W. Mallery	
James Nelson #198	black	65 or 70	Eastern Shore, Md.	Memphis	draying	signed with an "X"	
Columbus Polk #141	black	27	Franklin Co., Va.	Memphis	janitor at Freedman's Bank	signed with an "X"	member of the Finance Committee of Queen Esther's Court, No. 8
Horatio N. Rankin #1 & 167	mulatto	—	Madison Co., Ky.	Memphis	teacher	Horatio N. Rankin	formerly of Oberlin
Dr. Willis R. Revels #676	—	—	—	Memphis	pastor, A.M.E. Church	Willis R. Revels	
Richard Rickets #233	light	40	Henry Co., Ky.	Memphis	pastor of Phoenix Station	Richard Rickets [weak]	
Joseph Ross	—	—	—	—	—	signed with an "X"	treasurer of A.M.E. Church

Name	Complexion	Age	Birthplace	Residence	Occupation	Signature	Remarks
Samuel C. Silliman #206	white	–	Easton, Conn.	Memphis	pastor, Baptist Church & teacher	Samuel C. Silliman	
John Suskins #126	mulatto	27	Shelby Co, Tenn.	Memphis	bricklayer	signed with an "X"	
S. H. Toler #26	–	–	Ohio	Memphis	physician	Dr. S. H. Toler	
Rev. Page Tyler #13	medium dark	48	Butler Co., Ky.	Memphis	clergyman	Page Tyler	former slave of Brinkley Tyler

TABLE 11. Descriptions of Members of the Washington and Huntsville Advisory Boards (*ca.* 1868)

Name	Complexion	Age	Birthplace	Residence	Occupation	Signature	Remarks
Washington							
John H. Ferguson #1527	–	–	Fairfax Co., Va.	Georgetown, D.C.	carpenter	John H. Ferguson	opened account with $225
Rev. C. J. Johnson #1375	yellow	–	Kent Co., Md.	Washington	pastor, Asbury Church	C. J. Johnson	opened account with $185
Walker Lewis #3	[Negro]	–	–	–	messenger, U.S. Treasury	Walker Lewis	
Francis Madison #632	yellow	–	Louden Co., Va.	Washington	messenger, War Department	Francis Madison [weak]	opened account with $647
Griffin Sanders #580	light brown	–	King William Co., Va.	Washington	whitewasher	signed with an "X"	$700 in his account
O. S. B. Wall #715	mulatto	–	Richmond Co., N.C.	Oberlin, Ohio	Employment Agent Freedmen's Bureau	O. S. B. Wall	[former captain, USCT]
Huntsville							
Elias Donegan #248	brown	47	Madison Co., Ala.	Huntsville	farmer & wagon driver	signed with an "X"	
Howell Echols #50	black	50	Madison Co., Ala.	Huntsville	clergyman, Methodist	–	
Henderson Hill	yellow	–	Huntsville	Huntsville	register	signed with an "X"	
A. J. Hunt #893	dark	23	Huntsville	Huntsville	–	A. J. Hunt	
John Robinson	yellow	–	Virginia	Huntsville	at livery stable	–	
Sipio Simmons #486	dark	–	Beaufort, S.C.	Huntsville	plasterer	Sipio Simmons	

holding an annual fair. The Reverend N. G. Merry brought prestige and conservatism to the committee. A gifted leader, Merry had been influential in organizing the very popular First Baptist Church, which was attended by both whites and blacks. In 1873 he led in the construction of a new house of worship, the largest church then owned by Nashville Negroes; when he died in 1884, a Nashville paper commented that " 'no such demonstration was ever before or since made at a colored man's funeral in Nashville or perhaps anywhere else.' " Other Nashville committeemen of prominence were Randall Brown, political leader of a radical element; Jesse Woods, Republican political leader; B. J. Hadley, a prominent businessman and saloon operator; the Reverend Jordan W. Early, pastor of St. John's A.M.E. Church; A. S. McTier, politician; S. W. Keeble, justice of the peace, treasurer of the Colored Agricultural and Mechanical Association, politician, prosperous barber, member of the Thirty-eighth Tennessee General Assembly, and a fellow whom the *Union and American* described as "no uppity nigger"; William Sumner, an officer of the board of the Colored Agricultural and Mechanical Association and proprietor of Sumner House; and Peter Lowry, wealthy Nashville businessman and owner of property valued at more than $10,000.[126]

The Richmond advisory board also had able leadership. The chairman, John Oliver of Boston, was a notary public and a Republican politician whom the Richmond *Daily Enquirer* characterized as a "conservative radical"—a man who opposed the "insane policy of confiscation" of Confederate property. The *Daily Enquirer* felt that Oliver was far more intelligent, courteous, and dignified than most of his Republican colleagues. Fields Cook, a Richmond and Alexandria minister, and also a doctor and a politician of the "conservative radical" stripe, added prestige to the committee. For a while he was the Bank's cashier at Alexandria. At least four other ministers sat on the board, including the Reverend James H. Holmes, who, though born a slave, was now an officer of the Virginia Baptist State Convention and minister to a congregation of 3,800. The presence of the Reverend Scott Gwathney might have allayed some of the white concern over the reputed radical nature of the Bank, for upon his death the Democratic *Richmond Dispatch* eulogized him as a good and faithful Christian who eschewed politics and kept away from political meetings. Businessmen, too, sat on the board. Peter H. Woolfolk, a teacher, and Robert L. Hobson, a barber, were president and secretary, respectively, of the Virginia Home Building Fund and Loan Association, a cooperative organized to help Negroes

126. Taylor, *Negro in Tennessee*; Minutes A, p. 257.

buy land and homes. Committeeman Albert R. Brooks was a successful hackman, who was perhaps most esteemed because he was able to give his children a college education.[127]

In providing leadership for the masses, the churches, the most important social organizations in the Negro communities of the Reconstruction period, unofficially assumed much of the work of the advisory boards. When President Alvord and the actuary toured the South, they seemed to place equal emphasis on speaking to the advisory boards and to the churches and Sunday schools. Bank officials held public meetings in the churches and enlisted the support of Negro ministers in popularizing the company. Ministers frequently sat on the advisory boards, which they sometimes dominated, and their churches and church societies eventually deposited substantial sums in the Freedman's Bank.

Churches, beneficial societies, and business associations often set an example of thrift for the community.

> The first principle of organization after the war was the church organization, and every congregation began to assess its members, and that money was immediately carried and put into the Freedman's Bank, if there was one within reach. It was deposited there, sometimes in the name of the elder, as he was called, sometimes in the name of the class-leader . . . and sometimes it was put there in the name of the society, such as the Sons and Daughters of Jonaab, the Sons and Daughters of Ezekiel, and all kinds of names.[128]

A Mr. Hayes of Richmond recalled at a later date the activities of the churches and societies: "The preachers were speaking about it, and they were collecting from all the societies, churches, and Sunday schools. Every cent that they could rake and scrape was shoved into the institution with the idea that in the future we were going to live more like other men."[129] At Richmond by 1874 nearly every Negro society had something to its credit.[130] The Charleston branch also benefited from a great deal of church and society participation; over a period of twelve months, seventy-five church groups, societies, associations, and businesses opened accounts in Charleston (see Table 12).

Baltimore societies and businesses also patronized the Bank heavily. "Nearly every colored beneficial society and building association in the city," wrote the *Baltimore American*, "were depositors in the bank, and

127. Taylor, *Negro in the Reconstruction of Virginia; Boyd's Directory of Richmond City*, 1869.
128. U.S., Congress, Senate, Committee on Finance, *Interview of the Committee on Finance with Hon. W. L. Trenholm*, April 24, 1888, p. 13.
129. House, Committee on Banking and Currency, *Hearings*, 1910, p. 7.
130. *Richmond Dispatch*, July 3, 1874, p. 1.

TABLE 12. Charleston Societies and Businesses That Opened Bank Accounts, July, 1870–June, 1871

Acct. No.	Organization
5038	Veterans Republican Brotherhood
5039	Daughters of Jerusalem (sickness and death benefits)
5087	Lincoln Branch (charitable society)
5088	Union Lodge No. 1
5113	Daughters of Emanuel Watchman (sickness and death benefits)
5137	Young Calvary Union No. 2 (sickness and death benefits)
5165	Zion's Watchman Society
5183	Emanuel Sabbath School
5200	St. Theresa Charitable Association
5219	Israel Branch Society (charitable society)
5221	Benevolent Sociable Society (charitable society)
5231	United Fire Company
5319	Angel March Branch No. 2
5326	Good Hope Society (charitable society)
5346	Baptist Faith Society
5354	Young Watchman of Charleston Neck No. 2
5381	Christian Professor Society
5391	Faith, Hope, and Love (sickness and death benefits)
5456	Benford and Masyck "Ethiopia Troop"
5460	Young Centenary Branch No. 2 (sickness and death benefits)
5463	United Benevolent Compact and Sisters
5466	Emanuel Branch (sickness and death benefits)
5496	Charitable Home Association
5497	Club of the Sons of Jacob
5551	Young Interested Branch No. 2
5581	Liberia Branch Society (sickness and death benefits)
5610	Leaders Board of the Methodist Protestant Church
5635	Union Society No. 1 of the A.M.E. Church (sickness and death benefits)
5666	Lincoln Republican Guard
5670	Delany Rifles—Military Company of the City of Charleston
5672	Sons and Daughters of Daniel
5685	Class Union No. 19 (sickness and death benefits)
5708	Class Union No. 8 of Emanuel Church
5710	Ladies Historical Association
5716	Longshore Cooperative Association
5804	Class Union No. 17
5843	Sons and Daughters of Waymond
5852	Ladies Benevolent Society
5880	Zion Presbyterian Union No. 3
5909	Lincoln Tabernacle No. 1
5911	Laboring Union No. 2
5922	Young Wesley Branch No. 1
5933	Ladies Companion
5943	Young Mens Christian Aid
6051	The Emanuel Branch
6087	Charleston Branch Joint Stock Company

TABLE 12 (*Cont.*)

Acct. No.	Organization
6233	Wesley's Band
6243	Christian Social Nursery
6258	John Simmons Fish Company
6573	Sons and Daughters of Zareptha (sickness and death benefits)
6764	Class Union No. 9, Centenary M.E. Church
6778	Sons and Daughters of the Crops (sickness and death benefits)
6782	Ola Society of John the Baptist
6860	Lot Fund, Plymouth Church
6905	Class Union, Emanuel Church
6908	Class Union No. 9
6925	Lincoln Harp Society (sickness and death benefits)
6939	Protestant Gospel Society
6960	Beaufort Sons and Daughters of Love
7029	Plymouth Congregational Church
7059	Presbyterian Church, Wadisdo Island, S.C.
7065	Edisto Island Presbyterian Church
7111	Wesley Watchman Class No. 2
7116	Charleston Joint Stock and Jobbing Company (construction company)
7158	Spring Cart Association
7319	Charleston Land Company
7432	Good Samaritan Society
7440	Young Shebara Association
7500	Joshua Branch No. 2
7530	A.M.E. Church, Mt. Pleasant
7964	African M.E. Church, Edisto Island
8055	Mt. Olivet Independent Branch
8066	Union Star Fire Engine Company
8091	Enquiring Joshua Society
8181	Class Union No. 4

their deposits alone amounted to $50,000."[131] At least fifteen building and self-help associations, designed to help freedmen purchase land and homes, deposited $50 each per week in the Baltimore branch.[132] Similar building associations in other cities, such as the National Working Combined Savings Fund at Richmond and the cooperative of Longstreet, Cowen, and Fox at Shreveport, patronized the Freedman's Bank.[133]

The Bank's popularity and steady growth belied several handicaps, chief of which was the lack of an adequate loan policy. The Bank, being

131. September 15, 1874, p. 4.
132. *New York Tribune*, September 1, 1870, p. 2.
133. W. McKenna to the Hon. John Jay Knox, February 25, 1884, Letters Rec'd by the Commissioners, 1870–1914, FS&T Co.; advertisement for National Working Combined Savings Fund Society, in the Richmond Signature Book, FS&T Co.

a self-help institution, was always free with advice and propaganda but short on actual services, a characteristic typical of nineteenth-century American social service institutions. Until 1870 no loans could be made by the principal office or branch banks. The officials at Washington invested two-thirds of the deposits in U.S. securities and held the remainder as an operating fund. In 1870 the charter was amended to permit the central office to invest half of the money in loans on real estate security; but only two or three branches—Beaufort, Jacksonville, and probably Memphis—had this privilege.[134] Thereafter the home office began to lend a sizable portion of the available funds on a wide variety of security.

Because the Bank's loan policy after 1870 was aimed at earning profit, and because it was mainly restricted to Washington, relatively few Negroes were able to borrow money, and relatively little money was invested in the black community. Few Negroes had the necessary collateral, and so most of the loans went to the white community. A few black churches and societies, such as the Fifth Street Baptist Church in Washington ($10,000), the Fifteenth Street Presbyterian Church in Washington, a Norfolk Negro church ($3,000), the Zion Baptist Church of Portsmouth, Virginia ($1,300), the Dallas Street Church in Baltimore, and the Agricultural and Mechanical Association of Middle Tennessee, were able to borrow.[135] Among the score of Washington Negroes who received loans were two contractors, an attorney, and a few other people of substantial means.[136] The process by which money was lent to the Independent Baptist Church of Lexington, Kentucky, suggests that Negro applicants were scrutinized closely. In Washington in 1870 and 1871 the Bank made loans to many whites on little or no security, but when this particular church wished to borrow $4,600, putting up as collateral the entire church property (valued at $20,000) and the property of various church members, the loan was not readily granted. Cashier Hamilton forcefully presented the church's case: "The investment is a perfectly safe one and in making it we will relieve the church of a great embarrasment [*sic*] and do ourselves great good. . . . On every hand we are commended for our interest in them and they look

---

134. *Report of the Select Committee*, Senate, 1880, pp. 247–248, appendix, p. 63; *Report of the Commissioners*, 1874, p. 67; *Freedman's Bank*, House, 1876, p. 14.

135. *Baltimore American*, September 15, 1874, p. 4; Minutes A, Finance Committee, November 7, 1870; loan to Agricultural and Mechanical Association of Middle Tennessee, Letters Rec'd by the Commissioners, 1870–1914, FS&T Co.; *Freedman's Bank*, House, 1876, p. 100; *Report of the Select Committee*, Senate, 1880, p. 14; loan to the Zion Baptist Church, Letters Rec'd by the Commissioners, 1870–1914, FS&T Co.; *New National Era*, October 24, 1872, p. 2.

136. *Freedman's Bank*, House, 1876, pp. 136–139.

to *us* to help. I would not advise this loan if there was the slightest risk attending it or if it did not promise us greater confidence from the people and assure us increased deposits."[137]

As so many historians have shown—and as the freedmen obviously knew—wealth and prestige in the South were associated with land ownership. A soundly conceived long-term loan policy might have accomplished wonders for a group so eager to buy land, establish homes, and improve their businesses. But if the nineteenth-century American's respect for private property and the fear of charity's tendency to produce paupers precluded a general land redistribution, then how would poverty-stricken ex-slaves obtain homes or land? The extension of massive credit in the form of long-term, low-interest loans is an obvious, modern solution, but the Freedman's Bank was unequipped to meet this need and, at any rate, being enamored of self-help, could never accept this concept. For black people the Bank was mainly a teller's window through which their money was channeled to Washington; blacks who wanted to borrow at the branches found that they had to look elsewhere.

Had the charter permitted a portion of the funds to be used at the local level, declared one bank examiner, "the [St. Louis] bank would have been a success, as the colored population took pride in it, and among them is considerable enterprise, frugality, and wealth. But when needing money, and finding that the bank where they deposited could not loan, they had to withdraw their business, and it is regarded by the more intelligent as a 'drag-net' for the purpose of accumulating and sending off funds much needed at home."[138] A similar situation existed at Philadelphia. "The business portion of our people express their good will towards it [the Bank], but their business compels them to use the National Banks, where they can obtain private accommodations."[139] Probably for this same reason the Augusta cashier observed that "some of our richest men and women do not use this Bank, but prefer a National Bank, or a State-chartered Bank to our institution."[140]

There had always been some latent dissatisfaction with the Bank's limited scope. In 1866 Hewitt had observed that "in some of the larger Cities we have failed to get Branches established (instance N.O.) because the Col'd People wanted Commercial facilities."[141] Discontent

---

137. Hamilton to Col. D. L. Eaton, September 19, 1871, Letters Rec'd by the Commissioners, 1870–1914, FS&T Co.; copy of Resolutions Passed by the Church, September 14, 1871, *ibid.*
138. *Report of the Commissioners*, 1874, p. 66.
139. *New Era*, June 23, 1870, p. 3.
140. *Ibid.*, March 17, 1870, p. 3.
141. Hewitt to Col. W. H. Sidell, March 13, 1866, Bank Letters, BRFAL.

peaked in the 1870's, when more and more black depositors complained of the Bank's shortsighted loan policy and demanded that loans be made to Negroes. In mid-1873 the *New National Era* reported that depositors at several branches were being encouraged to demand the return of their money. While opposing this move, the paper revealed the intensity of the grievance:

> If the thousands of depositors in the Freedman's Banks desire that their money be invested in the South, in preference to other localities where greater safety and surer profits are to be obtained, it is to be presumed that they can be accommodated. For two hundred years they have toiled for the upbuilding of the South without compensation. The desire to contribute $4,000,000 more to that impoverished locality, with all the accompanying risks, is in keeping with the lifelong generosity of the race. We urge the colored people to consider well any efforts making to establish private banks, simply because the trustees of the Freedman's Bank do not regard Southern securities as safe.[142]

Three months later the paper noted that significant opposition to the Richmond branch had arisen among black real estate owners and others who wanted to borrow. There was even talk of establishing a rival bank.[143] Discontented Nashville and Memphis depositors went beyond words and sought to establish their own banking institutions. In February, 1867, the Tennessee assembly passed an act incorporating the Nashville Loan and Savings Bank, and a little later it incorporated the Tennessee Colored Banking and Real Estate Association of Memphis, which was empowered to discount notes, "buy and sell stock, bonds, deal in exchange, gold, silver and bullion, public and private securities, and negotiable paper."[144] Little else is known about these ventures, and it may be that they never went into operation. Nevertheless, their incorporation is evidence of the dissatisfaction with the limited usefulness of the Freedman's Bank.

To many, the demands for returning the money to the localities seemed only logical and fair. In outlining the case for change, John P. Sampson, a Negro employee of the Treasury Department, argued that because those who created the capital, the former slaves, were not able to borrow, they were actually working for the benefit of Washington citizens and financiers. "What good," he asked, "does investment do our people?"[145] Many others were asking the same question. A Baltimore

142. *New National Era and Citizen*, May 1, 1873, p. 2.
143. *Ibid.*, July 31, 1873, p. 2.
144. Taylor, *Negro in Tennessee*, p. 158.
145. *New National Era and Citizen*, February 19, 1874, p. 1.

bank committee, for example, petitioned Congress for an amendment to permit a branch board of trustees to control the investment of the Baltimore freedmen's funds, and the Augusta advisory board in February, 1874, unanimously adopted a resolution requesting that at least a portion of their funds be invested in their city.[146] Finally realizing the errors in their loan policy, the Freedman's Bank trustees persuaded Congress to amend the charter in June, 1874, so that money could be returned to the branch communities for investment.[147]

This decision, had it been implemented, might have changed the Bank by shifting its primary purpose away from savings and security and toward stimulating local business and economic development. The investments of all savings banks have always stressed security, as is seen in the priority given to bonds of federal, state, and local governments, schools and railroads, and mortgage loans and bank stock. Personal loans were fairly low on the list of priorities and were actually prohibited in the savings bank laws of New York, Minnesota, and perhaps other states in the late nineteenth century.[148] Personal as well as mortgage loans were probably what many Bank critics had in mind when they called for the return of funds to the locality, but personal loans clearly were not the traditional investments for savings banks. On the other hand, "local sentiment"—the desire to improve the area in which the bank was located—has always been "perfectly natural." According to William Kniffin, a savings bank "should, if possible, cater to the wants of the neighborhood in making mortgage loans and other investments."[149] Thus the Bank was impaled on the horns of a dilemma: it should have done more for the branch community, yet the Bank, a savings institution serving a poor clientele, lacked the proper form, leadership, or resources to undertake what would obviously be a risky project. Considering the Bank's inadequate inspection and the financial inexperience of many branch cashiers, it was perhaps fortunate that this liberalized loan policy of 1874 never went into effect. To implement this plan, almost all the branches would have required more experienced financial leadership, which it is doubtful that they could have obtained.

The Bank's obvious shortcomings and the complaints of black depositors disturbed the officers, who always worried about the Bank's popularity. They understood that in seeking to attract Negro depositors

146. U.S., *Congressional Record*, 43rd Cong., 1st sess., May 18, 1874, p. 3977; *New National Era*, May 21, 1874, p. 2.

147. *Report of the Select Committee*, Senate, 1880, appendix, pp. 1, 44.

148. Kniffin, *Savings Bank and Its Practical Work*, pp. 64, 67, 94; Welfling, *Mutual Savings Banks*, pp. 30–31.

149. Kniffin, *Savings Bank and Its Practical Work*, pp. 94–95.

they had to compete against other banking institutions. By 1868 the legal obstacles to Negroes using white banks had been set aside throughout the South, although it is true that where they had existed previously they had often been ignored.[150] Richmond had at least two competing stock savings banks, while the St. Louis branch had to contend with dozens.[151] "The thirty-nine Saving and other Banks in St. Louis, among the best in the country, have all had a liberal share of the patronage of the colored people. Our Bank has had to compete with these older and well established institutions."[152] The New York branch suffered from the competition of many mutual savings banks, and a branch intended for Wilmington, Delaware, was withdrawn because the Wilmington Savings Fund Society received all the Negroes' savings—about $25,-000.[153] Competition was also acute in Baltimore, where, according to the Agency Committee's report, Negroes had deposited almost one million dollars in the Baltimore Citizen's Savings Bank.[154] Likewise, Atlanta Negroes did not confine their patronage to one banking house.[155]

Other problems plagued the branch banks. A certain degree of white hostility was constant.[156] In addition, a few Negroes felt that the Freedman's Bank, a separate bank, was "a caste institution," opposed to the "integrationist" spirit of the age.[157] A more fundamental problem, however, arose from the economic position of black Americans in the first years after slavery: after paying for necessities, they simply had little or nothing to save. In New York (and certainly elsewhere) the basic expenses of living were so high that it was extremely difficult to save, particularly on the low wages of domestic service or day labor.[158] The *New Era* remarked how almost every profitable occupation was "shut against" Louisville Negroes;[159] that they could save small sums at this time was a credit to their diligence and thrift. Elsewhere, even this was impossible. The freedmen of Richmond, Kentucky, were refused a branch because, although they were industrious, their wages were too low for them to save anything.[160]

150. Keyes, *History of Savings Banks*, II, 383, 564.
151. Richmond *Daily Enquirer*, January 13, 1874, p. 2.
152. *New Era*, July 28, 1870, p. 1.
153. *Ibid.*, June 23, 1870, p. 3; Minutes A, July 11, 1867, p. 41.
154. Minutes A, June 10, 1869, p. 110. The Agency Committee did not indicate the length of time it had taken blacks to deposit this amount or how much remained on deposit.
155. *Atlanta Constitution*, September 27, 1873, p. 3.
156. See above, ch. 3.
157. *New Era*, June 23, 1870, p. 3.
158. *New National Era*, September 29, 1870, p. 3.
159. July 7, 1870, p. 3.
160. Alvord, *Letters from the South*, p. 36.

It would be quite impossible to say how much of the thrift, saving, and self-help which the freedmen showed in the postwar years was due to the propaganda and services of the Freedman's Bank. As has been noted, the disposition to work hard, save money, and get ahead in life may already have been characteristic of many blacks, and the Bank may only have reinforced the tendency and provided opportunities for the exercise of these virtues. Be this as it may, it is certain that many people at the time believed the Bank was extremely important in promoting the economic advancement of the freedmen. The Bank, they felt, was successful not only in attracting depositors and millions of dollars but also in influencing blacks to save money in order to purchase homes and land.

The *New Era*, spokesman and propagandist for Negro advancement and thus not an unbiased observer, carried frequent reports from southern branches testifying to the economic progress of thousands of freedmen. Most reports indicated that freedmen were struggling to fulfill the fondest dreams of Bank officials—saving to obtain the tools and symbols of economic security. Cashier I. W. Brinckerhoff reported in the columns of the *New Era* that Savannah freedmen, groaning under high rents, showed an increasing desire to purchase homes. Many, he declared, had already bought lots and built inexpensive houses with the money they had saved in the local branch bank.[161]

> The suburbs of Savannah are being dotted over with thriving villages of colored people who own, in whole or in part, the premises upon which they live. These villages are the first fruits of the Freedman's Savings Bank. But for the Savings Bank many of the occupants of those plain and comfortable homes would be to-day without a dollar.

The Freedman's Savings Bank in Savannah, claimed the *New Era*, was the cornerstone of the Negro's prosperity.[162]

Although somewhat exaggerated by the *New Era*, the Savannah success story was matched by the black communities in other branch cities. While most withdrawals at Wilmington were for immediate necessities, no less than one-third were used for the purchase of homes, lots, horses, and capital equipment.[163] The Raleigh cashier reported that local people, who testified that they never would have saved without the Bank's help, were purchasing homes. From Norfolk, H. C. Percy sent the *New Era* a subdued but hopeful report. During the first six months of 1870 he opened 328 accounts, most of them small, but, he rationalized, "just

161. *New Era*, June 9, 1870, p. 3.
162. June 23, 1870, p. 3.
163. *Ibid.*

the right kind of foundation on which to build." Large numbers of poor people were depositing small amounts every week, one washerwoman having saved $50 in a short period. Several draymen had saved enough to buy a horse and dray; others had bought lots and houses.[164]

When the *Memphis Ledger* stated that Negroes were fast becoming landowners and that about 500 owned well-cultivated farms in the vicinity of Memphis, the Nashville cashier, John J. Cary, claimed that many of these prosperous farmers were Memphis depositors. Through industry and economy, and by using the Freedman's Bank as a depository, these Memphis freedmen had become landowners. Some, said Cary, had assured him that until the organization of the Bank it had seemed impossible to save. But Cary also admitted that many others who were equally able to put aside small sums did not use the Bank.[165]

Other observers corroborated the reports in the *New Era*. Most maintained that Negroes saved earnestly for some important project.

> I met [wrote a Bureau superintendent of education] a little boy about eight years old last winter, in the savings bank in this city, making his small deposit of a few cents, on his way home from school, books in hand. Out of school hours this bright boy and his little brother, sons of a poor widow, did chores for ladies who paid them small sums, which they put away in the bank until each had about eight dollars; enough to buy coal for their mother, and beget in them a habit which has ever been the precursor of fortunes.[166]

A similar observation about the serious purposes of saving was made by Robert Somers at Charleston. "The negro begins to deposit usually with some special object in view. He wishes to buy a mule and cart, or a house, or a piece of land, or a shop, or simply to provide a fund against death, sickness or accident, and pursues his object frequently until it has been accomplished."[167] David Macrae noted in traveling through the South that Negroes were buying homes and lots in Atlanta, Augusta, and Charleston and had purchased 200 buildings in Macon. Like others, he attributed many of these achievements to the opportunity to save and to the Bank's influence.[168] "In hundreds of cases," concluded the comptroller of the currency, "the freedmen, through the influence of

164. *Ibid.*, July 7, 1870, p. 3.

165. *New National Era*, September 22, 1870, p. 3.

166. Alvord, *Eighth Semi-Annual Report on Schools for Freedmen*, July 1, 1869, p. 17.

167. Somers, *Southern States since the War*, p. 55.

168. David Macrae, *The Americans at Home* (Edinburgh: Edmonston & Douglas, 1870), II, 56.

this institution, have been taught habits of thrift, which resulted in their becoming the owners of small patches of land, and it is needless to describe the elevation of the man which this simple fact at once produces."[169]

Both the Louisville *Courier-Journal* and the Charleston *News and Courier* paid tribute to the thrifty habits the Bank induced,[170] while the *New York Tribune* cited the results of those habits: "They [the freedmen] assured me," wrote the reporter, "that many are buying land; others accumulating money in the Freedmen's Savings Bank with the intent to own homes at no distant day, and that nearly all are doing better from year to year."[171] Another New York paper, the *Herald*, pointed out that from the millions of drafts the freedmen purchased homesteads and cottages—humble ones, to be sure, but nevertheless often their first real homes.[172]

John Alvord of course publicized the Bank's accomplishments. "In a single day, in our Charleston Savings Bank," he wrote, "I took the record of seventeen Freedmen who were drawing their money to pay for farms they had been buying, generally forty or fifty acres each, paying about $10 per acre."[173] It was Alvord's firm belief that thousands of freedmen and the South generally benefited materially from the Bank. Many purchased land—ten, fifteen, or twenty acres—at low prices from money saved at the branches.[174] According to a report of the financial inspector who lived at Beaufort, nearly 2,000 families now settled on the Sea Islands owned their own land, and most had saved the purchase price at the Beaufort branch.[175] At all the branches, large numbers of freedmen withdrew small sums for seed, teams, and farming implements in order to increase their crops—and, inadvertently, the South's prosperity.[176]

Alvord's statements were not unfounded generalizations, for in 1867 and again in 1869 he had requested each cashier to send statistics concerning the purposes of bank drafts at his branch. How much had been

169. *Report of the Comptroller of the Currency*, 1873, p. 10.

170. *News and Courier*, August 1, 1873, p. 1; *Courier-Journal*, June 28, 1874, p. 1.

171. June 7, 1874, p. 4.

172. Undated clipping from *New York Herald*, Letters Rec'd by the Commissioners, 1870–1914, FS&T Co.

173. Alvord, *Letters from the South*, p. 9.

174. Alvord, *Eighth Semi-Annual Report on Schools for Freedmen*, July 1, 1869, p. 87.

175. Alvord, *Letters from the South*, p. 28.

176. Alvord, *Eighth Semi-Annual Report on Schools for Freedmen*, July 1, 1869, p. 87.

withdrawn for purchasing land, homes, businesses, seed, farm implements, and books and school supplies?[177] Alvord and the trustees hoped
to publicize the answers as evidence of "the civilizing and educating
influences of our Bank."[178] The results of this inquiry were quite satisfactory; Alvord was able to conclude that "the large amount drawn
from us and invested in important purchases is to us a matter of even
more congratulation than the balance which remains. Thousands of
families have been settled on permanent homes."[179] "No other thing
done for these people has so thoroughly stimulated industry."[180]

The statistics generally substantiated Alvord's conclusions, although
they are not as precise as one would wish. Indeed, they are more
noteworthy for the impression they create than for their exactness.
Most cashiers simply estimated the amounts withdrawn for the various
purposes, while several claimed that even an estimation was impossible.
Most of the data are incomplete. Then, too, the cashiers based their
assessments on the replies of those withdrawing money; how the
money actually was spent might have been entirely different.

In general, the cashiers' replies indicate that large amounts were
spent for purchases of land and homes and for farm and business improvements. In 1867 the Louisville cashier estimated conservatively
that $92,500 in drafts were spent in the following ways: $35,000 for
homesteads; $12,500 for mechanical and business improvements; $30,000
for seeds, implements, etc., for those working on shares; and $15,000
for education.[181] Although totals at the other branches in 1867 did not
approximate Louisville's, the cashiers nevertheless estimated that significant amounts were spent in the same categories. "Their chief object of desire," wrote the Tallahassee cashier, "seems to be to own a
house and their houses are going up in every direction. This is to me
one of the most encouraging signs of the improvement of the Colored
race."[182] Cashier Brinckerhoff at Savannah reported that soldiers generally withdrew their bounty money to purchase homesteads and engage
in business; the total amount drawn was about $30,000.[183] At Richmond
Charles Spencer made inquiries as to what the discharged soldiers
"were going to do with their money, and in many instances was in-

177. Alvord to cashiers, December 23, 1869, p. 307, Letters Sent, Book 15,
Educational Division, BRFAL.
178. Alvord to H. C. Percy, October 11, 1867, Bank Letters, BRFAL.
179. Minutes A, February 10, 1870, p. 145.
180. Alvord, *Eighth Semi-Annual Report on Schools for Freedmen*, July 1, 1869,
p. 87.
181. H. H. Burkholder to Alvord, October 24, 1867, Bank Letters, BRFAL.
182. F. W. Webster to Alvord, October 19, 1867, *ibid.*
183. I. W. Brinckerhoff to Alvord, October 18, 1867, *ibid.*

formed that they intended to buy themselves a place . . . but as they mostly lived many miles from the city, and had not fully made up their minds, I could get particulars in but few instances."[184] The examples Spencer provided, however, are noteworthy: one Alexander Robinson bought sixty acres of land at $10 an acre, paying $200 down; a Mr. McCam invested $125 in a store; and a David Walker invested $175 in teams, implements, etc.[185]

Details concerning withdrawals in 1870 were more abundant, though by no means more accurate. In 1867 H. C. Percy had estimated that approximately $8,000–10,000 had been drawn to buy land. "The people," he affirmed, "are rapidly becoming landowners, and the number of whites who are willing, or are obliged to sell land, is daily increasing."[186] In 1870 he estimated that of the total drafts one-eighth (about $54,000) were for land, while 250 freedmen purchased dwellings.[187] Unfortunately, the total picture presented by Percy was not so reassuring. The largest accounts belonged to Negroes who were engaged in the traffic in "ardent Spirits." "Our figures," Percy concluded, "look well at Norfolk; and some *have* done *nobly*, but compared with the vast field our institution is designed and ought to reach, our results are inconsiderable."[188]

Although the freedmen often used their withdrawals to purchase land, homes, and business improvements, they seem to have expended still more on consumer goods. For the period 1865–70, Horace Morris at Louisville recorded $16,000 spent for land (30 purchases averaging 75 acres each) and indicated that this figure would have been higher had rich landholders been more amenable to selling to freedmen. Fifty homes (about $25,000) had been purchased; $75,000 had gone for seed, teams, agricultural implements, mechanic's tools, and shops, and $50,000 for other business purposes. Ten thousand dollars had been spent for education and for "caring for distressed humanity." The largest part of the withdrawals was used for other important purchases for personal and family comfort; how much had been "squandered" Morris could not say.[189] The estimates for the Memphis branch resembled those for Louisville. The cashier guessed that very little, perhaps $5,000, had been spent for land, and perhaps $25,000 for business purposes. In the

184. Charles Spencer to Alvord, October 16, 1867, *ibid.*
185. *Ibid.*
186. Percy to Alvord, December 5, 1867, Bank Letters, BRFAL.
187. Percy to Alvord, February 8, 1870, Letters Rec'd, III, Educational Division, BRFAL.
188. *Ibid.*
189. Horace Morris to Alvord, February 16, 1870, Letters Rec'd, III, Educational Division, BRFAL.

other categories he offered no data but maintained that little had been squandered. Most of the money, he implied, had been withdrawn to improve the general living conditions of the freedmen. This is not surprising; emerging from slavery with so very little, and often earning the most meager wages, freedmen faced the challenge of rising above a bare subsistence level of living. One Bank official observed, "In the habits of the freed people there [is] a progression from the rudeness of slavery to the better conditions of civilized life, the desire to live better prompting them to expenses that largely absorb their surplus earnings."[190]

The most exact statistics were provided by the New Bern cashier, C. A. Nelson, who based his estimates on personal inquiries made over a period of several months and upon a detailed examination of the account of each depositor. At New Bern $9,240 was spent for land in 77 purchases averaging 15 acres each. Sixty-six freedmen used their money ($10,667.44) to buy houses, while $15,668.91 went for farm improvements and $87,068.28 for general business. Nelson listed $1,275 for education and $14,539.09 for personal and family comfort. Unfortunately, these impressive figures could not hide the fact that approximately $6,600 had been spent on liquor, tobacco, and "fast living," chiefly by ex-soldiers receiving bounties.[191]

On two separate occasions the Mobile cashiers furnished brief reports concerning the uses of the freedmen's drafts.[192] On October 17 and 18, 1867, A. M. Sperry recorded seven withdrawals for the following amounts and purposes:

$10 for sickness	$5 for trade and business
$25 for sickness	$125 for building
$5 for hard times	$40 for purchase of a boat
$19.25 for trade and business	

In 1868 the *National Savings Bank* printed an extract from the Mobile cashier's weekly report, listing total amounts withdrawn for various purposes:

$325 for building purposes	$325 for livestock
$200 transfer to New Orleans	$1,000 for trade
$30 for tuition at Oberlin	$1,919.21 for speculation and
$162 for traveling expenses	other purposes

Overall, most cashiers in 1870 reported that few depositors misspent

190. Sperry to Alvord, January 21, 1870, *ibid.*
191. C. A. Nelson to Alvord, February 12, 1870, *ibid.*
192. *National Savings Bank*, June 1, 1868, p. 2; Sperry to Alvord, October 18, 1867, Bank Letters, BRFAL.

their money. On the contrary, they were impressed by the desire to buy homes, businesses, land, and tools. Although it would be natural for the cashiers to exaggerate the successes of their endeavors, the correspondence between the branch leadership and Alvord suggests an honest attempt to assess the results of their work. In report after report, cashiers estimated that thousands of dollars had been spent constructively on useful purchases. One cashier stated that those who saved generally desired to own a home and were quick to do so when the opportunity arose. Another, C. A. Woodward of Mobile, said that 25 percent of his depositors had bought houses and land.[193] At Augusta the cashier reported that $20,000 had been spent for land; at New York $50,000 had been invested in real estate; at Nashville $75,000 was used to purchase land and homes; at Baltimore $35,000 was the estimated amount used to buy homes, while at St. Louis about 20 percent of the total drafts had been used to erect buildings (which included four Negro churches) and buy lots.[194] These figures did much to cheer the Bank's management and caused D. L. Eaton to estimate that 70 percent (or $7,650,000) of the Bank's total pre-1870 drafts had been invested in the soil and in "civilizing pursuits."[195]

Bank officials regarded the prosperity of the Freedman's Bank as a clear refutation of the popular ideas concerning the freedmen's improvidence and inability to take care of themselves. They felt that each additional black depositor served as an additional rebuttal to the conventional wisdom of white Southerners which claimed that the Negroes were dying off, that the whole population was diseased and degraded, that they could not rise, and that they were thriftless and idle and would not work.[196] In response to these widely accepted "principles," Bank officials, black leaders, and their friends quoted statistics on deposits, among other things. For example, the New Bern cashier argued that the $15,000 in deposits in his branch were "irrefutable evidence of the colored man's ability and intentions not only to take care of himself, but also to provide for the necessities of the future."[197] A southern

193. Spencer to Alvord, January 22, 1870; C. A. Woodward to Alvord, January 13, 1870, Letters Rec'd, III, Educational Division, BRFAL.

194. John J. Zuille to Alvord, January 15, 1870; David A. Ritter to Alvord, January 6, 1870; Willis N. Brent to Alvord, February 11, 1870; John J. Cary to Alvord, December 23, 1869, *ibid.*; Townsend to Alvord, January 8, 1870, Letters Rec'd, II, Educational Division, BRFAL.

195. Alvord, *Ninth Semi-Annual Report on Schools for Freedmen*, January 1, 1870, p. 68; "Freedmen's Savings Bank," *Old and New*, II, 2 (August, 1870), 246.

196. *New Era*, July 14, 1870, p. 2; see Gen. Howard's introduction to Alvord, *Letters from the South.*

197. *National Savings Bank*, June 1, 1868, p. 1.

traveler, David Macrae, observed that the funds of the Bank had increased by $558,000 in one year; "and yet," said he, "we are told that the negroes are incurably thriftless."[198] The *Louisianian* and the *New National Era* answered the charge of improvidence in a similar fashion:[199] "Let it be observed by those who have denied the capacity of the colored man to take care of himself, that in the last six years he has earned and put into this Savings Company alone more than twenty millions of dollars. The deposits for March were $1,038,870."[200] All in all, said the Savannah cashier, I. W. Brinckerhoff, black people could be confident that their deposits would be regarded as an indication of thrift and worthiness.[201]

White newspapers of both North and South also perceived that the successful record of the Freedman's Bank belied the popular ideas about thriftless and lazy ex-slaves. The *New York Tribune* observed that the Freedman's Bank "speaks volumes in favor of the freedmen's industry and economy," while the *New York Times* inquired in mock wonder (thus testifying to the freedmen's achievements) "how it was that they succeeded in keeping so large an amount in their own possession."[202] A reporter from the New York *Evening Post* described southern Negroes as working everywhere in full force and, as evidence of their progress, cited the deposits in the Freedman's Bank.[203] A financial statement in 1868 furnished, in the opinion of the *Charleston Daily Courier*, "very satisfactory proof of the usefulness of the Institution."[204] The $100,000 due depositors at Nashville, said the *Tennessee Tribune*, speaks well for "the industry, sobriety, frugality and intelligence of the colored people of Davidson county, and refutes the oft-repeated slander that colored people cannot take care of themselves."[205] Even one of the more rabid Democratic journals, the *Savannah Morning News*, observed that the local branch reflected the thrifty habits of some Savannah Negroes and foreshadowed prosperous times ahead.[206]

Although the Bank's success called into question a number of entrenched stereotypes, most people's way of thinking was probably little altered. In spite of the deposits being amassed by the branch banks, the

198. Macrae, *Americans at Home*, II, 56.
199. *The Louisianian*, March 2, 1871, p. 2.
200. *New National Era*, June 1, 1871, p. 2.
201. *Savannah Morning News*, May 14, 1869, p. 3.
202. *New York Tribune*, January 31, 1867, p. 2; *New York Times*, June 11, 1866, p. 8.
203. Quoted in Charleston *News and Courier*, August 16, 1873, p. 4.
204. April 11, 1868, p. 2.
205. Quoted in Taylor, *Negro in Tennessee*, p. 163.
206. April 13, 1870, p. 3.

Nashville *Daily Press and Times* noted with some amazement that many people still insisted on referring to the Negro's incapacity to take care of himself.[207] If unsympathetic whites were unmoved by the success of the Bank, the former slaves reacted in the opposite way. Black people readily accepted the Bank as a symbol of their new condition of freedom. They pointed to the Bank with pride, and community morale seemed to rise with every deposit.

Negroes discovered in the banking offices of the southern cities the visible evidence of the black man's progress since slavery. At first most branches were located in makeshift offices, but eventually all were remodeled to represent the best in business decor, while at several branches new buildings were purchased or rented.[208] Most branch offices were located in the white business district. For example, the second Louisville office, refurbished by Negro mechanics, was situated in a new building near the post office, and at this location enjoyed an immediate increase in business.[209] At Mobile Negro mechanics fitted up a new office because the old one looked more "like a policy [numbers] shop than a bank."[210] Illustrating the changes—symbolic and real —brought by freedom, the Augusta branch moved into the old Merchant's Bank, a granite building that had been used as a Confederate depository.[211]

Freedmen expected the banking office to have a creditable appearance, one that would induce confidence. Evidently the first office at Washington fell below this standard; Washington Negroes demanded that their bank be made to look like a bank. They wanted improved furnishings and a sign saying "Freedman's Savings Bank"; "for colored people like others require *show* as inducements and incentives," said Cashier Wilson, "and if it will accomplish the end we have in view [increased patronage], why not make it?"[212] Banking offices improved steadily. The Lexington branch moved into the building formerly occupied by the Fayette National Bank; at Vicksburg, the Vicksburg Banking House was remodeled, thus drawing compliments for its "beautiful appearance."[213] In November, 1871, Nashville Negroes participated in the dedication of an "expensive and well appointed edifice";

207. Quoted in Taylor, *Negro in Tennessee*, p. 163.
208. *Report of the Comptroller of the Currency*, 1873, p. 7; Minutes A, April 14, 1870, p. 157.
209. Minutes A, August 12, 1869, p. 128.
210. *Ibid.*, p. 119.
211. *New Era*, June 2, 1870, p. 3.
212. Wilson to Alvord, August 7, 1865, Bank Letters, BRFAL.
213. *New Era*, June 23, 1870, p. 3; Minutes B, October 10, 1872, p. 28.

at Jacksonville, branch leaders built a two-story building in the business district, supposedly the first separate banking house built in that city.[214] At Charleston the company purchased a handsome building on the city's principal street, and, according to the Agency Committee, the new office became the pride of the community.[215]

To the freedmen these events were great achievements; denied status for so long, they now saw their highest hopes realized. The feelings of many freedmen are represented by the Tallahassee community, which was particularly proud of its branch.

> The Freedman's Savings and Trust Company, to the great gratification of the depositors, and colored people generally of this city, has effected the purchase of the beautiful fireproof building known as the "Union Bank," in which it has been doing business for some time past. This is one of the finest, if not the finest, bank building in the state of Florida, and the people are almost lost in wonder at the turn events have taken.[216]

The construction in 1871 of the Freedman's Savings and Trust Company's four-story stone headquarters in Washington capped the building enterprises of the company. Facing the U.S. Treasury and situated across from Lafayette Park and thus close to the White House, the new building, which cost somewhere between $180,000 and $300,000, seemed to give national recognition to the achievements of the Freedman's Bank and assure future greatness. The *New National Era* praised it as one of the finest bank buildings in the country and one of the architectural adornments of the city.[217] Its marble counter, black walnut desks, massive fireproof and burglar-proof safe, and handsomely furnished trustees' rooms inspired confidence in all who entered its doors. The government enhanced this impression when it rented the upper floors for additional office space for the Department of Justice. The building, largely constructed by Negro mechanics and laborers, was, said the *New National Era*, a monument to the thrift and energy of the colored race.

> Truly we live in a changeful age. Who would have been so rash ten years ago, as to have prophesied that the colored people, then in a state of

214. *New National Era*, January 19, 1871, p. 3; Taylor, *Negro in Tennessee*, p. 290, n. 78.

215. Minutes A, February 10, 1870, p. 146.

216. *New Era*, March 17, 1870, p. 3.

217. *New National Era*, August 10, 1871, p. 3; December 14, 1871, p. 3; March 28, 1872, p. 1; Journal, October 14, 1869, and June 9, 1870; diagram of property of Freedman's Bank in Washington is in Letters of the Commissioners, 1870–1914, FS&T Co.; *Report of the Comptroller of the Currency*, 1873, p. 2; *New York Times*, October 18, 1869, p. 4.

abject slavery and destitution, regarded as degraded and incapable, would within a decade, through their industry in the condition of freemen, contribute by their prudent thrift, so fine a structure to the adornment of the capital of the nation, that so scorned and oppressed them.[218]

By 1870 the concept of a bank for ex-slaves had passed the experimental stage. Indeed, many judged the Negro bank a success, citing the significant achievements of its origin and rapid growth. As John Alvord noted, "It began without capital; not a dollar in the treasury; a scattered, ignorant people to be drawn together and instructed; confidence of depositors to be secured; supervision and plan of operation without precedent; great distances to be overcome; at the same time heavy expense was to be incurred for salaries, rentals, stationery, furniture, safes, etc. The task seemed hurculean [*sic*]."[219] By 1870 deposits totaled $1.6 million; in 1873 they would reach $4 million. The company had extended savings facilities to thousands of freedmen, establishing them in all thirty-seven branches in seventeen states and the District of Columbia. By contemporary standards, the Freedman's Bank was a flourishing institution. The *National Savings Bank* opined, "Surely there is hope for a people of whose total population nearly one-half are church members, more than one-tenth attend both secular and Sabbath schools, and over six hundred have in the [Savannah] Savings Bank an *average* deposit of sixty dollars each, with the number of depositors increasing rapidly."[220]

Credit for the Bank's success belongs to the freedmen. Regardless of the fundamental role played by white people in founding and organizing the company, only the freedmen could provide the money necessary for the Bank's continued existence. Black cashiers, assistant cashiers, advisory boards, and churchmen, as well as white cashiers, assumed the leadership of the Bank in the Negro community, and black people responded. The soldier fresh from military campaigns, the farmer from the fields, the day laborer, the hard-working artisan, the struggling washerwoman, and the careworn widow—all came to the bank counter to deposit ofttimes pathetically small sums. The Bank became the hope for these people—hope for a better life, economic advancement, status, and security. The Bank, as the *Memphis Daily Appeal* described it, was a

218. July 14, 1870, p. 2; Minutes of the Building Committee, June 20, 1870, FS&T Co.

219. Alvord, *Ninth Semi-Annual Report on Schools for Freedmen*, January 1, 1870, pp. 64–65.

220. June 1, 1868, p. 1.

great iron-safe of all the colored churches and societies of the city and surrounding towns and villages, some of which have accumulated immense amounts of money since their organization. This has been a source of much pride to the industrious classes of the colored population, and they loved to talk about it, and would dwell upon the great benefits to be derived hereafter from the proceeds of the deposits, which in the imagination of many had been wrought up to fabulous piles of wealth that would accumulate to them, that they might go down to their graves in peace, and with a consoling consciousness that their offspring left behind would be "well fixed" to combat the trials and vicissitudes of this life.[221]

The story of the Freedman's Bank shows that, when given opportunity and incentive, the people of the freedom generation worked and saved and planned for the future, revealing a capacity to deny themselves immediate gratification. Many bought land and homes. And what an achievement this was! Said C. A. Woodward, the Mobile cashier: "It seems almost incredible when we reflect that this money has been accumulated from the meager earnings of a people but recently emerged from slavery, who were necessarily in a condition of extreme destitution."[222]

The Bank became a cherished community institution enjoying widespread support. Even those who had no individual account might be brought into its sphere of influence through their church or society. At some branches Negroes were encouraged to visit the office whether or not they intended to deposit. "Friends in the city or from the country are invited to stop and write their letters, calculate the worth of their crop, and read the papers at all bank hours."[223] The local office served as a gathering spot and a center for news. It might be the center of community activity—or at least be a part of it—as at New Orleans, where at 114 Carondelet Avenue a black Republican organization, a freedmen's aid society, a black newspaper, and the Freedman's Bank all worked to advance the interests of black Americans.[224] In a few cases, reported Cashier Woodward, the Bank aided in reuniting families separated by slavery and war; for the Bank became a "vast intelligence network with ramifications extending to all its branches."[225]

Occasionally a whole community would be invited to a celebration

221. September 26, 1873, p. 4.
222. Woodward, *Savings Banks*, p. 56.
223. *New Era*, June 23, 1870, p. 3.
224. *New Orleans Tribune*, October 2, 1866; *Semi-Weekly Louisianian*, March 17, 1871, pp. 1, 2.
225. Woodward, *Savings Banks*, pp. 69–70.

at a local Negro church when deposits reached a certain figure.[226] The celebration actually was an affirmation of freedom's progress; since the Bank was essential to community progress, it could call forth sacrifices by the people. For example, at Martinsburg, West Virginia, where the Negro community was too poor to sustain a branch, the people made a valiant effort to keep their bank by offering to assume its expenses during a probationary period.[227]

Frederick Douglass described the feelings many Negroes must have experienced upon encountering the Freedman's Bank:

> In passing it on the street I often peeped into its spacious windows, and looked down the row of its gentlemanly and elegantly dressed colored clerks, with their pens behind their ears and buttonhole bouquets in their coat-fronts, and felt my very eyes enriched. It was a sight I had never expected. I was amazed with the facility with which they counted the money. They threw off the thousands with the dexterity, if not the accuracy, of old and experienced clerks. The whole thing was beautiful.[228]

With each deposit the freedmen hoped to advance themselves and their race—and to change the attitudes of the white community. Many Negroes believed it was the duty of every man, woman, and child who had a dollar to spare to deposit, not only because it was personally convenient, but also because the Bank was doing much to advance the cause of black people.[229] From Omaha a woman wrote about how she advertised the Bank to her friends and encouraged them to deposit. "I deposit . . . in your Bank," she informed the Washington officials, "as I wish to see our people try to elevate themselves, and to save their hard earnings."[230] And as William Whipper, Philadelphia's black cashier, affirmed, "the person who deposits in our Bank deposits his religion, his humanity, and his love of progress with his money."[231]

226. *New Era*, May 12, 1870, p. 3. At Savannah, blacks celebrated the fourth anniversary of Lincoln's signing the Bank's charter. *Savannah Morning News*, March 4, 1869, p. 3.
227. Minutes A, June 10, 1869, p. 126.
228. Douglass, *Life and Times*, pp. 409–410.
229. *New National Era*, June 29, 1871, p. 3.
230. Quoted in *New Era*, June 9, 1870, p. 3.
231. *Ibid.*, June 23, 1870, p. 3.

5

From Social Service to Speculation

"Like the Peabody fund, the Slater fund, the Freedman's Bank, and many other Institutions, nominally established for the benefit of these people, the hands are white that handle the money. The Germans have a proverb 'That they who have the cross will bless themselves.'" —Frederick Douglass (1890); quoted in Philip S. Foner, *The Life and Writings of Frederick Douglass*

The Freedman's Bank preached a message of thrift, patience, and honest enterprise throughout its existence, and it pleaded for the confidence of the freedmen as an institution especially created to serve their interests. John Alvord remarked in February, 1870, "Our institution has been the child of a protecting Providence . . . *the system* we have adopted seems as safe as anything of the kind in human affairs *can be*."[1] Unfortunately for the depositors, Alvord's optimistic self-congratulation almost exactly coincided with a transformation of the Bank's policies. In 1870 the Bank, at the national level, ceased to be primarily a savings institution for freedmen and became first and foremost a Washington business concern. While continuing to accentuate missionary zeal and moral exhortation in the branches, the officials at the headquarters turned to a pursuit of profit through speculative investment in real estate and business loans. In the process they sacrificed the safety and security of the freedmen's savings entrusted to their care.

Many of the decisions which made possible this change in the Bank's nature were made much earlier and often with the best of intentions. Probably the most crucial of these decisions was the transfer of the home office from New York to Washington in 1867. Quite clearly the transfer sprang from the financial difficulties inherent in the company's

1. Minutes A, February 10, 1870.

founding and expansions; the company's extensive organization and its large but poor clientele (necessitating more offices and paperwork for the many small deposits) involved abnormally heavy operating expenses. The transfer to Washington was an attempt to remedy a deteriorating financial situation in 1866–67 and had nothing to do with speculative ventures.

Early in 1867 John Alvord took the lead in advocating the transfer to the nation's capital. "A thought has struck me," he wrote to Hewitt, "that if the principal office was in Washington where everything could be done at less expense & where some of our friends, as you know, think the Charter required us to be, we might find the desired relief."[2] Alvord had been complaining to the several concerned trustees about how the others had given no attention to the company's affairs; in contrast, he emphasized, Washington men would have abundant time for the Bank.[3] In casting about for methods to tighten the organization and reduce expenses—how "our machinery can be screwed up and oiled," as he put it—Alvord criticized the record of many of the original trustees. Several of the most prestigious—Levi Coffin of Cincinnati, S. G. Howe, and William C. Bryant, for example—never attended a regular board meeting, and most of the others had been almost as negligent. Frequently in 1866 a quorum of nine members could not be assembled.[4] Furthermore, said Alvord, the trustees were too conservative, asking how and when the institution could be pared down rather than how it could be strengthened and made successful. Their actions revealed that they "do not know the ability and thrift which the negro, (under proper instruction) possesses."[5] Alvord cited five advantages to the proposed change of location: lower operating costs, more government patronage, Freedmen's Bureau help, proximity to the freedmen, and financial advice from friends in Washington.[6]

The first two arguments were really identical with the third: Bureau aid. General O. O. Howard's help was enlisted by the advocates of the transfer, and before the final trustees' vote he had promised Bureau support for the Bank. Additionally, bank officials hoped that the Bank would become the depository for all the Negro bounty money which

2. John W. Alvord to Mahlon T. Hewitt, January 21, 1867, p. 260, Letters Sent, Book 11, Educational Division, BRFAL.

3. Alvord to the Rev. George Whipple, January 3, 1867, p. 214, *ibid.*

4. Journal, 1866, *passim.*

5. Alvord to William A. Booth, January 23, 1867, pp. 273–274, Letters Sent, Book 11, Educational Division, BRFAL.

6. Alvord to Hewitt, January 21, 1867, p. 260; Alvord to Hewitt, February 23, 1867, p. 275, *ibid.*; Alvord to S. L. Harris, February 18, 1867, pp. 57–58, Book 12, *ibid.*

the Bureau was to receive and distribute.[7] That the Bank in Washington would be closer to the mass of freedmen in the South proved to be of no consequence, but the fifth advantage—the services of Washington financiers—turned out to be of extreme importance.

Alvord's dissatisfaction with the original trustees, plus his knowledge that Washington men such as bankers Henry D. Cooke, president of the First National Bank (the Washington branch of Jay Cooke and Company), and William S. Huntington, a Cooke employee and the cashier of the First National Bank, would agree to advise the Bank, loomed larger and larger in the plans for removal. In December, 1866, Alvord had suggested that "as our Deposits are with Jay Cooke & Co would it not be well, for our reputation, to have [on the board] either 'William S. Huntington' of the Bank or 'Henry D. Cooke' of the Brokers office . . . each of whom are excellent men of high business reputation, & *friends of the Negro*."[8] Huntington seems to have impressed people because of his close association with Cooke. The *Herald* described him as "a quick-witted, agile, humorous man, of small stature, keen features and occasional ministerial look, who hails from Penn Yan, N.Y."[9] Cooke was the real attraction, however; between 1865 and 1873, as banker and first territorial governor of the District of Columbia, he reached the pinnacle of political, commercial, and social prestige in Washington. Said the *Evening Star* in 1871 when Cooke was appointed territorial governor: "The name of Henry D. Cooke is synonymous with everything that is honorable, worthy, and public spirited; and he is so thoroughly identified with the interests of the District, and so well informed concerning the needs of the people that he is specially adapted to take the helm of our new government."[10] "In some ways," wrote the *New York Herald*, "he was even more talented than his internationally famous brother, Jay Cooke."[11] His Christian piety impressed Alvord, for Cooke was the treasurer of the Reform Society of Washington and a strong supporter of the local Y.M.C.A., and was renowned for his large contributions to charity. "He is," said Alvord, "an excellent Christian man, warmly the friend of the Freedmen, and much interested in the success of our institution."[12] In early January the corresponding secre-

7. Alvord to Harris, February 18, 1867, p. 57, Book 12, *ibid.*
8. Alvord to Hewitt, December 27, 1866, p. 199, Book 11, *ibid.*
9. Cited in a clipping from the *New York Herald*, January 4, 1872, in Scrapbook, Box 6, Alexander Shepherd Papers, Library of Congress.
10. February 27, 1871, p. 1. See also May 23, 1867, p. 3.
11. Cited in a clipping from the *New York Herald*, January 4, 1872, in Scrapbook, Box 6, Shepherd Papers.
12. Attorney General Williams to Shepherd, October 24, 1874, Box 4, Shepherd Papers; Alvord to Hewitt, January 8, 1867, p. 229, and January 21, 1867, p. 260, Letters Sent, Book 11, Educational Division, BRFAL.

tary strongly endorsed Cooke and requested President Hewitt to place his name before the board. "If you should not have the '10' affirmative votes needed [to elect him] at the next meeting, you can do, as I believe you have sometimes done, *find them in the street.*" This cavalier disregard of the charter's requirements for the selection of trustees indicates how casually Alvord could dismiss legal restrictions.[13]

The only argument of consequence against the move was that New York offered greater facilities for cashing drafts, and there was some worry as to the problems which would be raised by leaving such a convenient commercial center. Henry Cooke, however, persuaded the trustees that New York had no advantages over Washington as a center for their business. His own Washington bank had no difficulty in handling an account with a New York bank by telegraphic messages.[14] Before agreeing to become a trustee, Cooke requested a detailed financial statement, and afterward he assured the trustees that the Bank would prosper.[15]

On March 14, 1867, the trustees declared Washington to be the principal office and the site of their monthly meetings.[16] Only D. S. Gregory objected, and the others present defeated his motion to remain in New York by a vote of ten to one. Those favoring the removal seemed to be convinced that they could receive more help from the Bureau in Washington than in New York, and that the promise of financial advice from Cooke and Huntington and other friends of the Bank in Washington would be very valuable.[17]

The immediate consequences of the transfer to Washington were a rapid turnover in the trustees' membership and the loss of Hewitt as an active president, for he decided to stay in New York. After March, 1867, Alvord increasingly assumed the administrative and publicity functions of the president, and in 1868 he officially replaced Hewitt as president of the Freedman's Bank. The election of new trustees in March and April, 1867, because of the resignations of sixteen trustees from New York, Boston, and Philadelphia was potentially a welcome change, for many of these original board members had been very negligent. Although the original charter had listed no Washington trustees, by

13. Alvord to Hewitt, January 8, 1867, p. 229, *ibid.* For additional information concerning the officers' disregard of the charter, see pp. 150–166.

14. Hewitt to Alvord, February 10, 1867, Bank Letters, BRFAL; Alvord to Harris, February 18, 1867, p. 58, Letters Sent, Book 12, Educational Division, BRFAL.

15. Alvord to Hewitt, February 2, 1867, p. 63, Letters Sent, Book 12, Educational Division, BRFAL.

16. Journal, March 14, 1867.

17. *Ibid.*, April 16, 1867; Booth to Gen. O. O. Howard, April 29, 1867, Bank Letters, BRFAL.

1868 there were twenty. In addition to Cooke and Huntington, several financiers and government officials now became board members: General Charles H. Howard, a high-ranking Bureau official and brother of General O. O. Howard; J. M. Broadhead, second comptroller of the currency; George W. Balloch, chief disbursing officer of the Bureau; and E. B. French, second auditor of the treasury.[18] While the original trustees can be classified generally as philanthropists and successful, conservative businessmen, the new trustees on the whole were army men, politicians, and speculating businessmen (which is to say that they too had impressive credentials, though of a different kind).

Joining these trustees in 1867 were the Bank's first black trustees: the Reverend D. W. Anderson, pastor of the Nineteenth Street Baptist Church; Walker Lewis, messenger in the Treasury Department; the Reverend Sampson Talbot of the Zion Methodist Episcopal Church; and Dr. Charles Purvis.[19] Their election occurred seemingly without comment or publicity; later a few other blacks, most notably John Mercer Langston, a Howard University law professor and former Bureau official, were added to the board. Except for Purvis and Langston, who in 1872 and 1873 began to criticize the Bank's irregularities, the black trustees were content to let matters rest in the supposedly able hands of white businessmen and officeholders in Washington. Overall they played a minor role until 1873 and 1874.[20]

Because the remaining New York trustees had little intention of traveling 240 miles to attend the monthly meetings, control passed to the Washington members.[21] In April, 1867, a handful of active trustees made their newest and most popular member, Henry Cooke, chairman of the Finance Committee, which one month later was reduced by vote of the trustees from nine to five members, three of whom would form a quorum. Cooke's committee chairmanship seemed to pay off immediately. Whereas previous committees had made few reports, the Cooke committee now began to provide extensive reports for each board meeting.[22] The prestige of Henry Cooke gave prominence to the Finance Committee, and few questioned his judgment.

18. *Evening Star,* May 29, 1867, p. 3.
19. Journal, January 12, 1872. Purvis was a Washington physician and later surgeon-in-chief of the Freedmen's Hospital and a professor in the medical department of Howard University. In 1874 he became vice-president of the Bank. When the Bank closed, his father, Robert Purvis, became one of the commissioners.
20. See below, pp. 165, 183–186.
21. *National Savings Bank,* June 1, 1868, p. 2; *Freedman's Bank,* House, 1876, p. 92.
22. Journal, May 9, 1867. There are only two or three reports of the Finance Committee's meetings before Cooke and Huntington became active in mid-1867. See Minutes A, Finance Committee, 1865, 1866, 1867.

Although several of the new Washington trustees took an active interest in the Bank, the problem of the trustees' insufficient attendance at board meetings and neglect of business continued throughout the rest of the Bank's history.[23] For example, Major General B. W. Brice was one of several who accepted positions as trustees provided that they had no duties.[24] Seemingly unconcerned, Bank officials seldom attempted to compel the trustees to attend to their duties. One of the original trustees, Edward Harwood of Cincinnati, tried repeatedly to have his resignation accepted. In January, 1874, he admonished Alvord, "I declined several years ago (& so wrote) to act as one of the trustees of the Freedman's Savings & Trust Co. It seems a pity to be sending me notices of meetings causing expenses for nothing. I never have attended one of the meetings. Please discontinue sending me notices."[25] Only the most cursory inquiries into the qualifications and background of new trustees seem to have been made. After the U.S. commissioner of pensions—one of those who assumed that a trusteeship involved no duties—was elected to the board, the trustees received a note from their new appointee informing them that his name was Joseph, not George, Barrett.[26]

In spite of the transfer to Washington and the Freedmen's Bureau's timely contributions toward defraying the expenses of rent, transportation, and salaries, heavy expenses still forced the trustees to search for additional revenue. They turned their attention toward the possibility of investing in non-governmental securities. Actually, Hewitt had considered taking this step as early as 1866. He planned to use the Bank's available fund to loan money on call and in this manner earn 7, 8, or 9 percent interest, as opposed to the government's 6 percent.[27] Hewitt's opponents questioned whether the charter permitted such a plan. It provided that the available fund, which could be as much as one-third of the total deposits, "may be kept by the trustees to meet current payments of the corporation, and may by them be left on deposit at interest *or otherwise, or in such available form as the trustees may direct.*"[28] The vice-president complained to Alvord:

I feel anxious and sometimes blue, when contemplating the future. I know that expenses are out of Proportion to income. We are met with the remark that the Power given to the 9th Sec. of Charter never con-

23. Journal, 1867–71, *passim.*
24. *Freedman's Bank,* House, 1876, p. 115.
25. E. Harwood to Alvord, January 5, 1874, in Minutes B, Finance Committee.
26. Joseph H. Barrett to Alvord, April 29, 1867, Bank Letters, BRFAL.
27. Hewitt to Alvord, March 21, 1866, *ibid.*
28. U.S., *Statutes at Large,* XIII, ch. 92, p. 511. Emphasis mine.

templated business. That the ⅓ reserve fund was designated to meet Emergencies. Not for business. There is no controverting it. To urge upon the Trustees at this time, the use of that reserve fund for any other than to meet "Current Payments" would not be advisable.[29]

Generally the trustees felt that Hewitt's plan violated the spirit and intention of the charter, and the plan was rejected.

Nevertheless, just as expenses continued, so officials returned again and again to the idea of lending the freedmen's money. In June, 1868, the board discussed and referred to the Finance Committee a resolution that $50,000 of the company's available fund should be loaned on call on real estate under the terms of the charter.[30] Henry Cooke, replying for the Finance Committee, stated that the available fund was supposed to be kept on hand for current payments.

> Now it is manifest that a loan upon or investment in, real estate securities is not the "available form" of investments contemplated by the clauses referred to. My understanding of the clause is that it authorizes the leaving of a certain sum on deposit, which deposit may draw interest or otherwise, but it must be always subject to check and sight, and I think a careful reading of the clause will justify this interpretation.[31]

This passage is extremely important, for it reveals that in 1868 Cooke opposed a risky use of the available fund and a loose interpretation of the charter. It goes far to refute the subsequent charges that he joined the Bank in 1867 only to get his hands on the freedmen's money. Cooke's report put an end to plans to lend out the available fund under the existing charter.

The attention of some trustees, however, had already shifted to the possibility of Congressional action to amend the charter. In the early months of 1867 the Washington trustees voted to request Congress to legalize a more liberal investment policy.[32] With this end in view, actuary D. L. Eaton wrote to Senator Justin Morrill of Maine summarizing the Bank's case for a congressional amendment.[33] He argued that the expenses of the company, though strictly limited, amounted to $43,000, yet even under Henry Cooke's able management of the investments, the company's income came to only $42,000. The trustees

29. Hewitt to Alvord, March 21, 1866, Bank Letters, BRFAL. Hewitt actually meant section 6, which deals with the available fund.
30. Minutes A, Finance Committee, June 26, 1868.
31. *Ibid.*
32. Journal, January 9, 1868.
33. Eaton to the Hon. J. Morrill, February 3, 1868, Committee on FA, NA, RG 233.

believed that Congress was about to lower the interest rate on government bonds and thus cause an even greater deficit.

Although very practical considerations of profit and loss stood foremost in Eaton's letter, a humanitarian argument played no minor part. Eaton declared that the trustees would aid the poor, industrious freedmen by providing loans when other banks refused. Many freedmen had houses and some real estate which could serve as collateral, and they would benefit by "small but judiciously made" loans. Such people were continually applying to the Bank. The trustees did not intend to limit the loans to Washington, Eaton intimated, but hoped to extend this aid to the branch cities where Negroes labored under great handicaps.[34] A few months later the actuary took his appeal to the Committee on Freedmen's Affairs, asking its recommendation for an enlargement of the company's powers so that it could lend money on "unencumbered productive real estate." He hinted to the committee, "If the company has heretofore made good use of the privileges it possessed, that will perhaps be a reason why you will confer others."[35]

Congress took no action for two years; nevertheless, the company in early 1869 began to invest its funds in the government-guaranteed bonds of the Union Pacific and Central Pacific railroads, and early in 1870 began to make loans on Washington real estate.[36] Clearly in the case of real estate loans, the trustees exceeded the powers granted in the charter and rejected the conservative financial policy outlined by Henry Cooke in 1868. In January, 1870, the trustees authorized the Finance Committee to loan $100,000 on call or "at short time" as they might see fit. With no explanation other than the company's heavy expenses and the need for greater income, the Finance Committee, led by Henry Cooke, made an about-face—as did the other trustees—concerning the usage of the available fund, which it now called "idle money." The board's February report showed that during the preceding month $100,000 in sundry real estate loans had been made and no government bonds had been purchased. The board then set aside another $100,000 under the same instructions as in January.[37]

34. *Ibid.*
35. Eaton to Committee on Freedmen's Affairs, July 5, 1868, Committee on FA, NA, RG 233.
36. Minutes A, Finance Committee, February 27, 1869; Journal, January 13, 1870, February 13, 1868; Robert William Fogel, *The Union Pacific Railroad* (Baltimore: Johns Hopkins Press, 1960), pp. 46, 57.
37. Minutes A, Finance Committee, January 13, 1870; Journal, February 10, 1870. The actions of Cooke, Huntington, and others between 1870 and 1872 suggest that they were primarily concerned with speculation rather than with aiding the freedmen. See below, pp. 150–165.

The trustees redoubled their efforts to change the charter in late 1869 and early 1870, perhaps because they now felt the need to obtain legal sanction for their "irregularities," as Alvord euphemistically described them.[38] Certainly the company needed more profits to hold its own. As early as 1868 the New York advisory board had requested permission to pay its depositors 6 percent interest in order to compete with rival banks. The Finance Committee rejected the appeal because a profit over 6 percent could be obtained only through speculative operations or through constantly circulating deposits through loans on call, both of which involved risk.[39] When officials at Washington asked for this privilege in 1869, and when frequent demands for 6 percent interest arose in the South, where businessmen could lend their money at 6 to 9 percent interest, the trustees were impressed by the urgency of the situation.[40] Moreover, they still expected that Congress would fund the national debt at a lower rate of interest.[41]

A special bank committee organized the push for a congressional amendment in late 1869 and early 1870.[42] General Howard was persuaded to publicize the need for additional powers in the *American Missionary*; he argued that a higher interest rate was due black depositors, and that the Bank should be placed upon the same footing as banks chartered by individual states. While recognizing the implied risks, he felt that the "character, standing and energy" of the management guaranteed that the Bank's new powers "would meet with a satisfactory result."[43] D. L. Eaton again lobbied on behalf of the proposed legislation. To the Reverend George Whipple he wrote: "The proposed amendment to the charter I got before the District Committee today. It will enter upon its perilous voyage and will need the pilotage of all its friends. I write to ask that you will correspond with any member of House and Senate asking him to look into the committee & help it along. It is to us a matter of vital importance."[44] William S. Huntington visited the capitol to persuade prominent men on the Committee of the District of Columbia to expedite the matter.[45]

38. *Freedman's Bank*, House, 1876, p. 37.
39. Minutes A, Finance Committee, December 28, 1868.
40. *Freedman's Bank*, House, 1876, p. 38. After May, 1871, the Bank paid 6 percent interest. See Minutes A, Finance Committee, May 30, 1871.
41. *Freedman's Bank*, House, 1876, p. 38.
42. Journal, March 10, 1870.
43. O. O. Howard, "The Freedmen's Savings Banks," *American Missionary*, XIII (November, 1869), 244. This article may have been written for Howard by Eaton. See Eaton to Howard, October 4, 1869, Howard MSS.
44. Eaton to Whipple, March 17, 1870, AMA.
45. *Freedman's Bank*, House, 1876, pp. 37, 52.

In March, 1870, Congress at last took action. The House of Representatives passed without debate a bill permitting the trustees to invest the deposits in United States securities and, to the extent of one-half of all the deposits, in "bonds or notes, secured by mortgage on real estate in double the value of the loan."[46] When Charles Sumner introduced a similar Senate bill and attempted to rush it through, Simon Cameron of Pennsylvania objected strenuously. Cameron posed as a defender of the poor freedmen, "people who are ignorant and unable to take care of themselves." Shall we, he asked the Senate, "suffer them to be cheated if they have with implicit confidence selected directors of their institution who are not careful enough in protecting their interests"?[47] Actually, Cameron spoke more in defense of principles of sound banking. Although he would permit investments in city and state bonds, as the Senate bill provided, the Pennsylvania senator, a former bank organizer and cashier, sought to strike out that part of the bill authorizing the company to make loans on real estate security. Real estate speculation had been the downfall of hundreds of banks, Cameron argued, and no well-managed bank would tie up its money in real estate loans, which could never be collected immediately.

> For instance, the directors of this company may each one of them own real estate in this town. A man having property in a town like this or any other is very apt to believe that it is worth more than anybody else supposes it is, and he is imagining constantly that he is getting rich by the increase of the value of his property. So when he goes to the meeting of the board, and application is made by John Smith to borrow a certain sum upon John's house, he says, "Yes, that is good security; his house is better than mine; and I am sure mine is worth twice as much as he wished to borrow." But they forget how many other people may have borrowed money upon that same security all over the town.[48]

Cameron predicted—accurately, as it turned out—the consequences of the proposed change.

> ... the great objection is this: this money is made up of contributions by small depositors, and if there should come a panic to-morrow, as we have seen many a time, the depositors will rush in a fit of frenzy to claim their deposits; and if the money is invested in real estate it takes a long process to collect it; but if it be in the bonds of the United States or of any State the institution can sell them at some price, and thus save them—

46. U.S., *Congressional Globe*, 41st Cong., 2nd sess., April 28, 1871, p. 3064.
47. *Ibid.*, April 1, 1870, p. 2334.
48. *Ibid.*, p. 2333.

selves. But, depend upon it, the moment you allow them to put their money, under any pretense, in real estate that moment you weaken the credit of the institution and its stability.[49]

Only Senator George Williams of Oregon supported Cameron in opposition. Williams feared for the safety of the institution should wider powers be granted. The original charter had not provided for speculation in city and state bonds and in real estate, and he regarded this as a healthy protective rule without which the Bank might just as well be closed.[50]

The arguments of Cameron and Williams were to no avail. Sumner spoke for a large majority who saw little need for concern: the trustees, after all, could not borrow from the Bank, and they would certainly obtain adequate security for their loans. Senator Pomeroy stressed that the only reason for the amendment was to provide a surplus which could not be earned by investing in government securities.[51] The Senate concurred, but as a concession to Cameron and Williams the senators voted to amend the bill so that loans could be made only on real estate of double the value of the loan, exclusive of improvements on that real estate. The amendment passed as amended.[52]

The Senate bill never became law. To save time, on April 28, 1870, the Senate agreed to consider the House bill, which it passed on May 2. This bill permitted loans only on real estate security and said nothing about city and state bonds. Cameron, unmoved by pressure from Bank officers and depositors, again objected and voted in the negative.

> This amendment of the charter of this company I objected to some time ago. I think it will in the end probably destroy the institution; but the people concerned in its management and those most interested, the colored people, have written to me remonstrating against my course; and if they want to be cheated I do not know that it is worth while for me to make much trouble about it. It is a principle which ought not to go into any banking institution at all. It is endangering the depositors of the funds, the small depositors especially. They are in the hands of persons entirely irresponsible, except the responsibility given by their character. They will be led probably into speculations; and if this money is once invested in real estate it will be very difficult to get it back.[53]

49. *Ibid.*, p. 2334.
50. *Ibid.*
51. *Ibid.*, pp. 2333–34.
52. *Ibid.*, p. 2335.
53. *Ibid.*, April 28, 1870, p. 3064.

Cameron and Williams had little support in their opposition to the change in the Bank's charter. Not very surprisingly, both those favoring and those opposing the amendment claimed to speak in behalf of the freedmen.[54] The House version of the bill—to permit loans secured by real estate valued at double the amount of the loan—became law on May 6.[55]

A minor provision of the 1870 amendment permitted the trustees to improve their real estate—that is, to erect a bank building on Pennsylvania Avenue in Washington. It is doubtful that the charter originally gave the trustees the power to purchase real estate; nevertheless, they bought land, and once this was done they found it imperative to put it to use by building a multi-story home office. While the building may have been necessary to stimulate pride and confidence in the Bank's stability (at least this was how the trustees justified it), it was an extravagance which the Bank could ill afford and one which occasioned considerable criticism.[56] Some felt the Bank had no business diverting the money of hard-working freedmen into the construction of an elegant bank building. The *New York Times* expressed the belief that $80,000 (the original estimate) for a bank building was extremely unwise; "the savings of the depositors are not properly devoted to any such purpose."[57] Inspector Anson Sperry later declared that he had "damned" the new building from the foundation stone up: "The thing which practically helped to kill the bank was the erection of its banking-house in Washington, which was a piece of illegal and unjustifiable extravagance." Sperry went so far as to date the Bank's decline from the building's construction.[58]

The change in the charter was decisive in the Bank's history. The trustees had faced squarely the conservative policy of safeguarding deposits by contracting operations and retrenching in expenditures, and they had rejected it. Instead they committed the Bank to vigorous expansion, knowing full well that the speculative investments from which they would get the necessary revenue would involve serious risk if a severe crisis occurred. That other savings banks were changing their investment strategy in the same way at that time did not make the

---

54. *Ibid.*, April 1, 1870, pp. 2333–35.
55. *Report of the Comptroller of the Currency*, 1873, p. 1.
56. Journal, October 14, 1869, February 10 and June 9, 1870; *Report of the Comptroller of the Currency*, 1873, pp. 1–2; *New York Times*, October 18, 1869, p. 4.
57. October 18, 1869, p. 4.
58. *Freedman's Bank*, House, 1876, p. 15.

gamble less hazardous.[59] Thereafter the Bank would be vulnerable to exactly the same pressures as every other American business, and the wisdom, skill, and honesty of its officials would be tested by the same temptations. To an astute observer in 1870, these facts would offer grounds for worry, for the speculative nature of American business, the Bank's "irregularities" in lending in 1869 and 1870, and the fluctuation in its personnel at all levels gave little assurance of future safety or integrity.

The year 1870 marked the end of the Bank's conservatism. Previously almost all the company's investments had been in government securities, while the available fund, which could be as much as ⅓ of all deposits, had generally been kept in cash to meet any sudden demands. Beginning in May the trustees loaned substantial sums on Washington real estate of doubtful value, and the loans were not easily collected. They also loaned money on stocks and bonds of diverse companies and on personal security. Since the charter amendment permitted only loans on real estate security, where did they obtain sanction for these investments? They found it in a very liberal interpretation of the available fund clause—an interpretation formerly considered illicit by Henry Cooke and most of the trustees.[60] Now the Board of Trustees resolved that the available fund "shall be loaned only on collateral of govt. or railway bonds or other securities of a marketable value of at least 10% more than the loan."[61] Significantly, the trustee who proposed this resolution, publisher A. S. Barnes, was a large stockholder and director of a railroad that borrowed $175,000 of the freedmen's money.[62] Thus the available fund came to be, as Alvord admitted,

> a fund from which miscellaneous loans were made, and the actuary kept a certain sort of account which seemed to cover the balance on hand not loaned on real estate, which he called the available fund. It was an arrangement of his own, and when a loan came up that could not be

59. This argument was used in the Senate debate in 1870. See U.S., *Congressional Globe*, 41st Cong., 2nd sess., April 1, 1870, pp. 2333–34. See also *New York Times*, March 31, 1878, p. 4.

60. *Freedman's Bank*, House, 1876, pp. 38, 67; *Report of the Select Committee*, Senate, 1880, p. 27.

61. Journal, May 12, 1870.

62. Minutes A, Finance Committee, July 11, 1871; Minutes B, Finance Committee, December 10, 1872, p. 34. In 1879 Barnes received $125,000 for his stock in the Central Branch, Union Pacific Railroad. See Charles Edgar Ames, *Pioneering the Union Pacific* (New York: Appleton-Century-Crofts, 1969), pp. 522, 523, 524.

made on realty, he would say, there is an available fund not yet used, (that is, there is one-third of the total deposits which have not yet been consumed). If there was a balance not thus loaned from the one-third of the deposits, he called that the available fund. It was a distinction which he made himself.[63]

The available fund steadily became unavailable.

While the charter amendment and trustees' resolution made possible a certain amount of speculation, they were not entirely to blame for the speculative investment which ensued and for the Bank's failure. Had the Bank demanded real estate security of double the value of the loans, as the charter required, and had the available fund been kept in government securities or readily marketable securities, the Bank might have survived any crisis.[64] The problem, however, was that the management disregarded these safeguards, and the Bank was managed primarily for speculative purposes. The acquisition of profits (as opposed to safety) governed the Bank's loan policy, and in some cases it is even questionable whether the profits were intended for the Bank or for certain trustees. The actions of the trustees and officers in the period 1870 through 1872 (and to some extent thereafter) ranged from risky to unwise to starkly dishonest.

By the late 1860's control of the Freedman's Savings and Trust Company had narrowed to a few individuals. Cooke and Huntington of the Finance Committee, plus the members of the Agency Committee, were the same nine to eleven men who attended the Board of Trustees' monthly meetings. These Washington trustees regularly rubber-stamped the decisions that they as individuals or as members of committees had made during the preceding month.[65] President Alvord was still very visible in most administrative affairs and publicity functions, but his real power steadily dwindled. Happiest as an evangel spreading the good news, after 1868 he became increasingly ineffective; his interest in missionary matters and his many southern travels urging the freedmen to deposit diverted him from the Bank's financial management. Ignorant and naïve in financial matters, Alvord found himself completely out of place once the Bank had made its transition from a missionary organization to a financial empire. He seemed to have accepted

63. *Freedman's Bank*, House, 1876, p. 67.
64. *Ibid.*, p. 144.
65. See minutes and journals of the Bank's executive committees. Testimony before the House committee revealed that a small group of Washington trustees controlled the Bank (*ibid.*, p. 91). On one occasion the members of the Finance Committee served also as the Examining Committee. See Journal, May 20, 1867.

quite passively the expert financial leadership of Cooke, Huntington, and the actuaries. His health declined, and in the early 1870's he suffered a nervous breakdown and spent time in a sanitarium.[66]

To the commanding figures of Cooke and Huntington must be added a third, actuary D. L. Eaton, who entered the Bank's service after the transfer to Washington. As head of the American Building Block Company, an official of the First Congregational Church of Washington, and a former colonel, Eaton had won the friendship of O. O. Howard, the Christian general whose favor he used in his perpetual search for lucrative employment. Taking an avid interest in the Bank's work, Eaton took over the daily direction of the internal affairs of the company's home office and emerged with immense influence, doing much of the day-to-day work of the Agency and Finance committees. By 1869 he was the Bank's highest-paid official—which was probably only fair, for, according to a former bookkeeper, he seemed to run the entire company.[67]

Henry Cooke, William S. Huntington, and D. L. Eaton controlled the Bank's finances between 1867 and 1872. In January, 1870, when they and other trustees revolutionized the Bank's rules concerning investments, the three agreed that the Finance Committee, which often met at the Washington office of Jay Cooke and Company, and the actuary should make the company's loans. Over the next two years the "proposed loans" submitted to the Board of Trustees were loans that had already been made.[68] Some Finance Committee meetings, at which decisions to lend from $30,000 to $50,000 were reached, were merely personal conversations between Cooke and his employee Huntington.[69] Said actuary George Stickney, the nephew and successor of Eaton:

> The Seal-Lock Company's loan [which cost the company thousands of dollars] . . . was negotiated and approved by Mr. Huntington alone, who was one of the finance committee. When we had a meeting of the full finance committee these loans would be reported and approved. After

66. *Freedman's Bank*, House, 1876, pp. 33, 36, 89; Whyte, *The Uncivil War*, p. 255.

67. Alvord to Sauvinet, May 24, 1867, p. 316, Letters Sent, Book 12, Educational Division, BRFAL; Journal, August 12, 1869, and November 11, 1870; *Freedman's Bank*, House, 1876, pp. 50, 88; *Charges against General Howard*, p. 85; letters from Eaton to Howard, Howard MSS. The American Building Block Company was also known as D. L. Eaton and Company. Eaton knew many of the builders and speculators in Washington. See Paul Skeels Pierce, *The Freedmen's Bureau* (Iowa City: State University of Iowa, 1904), pp. 115–118.

68. *Report of the Select Committee*, Senate, 1880, p. 140; Journal, January 13, 1870; Minutes A, Finance Committee, January 13, 1870.

69. *Freedman's Bank*, House, 1876, pp. 42–43, 65; *Report of the Select Committee*, Senate, 1880, p. 56.

that they were reported to the board of trustees. I think that the record shows that all these loans were reported by the finance committee, after they were made.[70]

No one seemed to recall that the charter required the affirmative vote of seven trustees in order to invest the Bank's funds, and rarely did the trustees object to arrangements made by Cooke, Huntington, or Eaton. Alvord, who as president was to supervise the Finance Committee, only occasionally attended its meetings.[71] In fact, the Finance Committee denied him the vote on matters before the committee and encouraged him to concentrate on field work, which he seemed happy to do.

To Henry Cooke belongs much of the responsibility for speculative and probably dishonest undertakings. It later became apparent that Cooke's financial capacity had been ludicrously overrated by Alvord. Henrietta Larson, the biographer of Jay Cooke, summarizes succinctly the now somewhat tarnished image of Henry Cooke. He was valuable to Jay Cooke and Company as a lobbyist but for little else.

> Never can there have been a bank executive who was much less of a banker than Henry Cooke! He was an assiduous lobbyist, a profession in which he was adept. He proved to be a spendthrift, a "good fellow," easily influenced, lacking in business judgment, with an exaggerated opinion of his own importance, and inclined to tie up the business firm in speculative enterprises and loans to politicians.[72]

Lacking both integrity and financial acumen—as those who observed his Civil War speculation in quartermasters' vouchers knew so well—Henry Cooke was a born public relations man, and not a very honest one at that.[73]

Under the leadership of Cooke, Huntington, and Eaton, the Freedman's Bank, the safe depository for the savings of tens of thousands of ex-slaves, became a gold mine for speculators, enterprising stock companies, and the District of Columbia's Board of Public Works. The original purposes of the Bank now were of secondary importance. Foremost among the speculators was Cooke himself; as chairman of the Finance Committee he deposited much of the cash of the Freedman's Bank in Jay Cooke's Washington office, the First National Bank, whose president was, of course, Henry Cooke. At one time the amount totaled

70. *Freedman's Bank*, House, 1876, p. 110.

71. *Ibid.*, pp. 42–43, 65–66.

72. Henrietta M. Larson, *Jay Cooke, Private Banker* (Cambridge: Harvard University Press, 1936), p. 186.

73. *Ibid.*, pp. 153–154, 186.

$500,000, an enormous sum on which the Cookes paid only 5 percent interest, while the Freedman's Bank was paying its depositors 6 percent.[74] He also authorized several loans to organizations or companies in which he was materially involved. For example, Cooke was a member of the board of the Young Men's Christian Association, to which the Bank (i.e., Cooke and his friends) extended a loan on inadequate security. To make such a loan clearly involved a conflict of interest, regardless of pious motives.[75] Both the Finance Committee's chairman and William Huntington were major stockholders and incorporators of the Maryland Freestone Mining and Manufacturing Company (popularly known as the Seneca Stone Company) when the Bank extended to that company several loans totaling approximately $50,000, secured by the company's worthless bonds.[76] Cooke and Huntington favored these loans and maneuvered them through the Board of Trustees. One committee member who had no time to read the details of the transaction simply took Cooke's word that everything was in order and that the loan would be profitable.[77]

Cooke induced the trustees to take an agency to sell the bonds of Jay Cooke and Company's Northern Pacific Railroad; he was, as it happened, a full partner in Jay Cooke and Company. He also helped his brother's firm borrow $50,000 from the Bank on Northern Pacific bonds which the Cooke Company guaranteed to take back on five days' notice.[78] When Edgar Ketchum, one of the conscientious, conservative trustees, persuaded the board to demand that Jay Cooke and Company take back the bonds and that the Bank call in the $50,000 Seneca Stone loan, Henry Cooke, speaking for the Finance Company, objected.[79] He unblushingly argued that the Maryland Freestone Mining and Manufacturing Company was a well-known and solvent company; its business was profitable and its stocks and bonds found a ready market. Nor should the fact that the company employed over three hundred Negroes be overlooked. As for the railroad bonds, Cooke argued that they were more profitable than government investments and were entirely safe because of the five-day guarantee. Cooke concluded his one-man obstruction by conjuring up a rosy-hued financial future for the Northern

74. *Report of the Select Committee*, Senate, 1880, p. 179.
75. *Freedman's Bank*, House, 1876, p. 34.
76. *Ibid.*, p. 26; *Report of the Select Committee*, Senate, 1880, pp. 112–113.
77. *Report of the Select Committee*, Senate, 1880, pp. vi–vii, 112–113.
78. *Freedman's Bank*, House, 1876, p. 74; Journal, February 9, 1871; Minutes A, Finance Committee, February 7, 1871.
79. Minutes A, Finance Committee, May 3, 1871. Earlier in the year, in February, Cooke had objected. See *ibid.*, February 6, 1872.

Pacific Railroad.[80] Six months later another of the more conservative trustees, J. J. Stewart of Baltimore, ordered adherence to the board's resolution that Jay Cooke and Company take back the bonds; and, although redeeming the bonds proved difficult, the Bank eventually received all but $200 of its money.[81] Significantly, it was in February, 1872, when the board decided to get back its money, that Henry Cooke and his associate William S. Huntington resigned from the Finance Committee.[82]

Lacking conclusive evidence, we can only surmise the reasons for the Cooke and Huntington resignations.[83] True, their other business affairs were pressing; yet it is significant to note that the Finance Committee was at last being challenged, and it was clear that the committee would no longer have complete freedom in the manipulation of the Bank's funds. One cannot but wonder if Cooke and Huntington were beginning to fear the consequences of their risky and ethically questionable activities.

Even after his resignation, Cooke profited from his knowledge of the Bank and his friendship with the actuary. As governor of the District of Columbia he showed how Freedman's Bank loans might help finance the city's public works program. Cooke and Alexander Shepherd, the political boss of the District,[84] were quick to assure Bank officials that the Bank's loans would be repaid when Congress appropriated money for the Board of Public Works. But, as the New York *Sun* charged, "When that appropriation was made Cooke and Shepherd took care of the First National and the National Metropolitan Banks, and let the Freedmen's [*sic*] take care of itself."[85] On one occasion Cooke and

80. *Ibid.*, February 6, 1872.

81. Journal, January 11 and February 8, 1872; Minutes A, Finance Committee, March 11, 1872; *Freedman's Bank*, House, 1876, p. 75.

82. Journal, February 8, 1872.

83. Huntington left no papers, and there is no reference to the Freedman's Bank in the papers of Henry Cooke, Jay Cooke, or Jay Cooke and Company. It seems unlikely that these men would have let damaging evidence survive.

84. Shepherd was a Washington politician prominent in establishing the territorial government for the District of Columbia in 1871. When Cooke resigned in 1873, President Grant appointed Shepherd governor. As "boss" of the District, he was acclaimed for improving the capital, though the cost was staggering and the methods often unscrupulous. When Congress abolished the territorial government the next year and replaced it with commissioners, Shepherd was again proposed by Grant. The Senate, however, refused to confirm him because of the scandals associated with his regime. See *Dictionary of American Biography*, IX, 77–79.

85. April 29, 1874, p. 1; David M. Cole, *The Development of Banking in the District of Columbia* (New York: William-Frederick Press, 1959), p. 325; *Baltimore American*, July 8, 1874, p. 2.

Shepherd, being short of funds, hurried to the Freedman's Bank to borrow $50,000 on very doubtful security (a certificate of the Board of Public Works and a bad check on the First National Bank). With some effort, the actuary eventually got back the money.[86]

Cooke was hardly unique in abusing the Bank's funds; Huntington and Eaton were also involved in speculative and dishonest activities. Although by charter the trustees and officers were forbidden to use the Bank's money, Huntington found it convenient to borrow from the Freedman's Bank—a loan never repaid—to cover a shortage in his accounts as cashier of the First National Bank.[87] On another occasion Huntington negotiated a $13,000 loan from the First National Bank for R. P. Dodge, his landlord, in hopes that his rent would be reduced. The First National Bank held Dodge's notes until they were due and then, through Huntington's influence with Eaton, transferred them to the Freedman's Bank. Dodge refused to repay the loans when confronted by the Freedman's Bank, claiming that the money had actually gone to Huntington in the first place. There was no way to call Huntington to account, for by this time he was dead and buried.[88] This episode reveals a significant pattern; Cooke, Huntington, and other officers and trustees on occasion used the Freedman's Bank as a dumping ground for their bad private claims or the poor securities of the First National Bank. For example, George Balloch, a Finance Committee member in 1872 and a friend of many Bank officers, made a bad private loan in 1870; in 1872 he transferred the claim to the Freedman's Bank, reimbursing himself from the Bank's funds. In 1880 the commissioners concluded that the Bank would lose most of this money.[89]

Actuary D. L. Eaton always seemed ready to oblige his friends and was implicated in many unsavory transactions. Eaton and his wife both borrowed from the Bank.[90] The actuary seemed to violate the charter with impunity—among other things, he added names to committee minutes to establish a quorum and accepted fees for negotiating loans.[91] He also accepted a kickback from one of the Bank's largest borrowers.[92] Eaton's replacement, George L. Stickney, was no better; in one instance

86. *Report of the Select Committee*, Senate, 1880, p. 160.
87. *Freedman's Bank*, House, 1876, p. 18; *Report of the Select Committee*, Senate, 1880, p. 105.
88. *Report of the Select Committee*, Senate, 1880, p. 161.
89. *Ibid.*, pp. 176, 285.
90. *Freedman's Bank*, House, 1876, pp. iv–ix and *passim*.
91. *Report of the Select Committee*, Senate, 1880, p. 59; *Freedman's Bank*, House, 1876, pp. 138–139.
92. *Ibid.*, p. 131.

Stickney appropriated the collateral of a loan for his own use, and in 1877 he admitted that he owed the Bank a little over $4,000.[93]

Several trustees and officers other than the big three—Cooke, Huntington, and Eaton—became involved in conflicts of interest. Lewis Clephane, a contractor for the Board of Public Works and for a time a Finance Committee member along with Cooke and Huntington, was president of the Metropolis Paving Company (whose treasurer was Huntington) and the Seal Lock Company, speculative firms in which the Bank invested large sums.[94] Finance Committee member George W. Balloch was superintendent of streets under the Board of Public Works (which foisted its valueless certificates on the Bank) during the time when, as one trustee described it, Cooke and Huntington "were in the full vigor of their missionary work."[95] Zalmon Richards, a Bank trustee, was auditor of the Board of Public Works.[96] Even after Huntington and Cooke resigned, the Bank continued to help finance the District's building program, to the enormous profit of contractors and speculators.[97]

To grasp the full extent of the Bank officials' fraudulence, it is necessary to describe in greater detail some Bank transactions to which allusion has already been made: those with the Maryland Freestone Mining and Manufacturing Company (usually called the Seneca Stone Company). This Maryland concern, created in 1867, was originally a legitimate and potentially valuable business, but in 1869 its managers turned their energies toward speculative ventures in preference to developing the company's rich stone quarries.[98] Over the next three years, H. D. Cooke and William S. Huntington, both Finance Committee members and Seneca incorporators, and Charles W. Hayden, Seneca treasurer and Cooke's brother-in-law, negotiated a total of $50,000 in loans on inadequate Seneca security. When the debt fell due and the Bank wanted to collect, a $50,000 note of John O. Evans and Hallet Kilbourn,

93. "Memoranda as to the delinquencies of Geo. W. Stickney as Trustee and as Actuary FS&T Co. [n.d.]," Letters Rec'd by the Commissioners, 1870–1914, FS&T Co.

94. *Freedman's Bank*, House, 1876, p. 79.

95. *Ibid.*; *Report of the Select Committee*, Senate, 1880, p. 105.

96. *Freedman's Bank*, House, 1876, p. 79.

97. *Baltimore American*, July 8, 1874, p. 2. Other examples could be cited: A. S. Barnes was involved in an obvious conflict of interest; Cooke and Huntington loaned money to Howard University while Balloch was the school's treasurer and Alvord was on the board of trustees; Moses Kelly, Huntington's successor on the Finance Committee, was involved in public works speculation. See *Journal*, June 8, 1871; Minutes A, Finance Committee, July 11 and September 9, 1871; *Freedman's Bank*, House, 1876, p. 45; *Baltimore American*, July 8, 1874, p. 2.

98. *Report of the Select Committee*, Senate, 1880, p. vi.

Washington businessmen, was substituted as security at the insistence of Eaton, who probably hoped to change the form of the illegal loan and forestall uncomfortable inquiries. Through a secret agreement (never satisfactorily explained to congressional investigators or most of the Bank's trustees) the $50,000 note, with all its valid securities, was later surrendered to Evans and Kilbourn for $75,000 of perfectly worthless second mortgage bonds of the Seneca company. These bonds had no marketable value;[99] in fact, only Henry Cooke, who invested $5,000 in them, and the Freedman's Bank had ever purchased any. Later congressional investigators were much interested in this aspect of the transaction:

> Q: If Henry D. Cooke, with his supposed financiering ability and astuteness, was willing to pay and did pay par in cash for these second-mortgage bonds, how was it that they were unsalable in the general market?
> A: [*Hayden, the treasurer*] I really do not know. I had nothing to do with the sale of the bonds.
> Q: Have you any reason to believe or to know that, occupying the double relationship which he did to the Seneca Stone Company and the Freedman's Bank, that was a sham transaction, in order to give to the second-mortgage bonds an appearance of value which they did not possess?[100]

The answer was an unconvincing denial. A few moments later in this testimony it became clear that the Seneca Stone Company was a "monstrous fabric of credit." The company was doing business on a nominal capital stock of $800,000 and on bonds in the amount of $200,000 or more—all based on the value of the company's property. When the treasurer claimed that he did not know the actual assessed value of this real estate, the chairman of the committee made public an extract from the records of Montgomery County, Maryland, showing that the assessed value of the real estate in 1868 was $43,200.[101] When Cooke was asked about all of this, he claimed that he could not remember the Seneca transaction, for he had then been faced with many problems, doing the work of two or three men. Cooke swore he had assumed the Bank work voluntarily, "simply from a sincere desire to do good."[102] In 1880 a

99. Minutes B, Finance Committee, November 13, 1873, pp. 56–59; *Freedman's Bank*, House, 1876, pp. 58–65, 68–73, 118–121; *Report of the Select Committee*, Senate, 1880, pp. vi–viii.

100. *Freedman's Bank*, House, 1876, p. 59.

101. *Ibid.*, pp. 60–61.

102. *Report of the Select Committee*, Senate, 1880, pp. 100–103. Cooke's grand apologia before the Senate committee was intended to arrest charges of fraud and to evoke sympathy: ". . . I gave what time I could in assisting this company in its development and its growth and its success for a long time, until they were over-

commissioner of the Freedman's Bank raised the possibility of instituting legal proceedings against those responsible for the Seneca steal; but because of the deaths of Eaton and Huntington, the bankruptcy of others, the cost of litigation, and the difficulty in securing testimony concerning secret deals, those who desired to see justice done were thwarted.[103]

Just as disastrous as the Seneca loans were the Vandenburgh and Abbott Paving Company loans. On security such as certificates of the Board of Public Works of the District of Columbia and bills against the District for work on improving the streets, the Abbott Paving Company and J. W. Vandenburgh, the company's treasurer, borrowed $89,000 and $122,000, respectively.[104] Vandenburgh generally negotiated through the Bank's actuaries, D. L. Eaton and later George Stickney. The actuaries always seemed willing to defend these transactions before the Board of Trustees and to make additional loans, although the earlier ones were overdue.[105] On one occasion Vandenburgh received a loan which enabled him to complete a contract; then he and Eaton, who invested no money in the enterprise, split the profits.[106] After Eaton left the Bank's service in 1872, Stickney continued the accommodations, although somewhat reluctantly. Once when Stickney refused Vandenburgh a loan, fearing that the Board of Public Works could never pay the contractor, Vandenburgh took him to see Alexander Shepherd. Boss Shepherd assured Stickney that the Board of Public Works would have the money at a certain time, and on that assurance Stickney made the loan. Congressional investigators were unable to determine whether it was repaid.[107]

Loans made to Robert I. Fleming, the contractor for the Freedman's

---

taken by these hard times, which impaired and destroyed the value of its securities, as well as of itself, its standing. That company were the victims of a widespread, universal financial trouble, by which I myself, my firm, have been heavy losers, as well as others, and I have always regarded this trouble of the company as having been the result of a widespread, universal, sweeping financial disaster." In answering specific questions, Cooke was vague, pleading inability to remember. His memory lapses did not deceive the congressional investigators. "These indefinite answers and hypothetical suggestions amount to nothing," declared one senator. See *ibid.*, pp. 52, 57.

103. *Ibid.*, p. viii.

104. *Ibid.* Formerly Vandenburgh had been a Freedmen's Bureau official in the District of Columbia. See *Freedman's Bank*, House, 1876, p. 124.

105. Enoch Totten to Commissioners, January 12, 1878, Letters Rec'd by the Commissioners, 1870–1914, FS&T Co.; *Freedman's Bank*, House, 1876, pp. 48–49, 88–89, 126.

106. *Freedman's Bank*, House, 1876, p. 131.

107. *Ibid.*, p. 127. Shepherd was familiar with the Bank's loan-making process, for he personally had borrowed $20,000 on inadequate security. See Journal, May 11, 1871.

Bank building, aggregated $224,000. The securities Fleming offered frequently proved inadequate, in some cases being bills against the District of Columbia or stock of the Young Men's Christian Association.[108] As security for one note of $26,300 Fleming provided District of Columbia auditor's certificates, bonds of the Y.M.C.A., and two deeds of trust. These securities totaled $15,307.62 in 1875, and even valued at par they still fell $4,000 short of the original amount of the loan. Six years after the Bank closed Fleming still owed it $35,000.[109]

The Bank's most egregious loan, to Juan Boyle, was made secretly by actuary George L. Stickney a few days before the Bank failed—when the company was refusing to return the freedmen's deposits. In 1880 the Senate investigating committee reported:

> The books show that $33,366.66 was loaned Boyle on the 30th of June [1874]. . . . For one loan, viz, $4,366.66, no collateral whatever appears to have been taken, and for the other, viz, $29,000, collateral utterly worthless was accepted, in direct violation of the amended charter, which provided that the collateral in all cases should be of double the value of the loan. . . . The estimated loss on the Boyle loans is $31,000, which includes interest, costs, and expenses. These loans were not approved by the finance committee or the board of trustees. . . . This was not only an unlawful act, but one impertinently offensive, and made subsequent to the amendatory act of 1874, and subject to the penalties provided therein. Why Mr. Stickney has not been dealt with we are not advised, but he is certainly subject to criminal action for his conduct in this if not in other cases.[110]

In contrast to this remarkable spate of financial mismanagement and criminal fraud, the Bank's official reports always stressed the conservatism of the company's financial transactions. Eaton, obviously not the most trustworthy source, consistently reported to the trustees that loans had been restricted to small amounts, that only a small percentage of loan applications had been accepted, and that the value of the security was always substantially greater than the amount of the loan. Of the $2,993,790 due the freedmen when the Bank failed, approximately $1,200,000 was secured by notes on real estate, and column after column of real estate security created an image of solidity, at least in the minds of some trustees.[111] Apparently many of the trustees felt no concern

---

108. *Freedman's Bank*, House, 1876, pp. 18, 52–53; *Report of the Select Committee*, Senate, 1880, p. ix.

109. *New York Tribune*, June 14, 1875, p. 1; *Report of the Select Committee*, Senate, 1880, pp. 292–293, 301.

110. *Report of the Select Committee*, Senate, 880, pp. ix–x.

111. Minutes A, Finance Committee, June 8, 1870, January 10, 1871, and Feb-

because they were satisfied with the Bank's condition as presented by the officers. Granted that Eaton may have had ulterior motives in misrepresenting the Bank's loan policy, he may also have believed that most of the loans on real estate security were sound.

Before the panic of 1873 the value of real estate in Washington increased steadily, but not nearly as rapidly as real estate brokers' opinions of its value. As one of the commissioners of the Bank later revealed, "At the time when many of these loans were taken, real estate was at a high value, and high valuations were put upon it at the time of making the loans, and in many cases the properties were overrated in value."[112] Many of the Bank's loans were negotiated through real estate brokers who charged a commission of 2½ percent for their services (and this, of course, added to the already high cost of borrowing).[113] Some brokers were instrumental in placing high appraisals on the Bank's real estate collateral—an action which naturally facilitated granting the loan. Real estate brokers conducted business at the Bank until 1872, when the trustees voted to exclude them from the loan-making process.[114] Before this action, however, abuses had occurred. For example, the firm of Kilbourn and Latta had become real estate appraisers for the Bank while simultaneously negotiating Bank loans for their clients.[115] It is small wonder that in some cases the real estate security did not cover the loan.

The overvaluation, however, was not readily apparent; consequently, the Bank often had at least the appearance of making sound real estate loans. The reality was otherwise: when the Bank failed in 1874, most of the loans held by the Bank were overdue.[116] ". . . of the greater part of the assets of the company," reported the commissioners, "it will be seen that the loss in their conversion into cash will necessarily be large."[117]

Even if most of the real estate loans which the trustees made had been

---

ruary 7, 1871; "Report—To the Board of Trustees," Letters Rec'd by the Commissioners, 1870–1914, FS&T Co.; *Freedman's Bank*, House, 1876, p. 2; *Report of the Select Committee*, Senate, 1880, appendix, p. 22.

112. *Report of the Select Committee*, Senate, 1880, p. 38.

113. *Freedman's Bank*, House, 1876, pp. 96, 138–139; Minutes A, Finance Committee, September 9, 1871.

114. *Freedman's Bank*, House, 1876, pp. 138–139; Minutes A, Finance Committee, May 8, 1872.

115. *Freedman's Bank*, House, 1876, p. 19; *Report of the Select Committee*, Senate, 1880, pp. 146–147; Keyes, *History of Savings Banks*, II, 563. Hallet Kilbourn himself borrowed almost $4,000 without putting up any collateral. See *Freedman's Bank*, House, 1876, p. 40.

116. *Report of the Commissioners*, 1874, p. 7.

117. *Ibid.*, p. 8.

repaid, it is significant that the Bank's safety margin was so thin that it took only a relatively small number of bad loans to compromise the safety of the Bank. The Freedman's Bank lost thousands of dollars because of unwise (and perhaps illegal) loans on real estate and the speculative and dishonest use of the available fund, some of the worst transactions being the Seneca Stone, Fleming, Juan Boyle, and Vandenburgh cases. There were many others. The Bank loaned $12,000 to one man on $20,000 worth of valueless second-mortgage bonds of the Seneca Stone Company, invested $4,000 in Detroit Car Loan Company stock (which in 1877 brought fifteen to twenty cents on the dollar), and loaned money to hotels on chattel mortgage.[118] Much of the real estate security obtained by the Bank later proved worthless by reason of defective title, previous encumbrance, or other questions leading to litigation.[119] For example, one George Mattingly borrowed $15,000 on a piece of property to which he did not have undisputed title; in 1880, $16,000 (including court costs) was still due.[120] Litigation concerning loans began in the early 1870's and lasted well into the 1880's.[121] In 1879, $46,000, including interest and litigation costs, was still due on a loan to Evan Lyons; $15,000 was due on a loan to A. C. Bradley; and a large portion of an $8,000 loan to R. M. Hall (granted by the actuary) was still due.[122] In 1880 one authority concluded, "A large number of the loans made by the bank contrary to the provisions of the charter have been paid, but the books show that many of them were not paid at maturity, but ran considerably overtime, causing expense to the bank in collecting; others were not paid at all previous to the failure of the bank, but were collected by the commissioners of the company after they assumed control of the affairs, while many more remain unpaid at this date."[123] Six years after the Bank failed, the balance due on real estate loans was approximately $315,000, while the losses on other types of loans from the use of the available fund totaled $196,000.[124]

Many white Washingtonians benefited from the liberal loan policy of the Freedman's Bank, and it appears that several trustees worked

118. Minutes A, Finance Committee, November 18, 1870, March 26, 1872; R. H. T. Leipold to Cashier, First National Bank, November 7, 1877, Letters Rec'd by the Commissioners, 1870–1914, FS&T Co.; *Freedman's Bank*, House, 1876, p. 39.
119. *Freedman's Bank*, House, 1876, pp. 81, 101; Keyes, *History of Savings Banks*, II, 562.
120. *Report of the Select Committee*, Senate, 1880, p. 296.
121. Journal, November 14, 1870; *Report of the Select Committee*, Senate, 1880, pp. 289–309; Letters Rec'd by the Commissioners, 1870–1914, FS&T Co.
122. "Report of Accountants," in *Report of the Select Committee*, Senate, 1880, pp. 285–286.
123. *Ibid.*, p. 241.
124. *Report of the Select Committee*, Senate, 1880, pp. 299, 307.

more for their own "progress" than for the freedmen's. Scandals and the failure have cast suspicion on their motives. Was the amendment of the charter in 1870 part of a conspiracy to misappropriate the freedmen's money for personal profit? Various newspapers leveled this charge (a monstrous swindle by a Washington ring), as have later accounts such as Fleming's history of the Bank and David Cole's *The Development of Banking in the District of Columbia.* An 1876 political pamphlet, *The Washers and the Scrubbers: The Men Who Robbed Them,* purported to reveal the Republican plots which surrounded the Freedman's Bank.[125]

The accusation that a vile ring was filching the freedmen's money was all the more believable to contemporaries because in 1870 and 1874 scandals involving misappropriation of government funds tainted General Howard and the Freedmen's Bureau. Although on both occasions Howard and the Bureau were exonerated, evidence collected by obviously friendly congressional investigators revealed that some of his chief lieutenants were personally interested in ventures which the Bureau was financing. D. L. Eaton, John Alvord, Eliphalet Whittlesey, and Charles Howard were members of the American Building Block Company (the D. L. Eaton Company) which sold defective building blocks to Howard University. When the walls of the university's hospital collapsed and Congress decided to investigate, the idea of a "Freedmen's Bureau Ring" became public, and suspicions of wrongdoing were never allayed. A subsequent investigation into possible bounty frauds, which again exculpated Howard, revealed that George W. Balloch had made questionable investments. Both investigations uncovered the tendency of Howard and his aides and friends to construe liberally laws directing the expenditure of government money.[126] A similar attitude was most evident in the management of the Freedman's Bank.

A conspiracy—a combination of persons banded secretly together to accomplish an illegal or dishonest act—is necessarily difficult to prove. Excellent reasons existed in 1870 for amending the charter to permit a

125. Walter L. Fleming, *Freedmen's Savings Bank* (Chapel Hill: University of North Carolina Press, 1927), pp. 70–81; Cole, *Development of Banking,* pp. 342–343; F. C. Adams, *The Washers and the Scrubbers: The Men Who Robbed Them* (Washington: Judd & Detweiler, 1879). The New York *Sun* (April 29, 1874) called the actions of the Washington Ring a monstrous swindle. The *New York Tribune* (June 14, 1875) wrote that "having got possession of its Finance Committee, it [the Ring] lent out its money to Ring contractors and Ring operators on insufficient security or no security at all." The actions of the ring were "colossal in their meanness," thought the *Baltimore American* (July 8, 1874).

126. For the scandals and charges of scandal which surrounded the Freedmen's Bureau, see Bentley, *History of the Freedmen's Bureau,* ch. 14 and *passim.*

more liberal investment policy, and speculative ventures were quite common in the period known as the Gilded Age. There are no incriminating letters or documents extant to settle the case—but had there been, perhaps they would have been destroyed by the conspirators. It is hard to believe that Cooke, Huntington, and Eaton did not have their eyes fixed on glittering business opportunities in 1870 when they redirected the company's investment policy, and it was in 1870 that Jay Cooke and Company desperately began to market their Northern Pacific bonds. Eaton seemed only too eager to preside over the distribution of the freedmen's funds among his friends and business associates in Washington. The trustees' actions and their conflicts of interest point to a conspiracy to use the Bank's money in ways which would benefit the trustees; but this need not have involved the victimization of the depositors. Cooke, Huntington, Eaton, Stickney, and others quite possibly believed that their investments, no matter how speculative, would pay off. For example, they expected that the Northern Pacific would eventually return huge profits, that the District of Columbia Board of Public Works would soon receive substantial appropriations to cover its obligations, and that the value of city real estate would continue to increase.

Some of the worst cases, however, cannot be palliated by these charitable assumptions. The Seneca Stone transaction seems to be an unmitigated fraud, as was the action of George Balloch in transferring his poor security on a loan to the Freedman's Bank. Evidence here points not only to a conspiracy to use the money for a brief period, but also to criminal intent: Cooke, Huntington, Eaton, and Balloch must have known that they were in effect stealing from the Bank and, ultimately, from the freedmen.

Regardless of whether the motives were well intentioned or dishonest and criminal, the result was the same: bank officers and trustees violated the charter in numerous unwise, unethical, and illegal actions which resulted in the loss of thousands of dollars belonging to the freedmen. Those who labeled this a huge swindle could not have been far wrong.

The speculators and swindlers could not have succeeded in their objectives without the negligence of many trustees. LeRoy Tuttle, a Finance Committee member for a short while, testified, "They [Cooke, Huntington, and probably others] put me on the committee for a convenience, as they said, I telling them at the same time that I had not the time to assume any responsibility, as I was assistant treasurer of the United States."[127] Assured that everything was in order, Tuttle put his

127. *Freedman's Bank*, House, 1876, p. 104.

signature on transactions with companies of which he knew nothing—companies such as the Metropolis Paving Company, American Seal-Lock Company (sometimes called National Seal-Lock Company), Columbia Railroad Company, Morris Mining Company, and the Seneca Stone Company.[128] The Tuttle case suggests that such inappropriate appointments as his to key Bank offices might not have been an accidental misjudgment.

Through all this the role of John W. Alvord is ambiguous. There is no evidence that he profited from the use of Bank money, although occasionally he took part in decisions on loans which harmed the company.[129] Eventually he learned of the disreputable deals (especially the Seneca Stone transactions and the Vandenburgh loans) and the questionable financial stability; in fact, he may have been a stockholder of Seneca Stone when the loans were made. Although he protested about the doubtful loans and other irregularities to Bank officials and trustees, he remained silent publicly. To the end Alvord advised Negroes to support an institution that, as he knew, was using their money recklessly and illegally.[130] Perhaps his belief that the Bank could still perform useful work among the former slaves overrode his personal doubts about the institution. He may also have feared that, should the Bank's management suffer severe criticism or should the Bank close, he would lose his own job. This must have been a considerable worry to a man of slender means facing the forced retirement of old age.[131] But retirement was not Alvord's immediate fate, for after he left the Bank in 1874 he became president of the Seneca Stone Company. Alvord claimed to have taken this suspicious appointment because he hoped to work to get back the freedmen's money.[132] Was he hired to pay off past favors, or did the Seneca people want a figurehead as president? No answer can be given.

Only a few trustees, among them Edgar Ketchum, Joseph J. Stewart, and Dr. Charles B. Purvis—one of the first black trustees—opposed the activities of Cooke, Huntington, Eaton, and others. Ketchum placed resolutions before the board demanding that Jay Cooke and Company take back the Northern Pacific bonds and that the Bank cease risking its money on mining and manufacturing stock.[133] The New York attor-

---

128. *Ibid.*, p. 105.
129. *Ibid.*, pp. 33, 89; Whyte, *The Uncivil War*, p. 255.
130. *Freedman's Bank*, House, 1876, pp. ii, 66.
131. In 1871 Alvord's salary was $4,000, which Eaton thought excessive for the work accomplished. Eaton called the position a sinecure. Eaton to Howard, February 15, 1871, Howard MSS.
132. *Freedman's Bank*, House, 1876, p. 19 and *passim*.
133. Journal, March 9 and May 11, 1871; *Freedman's Bank*, House, 1876, p. 68.

ney also demanded (successfully, but after the harm was done) that the board stop lending on chattel mortgage security.[134] In a letter to General Howard, Ketchum revealed the principles which he and a few other trustees shared. "We *must* as just men get our affairs upon a right basis and we must banish . . . all loans without security (as at Jacksonville) and we must have no friendships *in the Bank* but only the hard rules of business."[135]

J. J. Stewart vigorously protested the misuse of the available fund and fought successfully for a resolution to repeal the bylaw that gave almost all financial power to the actuary and the Finance Committee. It was at this meeting in July, 1872, that Eaton resigned. Stewart himself resigned at the end of 1872, after failing to halt the ready acceptance of certificates of the Board of Public Works as security for loans.[136] While Ketchum, Stewart, and the others won occasional victories, they failed to restore honest and conservative management.

Poor investments were made not only at the central office but also at the branches. Similarly, the scandals surrounding the Bank were not confined to Washington. In the rigorous investigations following the Freedman's Savings Bank's failure, congressmen and bank officers uncovered instances of dishonesty and incompetence among the cashiers.[137] The shortcomings of some cashiers contributed to the Bank's tragic ending, and, unfortunately, the actions of a minority stigmatized the majority after the failure. Said Emerson W. Keyes in *A History of Savings Banks in the United States* (1878): "Where not themselves villains, they [the cashiers and agents] were too often ignorant, weak and incompetent, and became the victims, or rather the aids and tools of villains, who used them to get possession of the funds in their custody."[138] Charles Purvis, who called most of the cashiers "a set of scoundrels and thieves," charged some with making illegal loans and others with outright theft.[139]

Clearly, mismanagement at many branches hurt the Freedman's Bank. The Bank lost large sums of money through faulty loans on real

134. Journal, May 11, 1871. Ketchum resigned in 1872, probably because he objected to the Bank's irregular management. See *Freedman's Bank*, House, 1876, p. 57.

135. Quoted in William S. McFeely, *Yankee Stepfather: General O. O. Howard and the Freedmen* (New Haven: Yale University Press, 1968), p. 325.

136. Journal, July 11 and December 12, 1872; *Freedman's Bank*, House, 1876, pp. 91–92.

137. *Freedman's Bank*, House, 1876, pp. 4–6, 17, 22–23, 78.

138. II, 561.

139. *Freedman's Bank*, House, 1876, p. 78.

estate security. Only the Jacksonville, Beaufort, and perhaps Memphis branches had been authorized to make loans without special permission from the Board of Trustees, yet they, like other branches, abused their privileges or exceeded the instructions from the central office.[140] The Beaufort and Jacksonville branches tried to meet the financial requirements of communities that had no other banks, and each loaned over $100,000 on sundry securities.[141] Their losses were enormous. The Jacksonville branch became involved in sawmilling and, as the bank inspector said, in "anything else that anybody wanted done that no prudent banker would undertake."[142] On one occasion the cashier, who was a minister, loaned $6,000 to his son-in-law to help him conceal a deficit he had incurred as county tax collector.[143] Unauthorized loans were made at several other branches: Benjamin Lee at Vicksburg loaned $11,000-12,000 on city scrip, and N. D. Smith at Memphis made advances of $25,000-30,000 on cotton.[144] When in 1880 the Bank commissioners estimated a loss of nearly $1,000,000 in total assets, approximately one-third was attributed to the branches.[145] And in 1883 the annual report of the commissioners revealed that "the loans and investments at the branches outside of Washington have been found to be the most worthless of all."[146]

Individual cases of fraud, although less damaging to the Bank's solvency, were nevertheless harmful to its reputation. The two congressional investigations proved the guilt of a few cashiers such as Philip D. Cory of Atlanta, who was convicted of embezzling $8,000, and Nelson R. Scovel of Beaufort, who stole approximately $10,000.[147]

140. Minutes B, July 10, 1873; Journal, February 13, 1873; *Freedman's Bank*, House, 1876, pp. 4–6, 39 and *passim*; *Report of the Select Committee*, Senate, 1880, pp. 247–248, 250 and *passim*. Some cashiers claimed that the actuary gave them permission to make loans.

141. William H. Lockwood to Anson M. Sperry, June 20, 1874, Letters Rec'd by the Commissioners, 1870–1914, FS&T Co.; Sperry to Lockwood, October 6, 1874, Sperry Letters, Official Correspondence, FS&T Co.; *Freedman's Bank*, House, 1876, p. 88.

142. *Report of the Select Committee*, Senate, 1880, p. 250.

143. *Freedman's Bank*, House, 1876, p. 78.

144. *Ibid.*, pp. 6, 22–23, 88; Sperry to N. D. Smith, October 28, 1874, Sperry Letters, Official Correspondence, FS&T Co.

145. *Report of the Select Committee*, Senate, 1880, appendix, p. 58.

146. U.S., Congress, House, *Annual Report of the Commissioner of the Freedman's Savings and Trust Company for the Year Ending December 1, 1883*, 48th Cong., 1st sess., 1883, House Miscellaneous Document No. 10, p. 15.

147. Minutes B, April 10, 1873; "The FS&T Co. of Washington District of Columbia Plaintiffs against Nelson N. Scovel a Citizen of South Carolina," Letters Rec'd by the Commissioners, 1870–1914, FS&T Co.; Memorandum, July 1874, Sperry Letters, Official Correspondence, FS&T Co.; *Atlanta Constitution*, February 17, 1874, p. 3; *Report of the Select Committee*, Senate, 1880, pp. 259–260.

Cashier Macumber at Wilmington took almost $700, making false entries to cover his shortages; Cashier Bronaugh at Lynchburg made bad loans and appropriated money for his and his father-in-law's use.[148] The Bank brought suit against Cashier C. A. Woodward when he appropriated $3,375 of the Bank's money against a debt of the Freedmen's Bureau.[149] A more widely publicized case of fraud involved a Washington clerk, Thomas Boston, who withdrew $900 from the account of an illiterate depositor and duly recorded his withdrawals as the depositor's. When the defrauded depositor visited the Bank to inquire about his $900 on a day when Boston was absent, he discovered that his account contained only forty cents. There was quite a scene.[150]

Cashiers whose accounts were deficient (after several years and many thousands of dollars of transactions) were accused of fraud.[151] Indeed, after 1874, "being short in his books" became a euphemism for stealing. Since most cashiers lacked banking experience and bookkeeping skills, the evidence suggests that ignorance rather than criminal intent caused many of the shortages. Bank inspector Anson Sperry testified that many errors occurred before a standard, efficient system of accounting was adopted in 1872. As an example, Sperry noted the $40,000 deficit at the Washington branch.

> That there is fraud in it I do not know. The thing simply cannot be explained. There have been so many blunders in the accounts; so many duplications; so many wrong postings in the ledgers that the books are utterly and wholly unreliable. If that be fraud then it is fraud. When you find the book-keeping so bad that the debits and the credits are not always distinguished and that, when the account is carried forward, the reference marks are left off, and so a number of duplications have crept in what are you going to do about it? It may be fraud, and if the man [William J. Wilson] was smarter, I should say it was fraud, but I think he was too dull for fraud.[152]

A bank examiner stated that several branches carried no accounts for interest credited and paid on deposits.[153] These errors accumulated over

---

148. Sperry to G. W. Stickney, October 10, 1873; W. F. Bronaugh to Leipold, March 23, 1876; Sperry to Stickney, April 10, 1873, Letters Rec'd by the Commissioners, 1870–1914, FS&T Co.

149. Journal, April 9, 1874; Circular from the War Department—Bureau of Refugees, Freedmen, and Abandoned Land, April 16, 1869, Letters Rec'd by the Commissioners, 1870–1914, FS&T Co.; A. G. Riddle to Frederick Douglass, April 10, 1874, *ibid.*; *Freedman's Bank*, House, 1876, p. 5.

150. *Freedman's Bank*, House, 1876, pp. 9–10, 29–30.

151. *Ibid.*, p. 64.

152. *Ibid.*, p. 7.

153. *Report of the Commissioners*, 1874, p. 83.

the years, for bank inspections occurred infrequently if at all prior to 1874 at several branches of that far-flung enterprise.[154]

Clearly, many cashiers were poor businessmen and several made bad loans, but the evidence does not justify a blanket indictment that all, or even most, were thieves and scoundrels. The case of Cashier J. G. Hamilton at Lexington illustrates the problem of criminal culpability. Hamilton worked hard to realize the humanitarian principles which sent him to the post–Civil War South as a missionary. Unfortunately, he was not a banker. A bank examiner discovered a shortage of $1,305.84, but, having confidence in Hamilton's integrity, he concluded that the clumsy method of bookkeeping, which permitted errors in recording certain sums, had caused the discrepancy.[155]

Hamilton was accused of theft in the congressional investigation in 1876. His accusers charged that he had so skillfully manipulated the ledger books as almost to defy detection. Supposedly the depositors' passbooks exposed his clever maneuvers and revealed that he recorded only part of some people's deposits and pocketed the remainder. It should be added that Hamilton always denied the charges. (Investigators noted that Hamilton had moved on from the Freedman's Bank to become an Indian agent.[156])

It is not easy to generalize about the branch cashiers. Almost every branch showed unexplained differences between branch reports and the balances due depositors, but most of these were probably due to amateurish bookkeeping. The majority of the cashiers, it seems, were honest and reasonably competent; there were especially able cashiers at Augusta, Charleston, Macon, Louisville, New Orleans, Norfolk, Philadelphia, Richmond, and Savannah. The worst of the unauthorized and/or hazardous loans were made by white cashiers at Jacksonville, Beaufort, Memphis, Vicksburg, and Montgomery. It was also the white cashiers—such as Nelson Scovel (Beaufort), Philip Cory (Atlanta), C. A. Woodward (Mobile), C. A. Nelson (New Bern), and perhaps J. G. Hamilton (Lexington)—who were responsible for almost all the cases of embezzlement. Thomas Boston, who was not a cashier, and W. R. Bronaugh at Lynchburg seem to be the only blacks involved in

154. *Freedman's Bank*, House, 1876, p. 2.

155. *Report of the Commissioners*, 1874, p. 71.

156. *Freedman's Bank*, House, 1876, pp. 11–12. In 1876 Mrs. Hamilton informed the commissioners that the shortages were not her husband's fault, and that although he could not afford to make good the loss, he eventually would pay the amount owed. Hamilton thought he could pay his debt by extra work which would not compromise his duties as Indian agent. Apparently this did not work out, for the next year Hamilton was fired. See Mrs. J. G. Hamilton to Leipold, February 28, 1876; A. Bell, Ass't Sec'y, Department of the Interior, to Leipold, 1877 [?], Letters Rec'd by the Commissioners, 1870–1914, FS&T Co.

illegal activities. A few others, such as William J. Wilson and G. W. Brodie at Raleigh, simply had more responsibilities than their abilities warranted.[157]

The full extent of the company's losses in the 1870's remained undiscovered until after the failure. In 1872 a superficial report by the Bank's examining committee—one in which many statements by the officers were taken on trust—concluded that the company's financial position was basically sound. While the committee found little fault with the real estate securities and government investments, it did criticize the uses of the available fund. "The loans made should be only on such strong and reliable securities that in the event of an emergency requiring the use of the fund, they could be discounted or cashed by the Bank in the District. It is only necessary to name some of these securities such as—Stock of the Young Men's Christian Association upon property of which $33,000 is loaned [to show the Bank's weakness]."[158] The committee also cited stock of the American Seal-Lock Company and Metropolis Paving Company, Congregational Society bonds and Sacramento City bonds, and policies of life insurance companies as unsound investments.[159] Few trustees seemed disturbed by these revelations.

From time to time reports about questionable transactions and losses reached the public. In December, 1871, the *Savannah Morning News* publicized the company's loans to the Seneca Stone Company and to various paving companies.[160] That this report, which was reprinted in the Washington *Patriot*, did not stir up greater public interest is probably due to its obvious partisanship and racial prejudice. Cashier Wilson is "Daddy" Wilson, and Negro depositors are "Sambos" and "Chloes."[161] Public criticism of the Bank such as the *Patriot*'s muckraking was typically associated with anti-Negro sentiment. Tragically, the tendency to dismiss all criticism of the Bank as mere racial or political bigotry delayed public exposure of the Bank's weaknesses.

A report from the comptroller of the currency in 1873 had the ring of truth and briefly dented the complacency of a few trustees and depositors. In 1873 Congress authorized the Treasury Department to in-

---

157. *Freedman's Bank*, House, 1876, p. 181; *Report of the Select Committee*, Senate, 1880, pp. 56–58; *Report of the Commissioners*, 1874, pp. 56–83 *passim*.

158. Journal, October 11, 1872.

159. *Ibid.* The Congregational Society bonds were issued by the First Congregational Church in Washington, of which Howard and Eaton were leaders. See Eaton to Howard, September 30, 1868, Howard MSS.

160. *Freedman's Bank*, House, 1876, pp. 92–94.

161. *Ibid.*

vestigate all the savings banks in the District of Columbia, a routine practice already established for national banks. For the first time the Freedman's Bank received careful scrutiny from a disinterested agency. The report of the comptroller of the currency criticized the company's real estate loans; they were of a "character that should not appear on the records of a savings bank." It noted that only a small portion of the investments could be considered available to meet unexpected calls, that until 1873 the Bank had operated under a deficit, and that the books and records of the company had been kept too loosely. The report also revealed a deficiency of $16,000 at Beaufort, South Carolina.[162]

Notwithstanding the Bank's problems, the comptroller concluded by emphasizing what he believed to be the positive virtues of the company. He spoke of an upswing in business in early 1873 and noted the Bank's improved methods of bookkeeping. He considered the executive officers men of "undoubted integrity," "devoted to the best interests of a savings bank to a degree that promises a prosperous future for the institution."[163] With reforms, "the bank would be able to correct the mistakes already made, to retrieve its present and prospective losses, and be enabled to continue a business of great usefulness to the classes of depositors for whose benefit the institution was organized."[164]

Publication of the comptroller's report caused the Bank a good deal of embarrassment. Some newspapers, such as the Boston *Advertiser*, synthesized the negative aspects of the report and proceeded to denounce the Bank and its management.[165] The *New York Times* exposed this ploy, declaring that the comptroller's views were being "maliciously perverted."[166] When the Nashville *Union and American* summarized the report, it emphasized the Bank's weak points: the charter violations and the lack of a large available fund.[167] In this case, newspaper criticism led to a run on the local branch. The *Union and American* reported that "a considerable number of our colored citizens, who had money deposited in the branch bank of this place, became uneasy and determined to withdraw the amounts that had been deposited."[168] Tele-

162. *Report of the Comptroller of the Currency*, 1873, pp. 3, 9.

163. *Ibid.*, p. 9. Such a positive reaction despite obvious failings raises the possibility that the comptroller was politically motivated. One year later the comptroller and the speaker of the house tried to suppress another damaging report. See below, p. 187.

164. *Ibid.*, p. 3.

165. *New National Era*, March 13, 1873, p. 2.

166. March 11, 1873, p. 1.

167. March 13, 1873, p. 4.

168. *Ibid.* It is not known whether a run occurred at any other branch. The trustees, however, were concerned about the run at Nashville and the possibility

grams from the central office assured Cashier Cary of the Bank's solvency, and he was invited to draw on Washington for any amount. Cary paid all claims, which amounted to $10,000 out of a total of $110,000.[169] Within two days the fever had subsided, for, as the *Union and American* honestly observed, "When a bank can submit to a run upon its coffers, and meet promptly the demands made, this of itself will soon restore confidence."[170] The comptroller's report, the newspaper criticism, and the run at Nashville were rehearsals for the crisis of April and May, 1874.

---

of others elsewhere, and they authorized executive officers to sell the company's government bonds in case of excessive drafts. See Minutes B, Finance Committee, March 11, 1873, p. 43.

169. March 14, 1873, p. 4.
170. *Ibid.*

6

Panic, Reform, and Failure

When the Freedman's Bank failed on July 2, 1874, both its critics and its defenders sought a simple, satisfying explanation. Those who had always despised the Bank and the Reconstruction missionary movement of which it was a part, as well as those who wanted to vindicate the maturity, responsibility, and capacity of black Americans blamed the failure on the Bank officials. They agreed that the Bank had been betrayed by those at the top. Defenders of the Bank, on the other hand, attributed the debacle to the Panic of 1873 and treated the Bank as just another victim of national economic crisis. Obviously no single factor was decisive, and even a combination of fraud and national economic crisis leaves much to be explained. Certainly the Bank's special vulnerability to the pressures of 1873–74 owed much to its unsolved (and possibly insoluble) problems of structure, organization, and personnel.

With dozens of branches scattered over the South it was practically impossible to secure efficiency and accountability. Not until 1872 was an adequate system of daily branch reports begun, while inspections, which should have been made at least quarterly, occurred much too infrequently.[1] A new, undercapitalized institution paying minimal salaries and hiring, by choice as well as by necessity, men with missionary rather than banking credentials could expect to live with plenty of errors in bookkeeping.[2] The untrained cashiers, who often doubled as Freedmen's Bureau, AMA, or government employees, were grossly over-

1. *Freedman's Bank*, House, 1876, p. 4; *Report of the Select Committee*, Senate, 1880, p. 247.
2. New York *Sun*, April 30, 1874, p. 1; A. M. Scriba to Charles A. Meigs, February 14, 1874, Letters Rec'd by the Commissioners, 1870–1914, FS&T Co.; *Freedman's Bank*, House, 1876, pp. xi, xii.

worked.[3] At one time Christian A. Fleetwood, a Washington book-keeper and paying teller, was responsible for the accounts of 12,000 depositors scattered throughout seven ledgers.[4]

> I had no assistance in posting these accounts [said Fleetwood] . . . it [was] impossible for me to post these accounts during office hours. . . . It was to be expected, in fact it was unavoidable, that some errors should have crept into the books under those circumstances. No man who is born could have prevented it. It was my custom to work at the office from half past eight in the morning until nine, ten, and twelve o'clock at night, and frequently to carry work home with me.[5]

Anson Sperry, too, was overwhelmed by work—and by clerical mistakes.

> The blunders simply ran over me. . . . I stopped the business once and opened a new set of books. The new set of books was worse than the old set. . . . Why you could not settle the cash any night. Sometimes they [the Washington branch bookkeepers] were from five thousand to five cents one way, and sometimes they were t'other way. Everybody felt like going out and having a special oyster supper if the thing came out even.[6]

Sperry himself provides an excellent example of the Bank's personnel difficulties. No man worked harder for the Bank or for the freedmen; one need only recall his prodigious efforts in Texas after the war.[7] In 1870 Sperry became the bank inspector and set out on endless travels from branch to branch in the effort to straighten out the financial records.[8] Like so many of the Bank's employees, Sperry was well intentioned but lacking in qualifications. The man who claimed that the Bank needed a detective rather than an inspector admitted that he had had no experience as a bookkeeper "except theoretically." He once mused, "If I had had experience as a bookkeeper and a banker . . . I should probably have done differently; I should have known more and had less enthusiasm."[9] When Sperry attempted to balance the books at Washington, he found a $600 shortage; a few months later the national bank examiners assessed the deficiency to be a little over $40,000.[10] The inspector habitually certified ledger balances as "correct, E & O E." When congressional investigators found these balances incorrect, they questioned the inspector and learned that "E & O E" stood for "Errors

3. See above, ch. 3, esp. pp. 62–63.
4. *Report of the Select Committee*, Senate, 1880, p. 213.
5. *Ibid.*
6. *Ibid.*, p. 252.
7. See above, pp. 28–29.
8. *Report of the Select Committee*, Senate, 1880, p. 246.
9. *Ibid.*, p. 249; Minutes B, Finance Committee, May 8, 1873, pp. 55–56.
10. *Freedman's Bank*, House, 1876, p. 90.

and Omissions Excepted." "To err is human," Sperry pleaded. Replied the investigating committee, "it seems to have been not only human, but quite common in this bank."[11]

It was impossible to control the excessive operating costs. Indeed, these became more burdensome in the 1870's with the proliferation of branches and the cessation of Freedmen's Bureau help. At each branch the Bank paid heavily for salaries, rent or purchase of property, and furnishings. From ten to fifteen branches spent more than they earned, and it gradually became evident that small black communities such as in Lynchburg, Chattanooga, Raleigh, Atlanta, Montgomery, and Columbus (Mississippi) could not support branches.[12] Discussions of whether to reform or close the non-paying branches formed part of the trustees' regular business. Expenses during 1873 amounted to $155,000, of which $93,000 went for salaries.[13] The total expenses of successful Massachusetts savings banks equaled ¼ of 1 percent of their deposits, while those of England equaled ⅓ of 1 percent.[14] For 1873, when expenses were $155,000 and total deposits were below $5,000,000, the expenses of the Freedman's Bank were over 3 percent of the total deposits. Even this percentage was surpassed by several branches; indeed, in one cost-cutting reform plan, all branch expenses were to be reduced to no more than 4 percent of the branch's deposits. Thus the expenses of the Freedman's Bank were up to ten times greater than what the best banks of Massachusetts and England considered safe.

The Bank probably operated with a deficit during most of its nine-year history. In October, 1870, a special report of the actuary revealed an expected deficit of $18,000 by the year's end.[15] According to the testimony of Anson Sperry and Charles Purvis, between three and five million dollars in deposits were needed to counterbalance the heavy expenses.[16] If this is true, the Bank must have suffered deficits for every year except 1872 and 1873—and it will be recalled that the comptroller of the currency claimed that a deficit existed until 1873.[17] The mis-

11. *Report of the Select Committee*, Senate, 1880, p. 250.
12. Minutes A, October 12, 1871, p. 207, and December 14, 1871, p. 212; Minutes B, December 11, 1873, pp. 76–77; Journal, December 11, 1873; *Freedman's Bank*, House, 1876, p. 78; *Report of the Select Committee*, Senate, 1880, p. 255.
13. *Freedman's Bank*, House, 1876, p. 16; *Report of the Select Committee*, Senate, 1880, p. 181; Inspector's statement, Letters Rec'd by the Commissioners, 1870–1914, FS&T Co. The aid that the Bureau gave the Bank is described in ch. 4. See also, U.S., Congress, House, *Freedmen's Branch of the Adjutant General's Office for Year Ending June 30, 1875*, 44th Cong., 1st sess., 1875, House Executive Document No. 144, p. 5.
14. Woodward, *Savings Banks*, p. 30.
15. Minutes A, October 21, 1870, p. 179.
16. *Report of the Select Committee*, Senate, 1880, p. 255.
17. *Report of the Comptroller of the Currency*, 1873, p. 8.

managed loan and investment policy was aggravated by fraud, inefficiency, and fundamental weaknesses in organization and operation; the Bank was in no shape to try to weather a major crisis in the economy.

On September 18, 1873, the failure of the banking firm of Jay Cooke and Company started a severe financial panic in New York and led to economic upheaval throughout the country. Investors dumped their securities on the market, depositors withdrew their money, creditors called in their loans, and business came to a standstill. On September 20 the New York Stock Exchange closed for the first time in history.[18] Washington's Fifteenth Street, the capital's Wall Street, panicked; frightened depositors started runs at the Washington City Savings Bank and at the Freedman's Savings and Trust Company.[19]

"The crash of Jay Cooke and Company," said John Alvord, "turned us wrong side up."[20] Heavy runs forced the Bank to sacrifice its good securities and pay hundreds of thousands of dollars. When the Cookes' First National Bank closed, Alvord rushed to New York in order to sell $200,000 in government bonds, leaving (supposedly) $400,000 in bonds behind. Every two or three days the trustees met in unrecorded sessions to authorize the executive officers to sell the bonds, $100,000 or so at a time.[21] The company was even forced to borrow, and to gain time it announced that sixty days' notice would be required to withdraw money.[22]

The ordeal pitilessly exposed the Bank's inability to realize quickly upon its assets. John Alvord and Charles B. Purvis later testified that before the panic the Bank's vaults contained $700,000 or $800,000 in government securities. A July, 1873, financial report, the latest available, contradicts them, showing but $487,000.[23] In any case, the fact is that the Bank's available funds and easily negotiable securities barely covered depositors' demands, and the Bank barely managed to flounder through the panic.

Although the Bank had practically severed its relationship with Jay Cooke and Company in 1872, the public believed otherwise. Not even

18. Larson, *Jay Cooke*, p. 409.

19. *Daily Critic* (Washington), September 19, 1873, p. 1; September 23, 1873, p. 1.

20. *Freedman's Bank*, House, 1876, p. 55.

21. *Ibid.*, pp. 68, 75, 78. Purvis claimed that the amount withdrawn immediately after the failure of Jay Cooke and Co. was $800,000.

22. *Ibid.*, pp. 38, 142, 144.

23. *Ibid.*, p. 68; "Report of the Condition of 'The Freedmen's Savings and Trust Company' at Washington . . . on the First Day of July 1873," Letters Rec'd by the Commissioners, 1870–1914, FS&T Co.

the most fervent denials could allay the fears. "It has been rumored," reported the *Evening Star*, "that the Freedman's Savings Bank was a heavy loser by the suspencion [*sic*], but this is a mistake. . . . [It] had only about $800 on deposit there."[24] Few believed this disclaimer, and the run continued. "Knowledgeable persons" in the street predicted the Bank's imminent suspension; "every man you talked with knew all about it."[25] In the confusion, Bank employees did their best to calm the depositors. The clerks of this "extensive and popular institution," the *National Republican* said, seemed not in the least nervous; they handled the cash and paper with their "usual *sang-froid*."[26]

The run on the Washington branch continued from September 18 through 20, gradually lessening in intensity. By noon of the third day $65,000 had been withdrawn and approximately fifty persons remained in line.[27] The *Evening Star* gleefully reported the "droll scenes" outside the Bank's doors:

> Much time is necessarily expended on each depositor, as nine out of ten are unable to write, and the checks are prepared by the paying teller, who witnesses the mark made by each. It is expected that by the time of closing the bank this afternoon that all making demands will have been satisfied. The usual droll scenes were to be witnessed today. The check-books are sometimes wrapped in bandanas, towels, brown paper, etc. The hat seems to be the favorite receptacle with many; the older dames carry "dat book" in their bosoms; but one old "Aunt Dinah," when her turn arrived to receive her cash, grinned all over with evident satisfaction and produced the evidence of the bank's indebtedness from within a black stocking, which encased a leg of attenuated dimensions. Upon receiving the "cash money," it was substituted in the place vacated by the check-book, and she skipped out, as lighthearted as a school-girl at recess. Many who fall in at the rear end of the line, drag slowly about half way, take a look ahead, and reason perhaps that the bank is all right, and drop out and go their way.[28]

The immediate crisis ended in a few days. The lines of mistrustful depositors disappeared, and some people even returned to hand over their funds once more to the bank for freedmen. Things were as dull as

24. *Evening Star*, September 18, 1873, p. 1; *Atlanta Constitution*, September 24, 1873, p. 2; *Republican Banner* (Nashville), September 23, 1873, p. 2; *Daily Critic*, September 19, 1873, p. 1.
25. *National Republican* (Washington), September 19, 1873, p. 1.
26. *Ibid.*
27. *Evening Star*, September 19, 1873, p. 1; September 20, 1873, p. 1; *National Republican*, September 20, 1873, p. 1.
28. September 19, 1873, p. 1; September 20, 1873, p. 1.

ever at the Freedman's Savings Bank, the *Daily Critic* announced on the twenty-third; reason and judgment had resumed sway.[29] But just in case the "good judgment" of depositors did not last, Bank managers the next day felt it necessary to announce that thereafter a sixty-day notice would be required, as a "matter of prudence," to withdraw funds. The actuary explained that this requirement constituted a conservative move which should in no way reflect upon the Bank's safety.[30]

The telegraph had quickly spread news of financial distress to all the branch cities. Repercussions came swiftly in the form of branch demands for cash, for people everywhere questioned the Bank's solvency and its relationship with Jay Cooke and Company.[31] Actuary Stickney and the New York manager, S. L. Harris, sent telegrams to all cashiers reassuring them that the Bank would lose very little by the failure of the Cookes. Southern newspapers in some cases cooperated with Bank officials by reprinting favorable news items from the capital.[32]

Verbal assurances did not suffice in many cases. Runs occurred at Augusta and Savannah,[33] and the Montgomery depositors besieged their Bank for two days before calm was restored by the prompt payment of every demand.[34] All the banks cooperated in the emergency, the *Alabama State Journal* (Montgomery) reported; the Merchants and Planters National Bank "sent over an armful of greenbacks," and other firms informed the Bank that it could have all the money it needed— for a price, of course. Two days after the first disturbance at the Washington office, the Montgomery branch had to borrow large sums to carry it through the panic.[35]

Atlanta's difficulties fell short of a run, but withdrawals increased alarmingly while deposits declined. At a depositors' meeting arranged at the city hall by the advisory committee, Cashier Philip Cory, President E. R. Ware of Atlanta University, and several Negroes urged patience and reaffirmed their confidence in the Bank. Cory also took his appeal to the columns of the *Atlanta Constitution*, where he argued

29. *Ibid.*, September 22, 1873, p. 1; September 23, 1873, p. 1; *National Republican*, September 23, 1873, p. 1; *Daily Critic*, September 23, 1873, p. 1.

30. *Evening Star*, September 24, 1873, p. 1.

31. *Ibid.*, September 18, 1873, p. 1; *Atlanta Constitution*, September 24, 1873, p. 2; *Republican Banner*, September 23, 1873, p. 2.

32. *New Berne Times*, September 20, 1873, p. 1; Charleston *News and Courier*, September 20, 1873, p. 4.

33. Charleston *News and Courier*, September 27, 1873, p. 1; September 26, 1873, p. 1.

34. *Alabama State Journal*, September 21, 1873, p. 3.

35. *Ibid.*, September 20, 1873, p. 3; September 21, 1873, p. 3; Edwin Beecher to "Dear Sir," September 20, 1873, AMA.

that no bank would fail and that depositors should leave their money in the Freedman's Bank.[36]

At Memphis, too, depositors showed signs of panic. As described rather unsympathetically by the *Memphis Daily Appeal*, they clamored for their money and felt the most intense anxiety upon announcement of the sixty-day rule. Cashier N. D. Smith attempted to restore confidence by denying the rumors of suspension in a public circular. He explained that the sixty-day requirement was necessary to enable things to quiet down and to give the Bank time to liquidate its securities. All the money was in government bonds and securities, he incorrectly assured them, and he rashly promised, "No depositor can or will lose a cent by this company."[37]

There was much excitement at Nashville, which Cashier John J. Cary contained by disregarding the sixty-day requirement and paying all those who needed money.[38] Several months later, one advisory board member asserted that only the pride of the depositors together with the cashier's readiness to pay withdrawals had prevented a crippling run. "Shortly after the great 'run' was made on all the savings banks in New York[,] one was started on this institution which was saved by an appeal to colored pride. They refused to draw their money, notwithstanding that much was said in public print about the unsoundness of the institution."[39] On September 27 Cary had the *Republican Banner* print a two-day-old telegram from S. L. Harris, which had advised him to "Say to your committee, and those who know me, my word for it, that we are sound. . . . Our committee [the New York committee] stood faithfully. Ministers of colored churches prevented a run. Deposits are increasing daily. Only twelve notices at Washington under the sixty day rule."[40] Calm again returned to Nashville, and plans were made for a campaign to increase deposits.[41]

Despite the Charleston *News and Courier*'s accurate coverage of the Washington runs, the panic had little effect upon the Charleston branch. "The business went on yesterday as usual, the deposits being if anything in excess of the drafts, which were about as heavy as they generally are at this season. The manner in which the branch bank here is conducted has inspired the depositors with much confidence in the

36. September 26, 1873, p. 3; September 27, 1873, p. 3.
37. September 26, 1873, p. 4.
38. *Republican Banner*, September 26, 1873, p. 4.
39. Nashville *Union and American*, July 4, 1874, p. 2.
40. September 27, 1873, p. 4.
41. September 28, 1873, p. 1.

institution."[42] Nor did the sixty-day rule frighten the Charleston depositors. "It is somewhat singular that the colored element in the community seemed to be entirely free from all panicky feelings, and during the entire day there were no more than the usual number of applicants for money."[43]

The Charleston reaction was exceptional, for the panic generated runs on most of the branches. The announcement of the sixty-day rule dealt another body blow to depositors' confidence, which never again reached pre-panic levels. This crisis in confidence lasted from mid-September until the closing and resulted in the loss of over $1,000,000 in deposits.[44] As depositors closed their accounts, the trustees sold securities to meet their demands. In February, 1874, they had to borrow $25,000 from a Boston bank.[45] The last entry (April 3, 1874) in the minute book of the Finance Committee recorded authorization for the actuary to borrow $10,000.[46] The collapse of Jay Cooke and Company had precipitated so many crises that many were led to conclude with Charles Purvis that the panic "killed the Bank."[47]

After the Comptroller's Report of 1873 and the panic, many of the trustees belatedly realized that the Bank would have to be reformed if it were to survive. Before this time reformers like Stewart and Ketchum had achieved only minimal results because they could not budge Alvord and the other trustees from their flaccid dependence on dominant figures like Cooke, Huntington, and Eaton. But in 1873 and 1874 the big three were gone, and the initiative shifted to a group which included a handful of concerned black trustees. In addition to Dr. Charles Purvis, who was especially concerned about collusive lending,[48] John Mercer Langston became in 1872 one of the new black trustees who could be counted on to look after the Bank's interests with great care. Langston had won a seat on the Finance Committee when Cooke resigned; because of this influential position, as well as his Bureau credentials, he was able to lead the forces of reform in 1873 and 1874. At times proposing radical solutions for the Bank's problems, Langston

42. September 24, 1873, p. 4.

43. *Ibid.*

44. *Report of the Commissioners,* 1874, p. 63; "Financial Statement" (January, 1874), Letters Rec'd by the Commissioners, 1870–1914, FS&T Co. This is the official report of bank examiner Charles Meigs; it is beter known as *Report of the Comptroller of the Currency,* 1874.

45. *Report of the Commissioners,* 1874, p. 3.

46. Minutes B, Finance Committee, April 3, 1874, p. 69.

47. *Freedman's Bank,* House, 1876, p. 78; "Banking and Financial Items," *Banker's Magazine,* XXIX (August, 1874), 154.

48. Journal, February 8, 1872.

generally worked for conservative goals: to limit expenses and to restore cautious, honest management. No doubt Langston shocked the
trustees when in March, 1873, he advocated the company's dissolution
by closing the weak branches and establishing the strong ones as independent banks.[49] Although his proposal did not even receive a hearing
at that time, its basic principle—to give more power to the branches—
emerged as an important reform one year later.

Immediately after the first runs in September, 1873, Langston proposed three resolutions designed to limit expenses at the principal office
and branches in proportion to the Bank's income. The board accepted
his resolutions and eventually limited the expenses of ten branches to
4 percent of their deposits and reduced expenditures at Philadelphia,
Vicksburg, New Orleans, New York, and Washington.[50] Meanwhile,
as heavy withdrawals continued, Langston moved successfully in November to have the officers sell the company's securities "to relieve the
Bank of its present embarrassment."[51] He also presented to the board
a detailed report on the notorious Seneca transaction and the $50,000
note of Kilbourn and Evans.[52]

Anson Sperry also worked hard for reform. In close cooperation with
Langston and the actuary, George Stickney, he made persistent efforts
to reduce expenses and remove unsatisfactory officers; at long last
Washington cashier Wilson was demoted to traveling agent in January,
1874.[53] Sperry also took up the idea of gradually phasing out the Freedman's Savings Bank and establishing the branches as independent black
banks. He proposed, first of all, to reconstruct the board of trustees,
two-thirds of whom were to be elected from the branch cities by the
advisory committees. Almost as important, he wanted to make trustees
liable for actions harmful to the company.[54] Like Langston, he sought
to return power to the localities—the source of all the money.

> The ultimate purpose [of his proposed legislation] . . . was to provide
> for the disintegration of the institution without loss. The trustees were
> to be changed so as to get the branches under local control; these Wash-
> ington investments were to be called in and re-invested at the branches.
> The institution was gradually to be hedged in and drawn down to a
> paying basis, in the hope that at some future time we might be able to

49. *Ibid.*, March 13, 1873.
50. *Ibid.*, September 25, 1873.
51. *Ibid.*, November 13, 1873.
52. *Ibid.*; Minutes B, Finance Committee, November 13, 1873, pp. 56–59.
53. Journal, January 10, 1874; *Freedman's Bank*, House, 1876, pp. 179–180.
Thomas Boston, the Washington clerk who helped himself to a depositor's account,
was also removed at this time.
54. *Freedman's Bank*, House, 1876, p. 179.

turn the whole concern over to local organizations under State charters, and so dissolve the Freedman's Savings and Trust Company without loss, still keeping the good results which we had already attained.[55]

The "radical" ideas first put forward by Sperry, Langston, and others would reach fruition in the charter amendment of June 20, 1874, too late to save the Bank.

The reforms of 1873 and early 1874 did reduce expenses. The 4 percent plan went into effect, and several high-salaried cashiers, assistant cashiers, and clerks were released, thus bringing the expenses of certain weak branches within tolerable limits. Chattanooga was closed permanently.[56] The trustees also disengaged the company from its unprofitable Montgomery branch by selling it to the cashier, Edwin Beecher.[57]

The trustees in 1873 and 1874 were much more successful than earlier reformers in returning to a conservative lending policy. As early as 1872 the Board of Trustees had placed restrictions upon the Finance Committee and attempted to bring the Bank's loan policy under control; in the following two years, although some poor loans were made, few of the egregious errors of the earlier period were repeated. Stickney's secret loans to J. V. W. Vandenburgh and Juan Boyle were, to be sure, glaring exceptions. Said John Mercer Langston, writing in the third person about his responsibility for the loan policy, "It is a matter of great satisfaction to him to be able to state, that every considerable poor and doubtful loan of the bank was made before he became a member of the Board of Trustees, and every practice calculated to work its ruin had been made a part of its management without his knowledge or participation, before he had any concern in its control."[58] Although

55. *Ibid.*
56. Journal, October 3, 1873.
57. Beecher was a member of the mission community in good standing. A former major and paymaster from Illinois, after the war he became a Bureau assistant commissioner and superintendent of education. As cashier he had directed a considerable banking business in Montgomery, making unauthorized loans on which the estimated loss was $5,000. To settle matters with the Bank, he proposed, shortly before the Panic of 1873, to buy the Montgomery branch. The trustees probably felt that this was a good way to dispense with a costly branch. Thus Beecher, with the backing of his brother, C. A. Beecher, and probably others, formed Edwin Beecher and Co. and contracted to buy the branch bank and put up a bond of $60,000 as guarantee for fulfillment of the bargain. As soon as possible they were to substitute their deposit books for those of the Freedman's Bank. Although Beecher claimed that all the old Montgomery depositors received their money, he defaulted on his obligations to the Bank, and his enterprise failed in 1874 or 1875. See *Report of the Commissioners*, 1874, pp. 77–78; Minutes B, September 16, 1873, pp. 71–72; Minutes B, Finance Committee, March 3, 1874, pp. 65–67; Beecher to Anson Sperry, December 30, 1875, Letters Rec'd by the Commissioners, 1870–1914, FS&T Co.
58. John Mercer Langston, *From the Virginia Plantation to the National Capitol* (Hartford: American Publishing Co., 1894), p. 341.

Langston's leadership is notable for causing a marked improvement in the Bank's loan policy, he did overstate his case a bit; a number of loans made under his aegis were not readily collectable and occasioned loss to the Freedman's Bank.[59] The branches left behind the reckless lending of the pre-panic days and extended very few loans in 1873–74. Yet the success of this reform may perhaps be attributed as much to the paucity of available money as to the trustees' diligent pursuit of conservative banking practices.[60]

The most visible mark of the reform movement was a change in the Bank's top personnel. At least four blacks had been elected to the Board of Trustees as early as 1867; by 1873 there were several more, among them Dr. Alexander T. Augusta, William H. A. Wormley, and of course John Mercer Langston. As whites dropped out, the number of blacks increased.[61] Like most of the white trustees in the heyday of Cooke, Huntington, Eaton *et al.*, they were convinced of the Bank's soundness. As Dr. Purvis later testified: "As the thing was, we, trustees—meeting but once a month, and then only hearing statements—could really know nothing about the affairs of the bank."[62] Then came the panic and the rude awakening of the trustees. As the March, 1874, elections of the Bank officers approached, several black trustees determined to restore confidence in the institution and rid the Bank of what they called "an element which was believed to be the cause of all our disasters."[63] They decided to depose the president, John Alvord. Alvord, they fully realized, was the Bank's founder, and he still had strong church connections in Washington; nevertheless, they thought he was old and incompetent. "All the colored trustees [said Purvis] . . . discussed the matter and determined to change the president. . . . We found that we were losing our control among the colored people, and we had hopes to get it back again, and to control the bank as well."[64] They had a candidate in mind who would suit the purpose perfectly: Frederick Douglass.

The identity of the Negro trustees to whom Purvis refers can only be surmised. Among the *active* Negro trustees in 1874 were the following: Purvis himself, John Mercer Langston, Dr. A. T. Augusta, the Reverend Sampson Talbot, Walker Lewis, O. S. B. Wall, and perhaps William

59. See schedules of overdue loans in *Report of the Commissioners*, 1874, and *Report of the Select Committee*, Senate, 1880.

60. Journal, October 11, 1872, and March 13, 1873; Minutes B, Finance Committee, October 9, 1872, p. 17; *New York Times*, July 4, 1874, p. 1.

61. The trustees who resigned were W. J. Albert, E. A. Lambert, Eliphalet Whittlesey, E. P. Smith, L. R. Tuttle, and George Whipple. See below, pp. 184–185, 192.

62. *Freedman's Bank*, House, 1876, p. 76.

63. *Ibid.*

64. *Ibid.*

H. A. Wormley and the Reverend D. W. Anderson. In many instances these trustees probably constituted a majority at the board meetings. It was largely their votes in the trustees' meeting on March 14, 1874, which assured a majority for the motions to thank Alvord for his long and faithful service and to elect Frederick Douglass president, a move which won favorable comment in the press. Purvis became first vice-president and Langston chairman of the Finance Committee.[65] At last blacks had claimed and won the company's top positions; just four months before the failure, the company lived up to its reputation as a black bank.

Later it was alleged that Douglass was elected president so that a black man would be in office when the Bank failed.[66] White America would then be able to attribute the Bank's failure to the inherent in-capacity and irresponsibility of blacks. But clearly, in the case of Douglass, black trustees voted to replace Alvord with a man who had the confidence of blacks. Certainly Douglass always felt that it was his friends who had elected him.

In 1880 a Senate investigator discovered repeated assertions that "more than once, when it was found that the institution was about to fail, or had got in serious trouble, that some colored man was called forward to take the helm at that critical time; I will not say for what cause."[67] The assertion has no validity as regards Douglass, but there is a certain superficial plausibility to its application to other personnel changes. Most blacks entered the Bank's employment late in its history; seventeen of the twenty-one black cashiers hired were in the Bank's employment when the Bank failed. At Atlanta a black cashier took over in 1874 to restore confidence after Philip Cory had developed exces-sively close ties with white businessmen. Then Cory's embezzlement was discovered. The Atlanta branch faced numerous problems, and it was hoped that a black cashier could restore faith in the branch. Turn-ing to the central office, it can be seen that by 1872 and 1873—after the harm was done—Cooke, Huntington, Eaton, and others had severed their ties with the damaged institution. Between December, 1873, and February, 1874, six white trustees resigned, George Whipple among them. Whipple said that he resigned because it was impossible for him to attend the board's meetings, yet he had been a trustee from the

65. Journal, March 14, 1874; Commissioners to the Hon. Clinton L. Merriam, January 27, 1875, Official Correspondence, III, FS&T Co.

66. Fleming, *Freedmen's Savings Bank,* p. 85, makes this statement but fails to document it.

67. *Report of the Select Committee,* Senate, 1880, p. 262.

beginning and had seldom—in some years, never—attended the meetings.[68] It seems evident that some white trustees—those who had used it and those who had been negligent—were escaping from a doomed institution. They did not arrange for their successors to be black, but this followed in the natural course of events.

Because of white default and the increased concern of blacks, the March election reflected the new power of the black trustees who were in the forefront of the last reform movements. The *Evening Star* was quick to perceive a new spirit behind the trustees' reorganization. Noting that Douglass and Purvis had won the two top positions, it reported that "Forty out of seventy clerks are likewise colored. The new board of management appeared before the House Committee on Banking and Currency yesterday, and said it was their desire to make the bank an institution exclusively for colored people, and one which they would regard as their own."[69] That Douglass did not agree with this idea appears from another brief notice in the *Evening Star*: "A *Report* in circulation that the Freedman's Savings and Trust Company was to be run exclusively as a colored institution is authoritatively denied by Mr. Frederick Douglass, its president, who says it will always welcome its friends and depositors of all colors."[70]

If anyone could restore confidence in the Freedman's Savings Bank, that person was Frederick Douglass, who was widely recognized as the spokesman for all Negro Americans. Obviously Douglass was chosen because of his prestige and integrity.[71] He himself did not seek the presidency or, indeed, even wish to accept it, for he felt that his time could be spent more profitably elsewhere. He even doubted his fitness for the position because, as he later said, his life's work had been theoretical rather than practical.[72] Friends felt that it was a pity for him to hazard his property and reputation, while Langston, who actively and perhaps single-handedly opposed Douglass's election, predicted that he would find his new duties "difficult, trying, and disappointing."[73] Others, such as Purvis, William J. Wilson, William Whipper, and Al-

68. Journal, December 11, 1873, and February 12, 1874; George Whipple to John Alvord, December 10, 1873, Minutes B, Finance Committee. See p. 183, n. 61.

69. March 21, 1874, p. 4.

70. April 7, 1874, p. 1.

71. *Report of the Select Committee*, Senate, 1880, p. 236.

72. Frederick Douglass to the Rev. Henry Highland Garnet, March 19, 1874, Douglass MSS, Library of Congress; *Report of the Select Committee*, Senate, 1880, p. 239.

73. R. L. Carpenter to Douglass, June 4, 1874, Douglass MSS; Ottilia Assing to Douglass, May 1, 1874, Douglass MSS; Langston, *From the Virginia Plantation to the National Capitol*, p. 343.

vord, urged him to accept.[74] Because of his sense of duty he acceded to their wishes. Douglass described his sudden election in this manner:

> So I waked up one morning to find myself seated in a comfortable arm chair, with gold spectacles on my nose, and to hear myself addressed as President of the Freedmen's [*sic*] Bank. I could not help reflecting on the contrast between Frederick the slave boy, running about at Col. Lloyd's with only a tow linen shirt to cover him, and Frederick—President of a bank counting its assets by millions. I had heard of golden dreams, but such dreams had no comparison with reality.[75]

Whatever his personal feelings about the golden dream, Douglass was well aware that the Bank had plenty of troubles and was rumored to be insolvent and on the verge of dissolution. On his first day as president he wrote, ". . . you may deny in my name any assertion from any quarter, that I am in favor of abandoning the Institution or any of its useful branches. I believe that the Institution has done a good work and has yet a good work to do—I have no sympathy with my daughters [*sic*] idea that now is a good time to wind up the concern."[76] On the same day, he informed S. L. Harris in New York that he could depend on two things: that he, Douglass, stood for honesty in management and for continuing the work of the Freedman's Bank.[77] In March and April he believed the Bank to be basically sound and still capable of doing much good work among his people. As more and more money would accumulate in the Bank, more and more respect would be shown Negro Americans.[78] Later, as his doubts about his ability and the Bank's condition grew, enthusiasm was tempered by knowledge of the hard tasks ahead.

> . . . I have been elected to a position of which you [Senator Frelinghuysen] would little dream and one of which I had no dreams a few weeks ago. I have been made President of the Freedman's Bank. In placing me here my friends have conferred upon me such honor and imposed upon me much labor. The truth is, I have neither taste or talent for the place and when I add as I must, that the Condition of the Bank is not prosperous and possibly not even sound you will appreciate my ill fortune. I am only persuaded to remain in it for the present with a view to restore confidence and save the depositors from themselves.[79]

---

74. *Report of the Select Committee*, Senate, 1880, p. 240; *Freedman's Bank*, House, 1876, p. 76.
75. Douglass, *Life and Times*, pp. 410–411.
76. Douglass to "Sir," March 30, 1874, Douglass MSS.
77. Douglass to Harris, March 30, 1874, Douglas MSS.
78. Douglass, *Life and Times*, p. 410.
79. Douglass to Senator Frelinghuysen, May 23, 1874, Douglass MSS.

The comptroller's report of March, 1873, had exposed abuses in the Bank and had given it a salutary shock. The comptroller's report of March 10, 1874—which was not made public until the end of April—revealed a huge deficit and dealt a deathblow to the Bank's efforts to remain open. Indeed, the report was so damaging that the Comptroller and the Speaker of the House, fearing that it would cause panic among the depositors, may have tried to suppress it. At least the New York *Sun* thought so, and the six-week delay in its release tends to corroborate the *Sun's* interpretation. The report became public only when Representative Frederick G. Bromberg of Alabama, a former Mobile advisory board member who bore a grudge against the Bank, got a resolution through the House calling on the secretary of the treasury to forward all reports of the national bank examiners.[80]

While offering a frank account of the Bank's assets and liabilities, the comptroller's report tried to put the best possible interpretation on the Bank's financial position. The comptroller noted that after his report of the previous year the trustees had worked toward liquidating liabilities and had made very few loans, but they could hardly work miracles in a time of financial depression. The panic of the fall had reduced deposits by more than $1,000,000, with a consequent loss in profits. Hence there was no material change in the general character of loans and investments since that report. One fact stood out above all the others: the Bank had a deficit of $217,886.15. How to explain that? The comptroller emphasized misfortune rather than mismanagement. The deficit was attributed primarily to the excessive overhead costs of the Bank and to the unfortunate financial disturbances of the country. Specifically, the comptroller pointed to the burdensome expenses of the unprofitable branches, the high rate of interest (6 percent) which had been adopted to make the Bank competitive, and the sacrifices made to raise money during the late panic and the shrinkage in value of the company's investments. While assigning some blame to unwise loans at the branches, the comptroller surprisingly ignored the poor loans made in Washington. On this matter he merely cautioned that the managers should ad-

80. New York *Sun*, April 29, 1874, pp. 1, 2; U.S., *Congressional Record*, 43rd Cong., 1st sess., April 18, 1874, p. 3172. Abby L. Gilbert praised the work of the comptrollers in defending the interests of black depositors. The comptrollers, writes Gilbert, "first discovered the insolvency of the bank and the accompanying scandal." See "The Comptroller of the Currency and the Freedman's Savings Bank," *Journal of Negro History*, LVII, 2 (April, 1972), 125–143. This may be misleading, for the comptroller may have tried to withhold the report from Congress and the public, and the report itself certainly underestimated the deficit. It was not generally known that figures for the report were compiled in January, 1874, but that some branches were not examined until February and March. Trustees, depositors, and the public became aware of larger losses only after the failure. See below, p. 199.

here more closely to the charter's restrictions in making loans and securing sound investments. Like the first report, the 1874 report, noting the reforms under way, concluded with an optimistic summation. Non-paying branches were being closed; no loans were now made at the branches without permission from the trustees; and interest would be lowered to what the profits would permit. Additionally, the deposits of deceased soldiers, a sum estimated to be $100,000 or $200,000, would not likely be claimed by survivors and could be used to reduce the deficit.[81] Consequently, if the depositors exercised reasonable forbearance in the next six to twelve months, the comptroller asserted, the Bank could recuperate from past misfortunes and provide greater safety in the future. In concluding, he asked the fostering care of Congress for an institution which had greatly benefited the freedmen by inducing habits of thrift among them.[82]

The press, however, did not accept the optimism of the comptroller's report; in a time of financial disturbance—or any time, for that matter—a deficit of $217,000 could not be explained away. Earlier newspaper criticism had been annoying and embarrassing; now it was disastrous. The Bank provided good copy for the Democratic press, North and South. These journals listed the bad loans, predicted failure at any moment, and chorused a one-word refrain: swindle. Perhaps the most vitriolic criticism appeared in the New York *Sun*, a Democratic paper lustily fighting Radical Reconstruction. It sneered at the "concern's rottenness" and hinted that "one well-informed gentleman" said there would be a $1.5 million deficit.[83] In an era replete with more or less exaggerated tales of corruption of carpetbaggers, scalawags, and "black-dominated" southern legislatures, to say nothing of the Tweed Ring and Grant scandals, any charge against the Bank found a credulous audience. Charges against General Howard's use of Freedmen's Bureau funds in 1870, although disproved, had publicized questionable financial transactions by Howard's subordinates, while in 1874 new charges about the misuse of bounty-fund money—which were similarly rejected —were aired.[84] On April 30, 1874, the *Sun* editorialized:

81. Generally, unclaimed deposits are taken by the state, but in this case a charter provision required the Bank to place them in a separate trust fund to be used for the education and improvement of ex-slaves. The unclaimed funds were actually used to pare down the deficit.

82. "Financial Statement" (January, 1874), Letters Rec'd by the Commissioners, 1870–1914, FS&T Co. This is the official report of the bank examiner which became the *Report of the Comptroller of the Currency*, 1874.

83. *Savannah Morning News*, April 30, 1874, p. 2; U.S., Works Projects Administration, *Annals of Cleveland*, LVII, Part 1 (1874), 39; New York *Sun*, April 28, 1874, p. 1.

84. See above, p. 163.

The sordid and pernicious influences which disgraced the management of the Freedmen's Bureau under Gen. Howard have discredited and seriously damaged the Freedmen's [*sic*] Bank at Washington. In the former case bounties due to colored soldiers were venally misapplied; and in the latter the small savings of poor colored men and women have been stolen. Professed friends of humanity, who shouted loudest for the Civil Rights bill, who demanded social equality for the negro, and who would hear no voice of moderation, have not scrupled to pick his pockets and to carry off his hard earnings intended for his children.[85]

The papers harped on their favorite theme: Republican swindlers duping their confiding wards. Like the *Sun*, the Charleston *News and Courier*, in articles such as "Lo! the Poor Negro!" and "Frauds on the Freedmen," pointed out a lesson for freedmen who trusted professed Republican friends:

Once more the poor negro has been the prey of a batch of so-called philanthropists, who have either squandered his money, or, which is about the same thing, lent it out upon worthless security. In the hands of the State savings banks, such as we have in Charleston, the money would have been entirely safe. They are not conducted on "political and philanthropic" principles, but they are managed with honesty and prudence, and the depositors run no risk of losing their little hoards.[86]

It was particularly tragic, noted the *Rochester Democrat* in a typical passage, that the former slaves should be swindled by their so-called friends. "If any citizen should be specially guarded from imposition and rapacity they are these wards of the nation yet ignorant and defenseless —incapable of properly taking care of themselves. It were a burning reproach if the freedmen were plundered in the house of their friend."[87]

Republican journals now responded in patently defensive tones. For example, the *Baltimore American*, trying not to be overly excited, pointed out that the irregularities had occurred prior to the election of the new president, Frederick Douglass, a man of honesty. Douglass would see to it that the Bank paid due regard for safety. Still, the paper had to admit that substantial losses had occurred.[88]

The release of the comptroller's report and the storm of criticism it

---

85. April 30, 1874, p. 2.
86. April 28, 1874, p. 2. For similar material, see the issues of April 27 (p. 1) and April 30 (p. 2). According to Welfling, there were no mutual savings banks in South Carolina; the quotation probably refers to regular banks, often called savings banks.
87. Quoted in *New National Era*, May 21, 1874, p. 2.
88. *Evening Star*, April 27, 1874, p. 2. For similar attitudes, see *New York Herald*, April 28, 1874, p. 5.

unleashed created panic among the depositors. Heavy runs occurred at Washington, New York, Charleston, and several other cities, while all the branches experienced anxious moments.[89] From Washington and New York rumors that the Bank had suspended payments spread to other branches. Before the New York branch opened on April 29, a crowd composed of Negro waiters, washers, and servants gathered to demand full payment. Because $15,000 had been withdrawn on the previous day, the sixty-day rule was invoked, and upwards of two hundred depositors, among them a man who claimed to have a $900 account, were denied their money. The only funds paid out were special deposits made since Saturday, drafts from southern branches, and money for those who needed to buy food. Twenty-two people in this last category each received five dollars or less.[90]

As soon as news of the comptroller's report reached Charleston, a crowd besieged the local bank. The cashier was kept busy explaining and paying—probably doing more of the latter, as $5,000 was withdrawn on April 28. A few alarmed depositors discovered that the company was fully able to pay, and, their faith restored, left their funds on deposit; others expressed a profound distrust and demanded their money.[91] On April 30 the run forced the cashier to require the sixty-day withdrawal notice, and though depositors continued to gather before the bank and demand what was owed them, the cashier paid no more than two dollars to any one person. Said the *News and Courier*: "There being no help for it, the colored people have subsided into a calm but disgusted resignation to this condition of affairs; but the crowd still lingers around the bank awaiting developments."[92]

Frederick Douglass sought to restore calm to the Bank by sending reassuring telegrams to all the branch cities. Relying on presentations by Anson Sperry and George Stickney, Douglass stated that the depositors should have no uneasiness and should not dispose of their passbooks at a sacrifice.[93] In a letter to the editor of the *New York Herald*, Douglass admitted the deficit but added: "Every business man will see at once that with assets amounting a[s] they do to more than

89. *Evening Star*, April 29, 1874, p. 1; *Little Rock Daily Republican*, April 29, 1874, p. 1; *Washington Chronicle*, April 29, 1874, p. 1; 60-day notice of withdrawal of deposits at Vicksburg branch between May 2 and May 16, 1874, Letters Rec'd by the Commissioners, 1870–1914, FS&T Co.
90. New York *Sun*, April 29, 1874, p. 1.
91. Charleston *News and Courier*, April 29, 1874, p. 4.
92. *Ibid.*
93. *Report of the Select Committee*, Senate, 1880, p. 238; Philip S. Foner, *The Life and Writings of Frederick Douglass* (New York: International Publishers, 1955), IV, 88.

$3,000,000, if only tolerably well managed and let well alone, a few months only would be required to enable it to overcome this small excess of liabilities and pay all its depositors a small amount of interest."[94]

In his biography of Douglass, Benjamin Quarles claims that in early May Negroes took heart, feeling that the Bank could ride out the storm with Douglass as president.[95] No doubt he did raise the hopes of some. Upon reading the comptroller's report, the *Christian Recorder* declared its thankfulness that Douglass was president, for a load so mighty must rest on strong shoulders. And Douglass, the Negro newspaper added, "superabounds in a well earned and well preserved character."[96] The runs subsided, but anxiety remained. Exactly how much Douglass's reassuring appeals affected the situation cannot be measured. Perhaps his presence and actions helped to restore calm; yet the implementation of the sixty-day rule probably had more effect, for there is no purpose in a run if the bank refuses to pay. As Quarles himself admitted, those "who believed that the presence of Douglass at a glass top desk was superior to the working of economic law"[97] were soon disillusioned.

In spite of his confident public statements during the runs on April 28 and 29, Douglass was deeply disturbed by the Bank's financial position. Upon assuming the presidency, he had set out to learn as much as he could about the Bank—which was not an easy task. He later wrote: "Standing on the platform of this large and sophisticated establishment, with its thirty-four branches, extending from New Orleans to Philadelphia, its machinery in full operation, its correspondence carried on in cipher, its actuary dashing in and out of the bank with an air of pressing business, if not bewilderment, I found the path of enquiry I was pursuing an exceedingly difficult one."[98] On paper the company had looked sound; its deposits totaled nearly $3 million, with assets equaling liabilities. By pursuing reforms which the trustees had already undertaken, Douglass had felt the company could survive the financial strain. So confident was he that he loaned the company $10,000 to meet a temporary emergency. When his money was not repaid as rapidly as it should have been, his fears increased.[99]

Then the comptroller's report was made public and the runs ensued. Douglass learned in May that the only other trustees who had deposits in the Bank, William H. A. Wormley and probably Dr. Alexander T.

---

94. Quoted in *Report of the Select Committee,* Senate, 1880, appendix, p. 44.
95. Benjamin Quarles, *Frederick Douglass* (Washington: Associated Publishers, 1948), p. 270.
96. Quoted in *New National Era,* May 7, 1874, p. 1.
97. Quarles, *Douglass,* p. 270.
98. Douglass, *Life and Times,* p. 412.
99. *Report of the Select Committee,* Senate, 1880, pp. 238–239.

Augusta, had withdrawn their savings during the recent runs and had induced several friends to do likewise.[100] Additionally, several trustees had recently resigned, which looked suspiciously like a desertion of a sinking ship.[101] Douglass's suspicions quickened when he inquired about the Bank's telegraphic correspondence, which was carried on in code. When the Bank's actuary said he was too busy to provide the president with the key, Douglass deduced that he was not supposed to read the dispatches. He may have been correct.[102] Anyone might have been suspicious upon reading a transcription, for a large portion of the code was adopted after the failure of Jay Cooke and Company and was designed to handle a crisis situation. The following code words are suggestive:

Spruce = There is a heavy run at this branch.
Poplar = How are things at your branch?
Plum = All quiet. Business as usual.
Pear = Excited. Anticipate a run.
Cherry = Bad. Can you help us?
Walnut = Apply the sixty-day rule.
Linden = Cannot spare currency.
Birch = No currency at banks here.
Prune = Remit all the funds you can spare.[103]

By mid-May at the latest, Douglass had learned of the losses at the southern branches, the $40,000 shortage in Wilson's accounts at Washington, and the scope of the Bank's deficit. He was forced to conclude that the institution was no longer "a safe custodian of the hard earnings of my confiding people," and that the money was already gone when the trustees had elected him president.[104] His friends, he later wrote, had married him to a corpse, which "by some drugs, some charms, some conjuration or some mighty magic" he was to revive.[105] The man who took office to restore confidence turned all his prestige to the efforts to close the Bank.

Seeking to prevent depositors from suffering further losses, Douglass immediately informed Senators John Sherman and John Scott of the Committee on Finance that he considered the institution insolvent and

---

100. *Ibid.*, p. 222; *Freedman's Bank*, House, 1876, p. 180.
101. *Freedman's Bank*, House, 1876, p. 180; *Report of the Select Committee*, Senate, 1880, p. 257; *Journal*, February 12, 1874; Whipple to Alvord, December 10, 1873, Minutes B, Finance Committee; see above, n. 61.
102. *Report of the Select Committee*, Senate, 1880, p. 237.
103. *Ibid.*, appendix, p. 49.
104. Douglass, *Life and Times*, pp. 412–414.
105. *Ibid.*, p. 414.

hopeless and that he could no longer ask the freedmen to support it.[106] Several officers and trustees (George Stickney and others, presumably among them Sperry, Purvis, and Langston) objected bitterly to their president's actions and went before the committee to refute his account of the Bank's condition. "Some of them," Douglass said later, "who had assisted me by giving me facts showing the insolvency of the bank, now made haste to contradict that conclusion and to assure the committee that it was, if allowed to go on, abundantly able to weather the financial storm and pay dollar for dollar to its depositors."[107] The Senate committee accepted Douglass's views and began to prepare legislation to close the Bank.

Meanwhile, several officers and trustees, among them Stickney, Sperry, Purvis, Langston, and Cashier C. A. Woodward, went to the House Committee on Banking and Currency with a plan to save the Bank by a radical restructuring. If they failed, they intended to obtain power to close it in an orderly fashion.[108] Spurred on by revelations of bad loans and approaching failure, they sought to return the deposits to the branches for investment in the branch cities. Returning money to the branches would mean that larger numbers of Negroes, who were receiving only minimal benefits from the Bank's loan policy, could obtain loans, and perhaps this might restore the freedmen's confidence in the Bank's good faith. The trustees' desire to reform the Bank and to restore confidence thus coalesced with the demands of black depositors (and some white critics of the Bank) for the extension of credit to blacks.[109]

The bill which the House Committee on Banking and Currency drew up authorized the Bank to invest half of the deposits in the branch communities and specified that the other half was to be invested by the Washington officers in United States bonds or kept on deposit in a national bank. The depositors' money controlled by the home office would henceforth be absolutely safe and always available. The trustees were well aware of the Bank's previous structural problems and heavy expenses at the branches, the lack of trained bankers, and the lack of success of the branch's attending committees. Several provisions of the bill reflected their attempt to remedy the Bank's acknowledged

106. *Report of the Select Committee*, Senate, 1880, p. 237.
107. Douglass, *Life and Times*, p. 413.
108. *Report of the Select Committee*, Senate, 1880, pp. 186, 254; C. A. Woodward to Committee on Banking and Currency, April 13, 1874, Papers of the Committee on Banking and Currency concerning the Freedman's Savings and Trust Co., 43rd Cong., Legislative Records, NA, RG 233.
109. See above, pp. 120–123.

weaknesses: the bill granted permission to close non-paying branches, specified that officers harming the Bank would be held liable for a misdemeanor, limited loans to any one person to $10,000, and restricted interest to 5 percent or less. The bill also established procedures to close the Bank by empowering the trustees to appoint three commissioners who would take charge of the company, collect the sums due, and distribute them to the depositors pro rata as fast as practicable.[110] If the reformist sections of the bill could not save the Bank, the trustees could implement an orderly and equitable procedure to wind it up.

The congressmen who guided the bill through the House (Milton Durham of Kentucky, Horace Maynard of Tennessee, and Clinton Merriam of New York) argued the Bank's case on the basis of the comptroller's report of 1874: the Bank had sustained losses due to its previously irregular management, yet its prospects for recovery and for future benefit were excellent.[111] Durham maintained that the trustees' unprofitable investments and errors of judgment formed only a small part of their largely favorable record. The Bank, he stressed, had conferred many benefits upon the freedmen, who were proud of their own banking institution.

> I undertake to say that he who devised these savings institutions for the colored men in the Southern States conferred a great blessing and a great good upon that race. It has taught them habits of economy; it has taught them to lay up their little pittance. . . . And I am credibly informed by the managers of this institution that they had collected and distributed through these agencies over $58,000,000 since they were established. . . . These individuals are proud of their race; I use the word "proud" knowingly. They desire to encourage their own institutions. And I have no hesitation in saying that they will lay up and accumulate two dollars in one of these institutions, conducted under the charge and control of their own men, as is now done, to where they would lay up one dollar in institutions that are conducted as the national banks are.[112]

The only objection to the bill—and a forceful one it was—came from Representative Frederick Bromberg, who was being sued by the Bank. Bromberg had signed the bond of his friend, Cashier C. A. Woodward; when Woodward appropriated $3,375 from the Bank for services rendered to the Freedmen's Bureau, Bank officials took Bromberg to court

110. *Report of the Select Committee*, Senate, 1880, appendix, p. 13; *Evening Star*, May 8, 1874, p. 1.
111. U.S., *Congressional Record*, 43rd Cong., 1st sess., May 14, 1874, pp. 3893–3901. This report was very similar to that of a year earlier.
112. *Ibid.*

to make good the loss.[113] However malicious his motives may have been, Bromberg's analysis turned out to be more accurate and prescient than any other congressman's. Criticizing the overly sanguine nature of the comptroller's report of 1874, the Mobile representative correctly pointed out that the company's losses were far greater than the comptroller had stated because the national bank examiners had not visited all the branches before the comptroller's statistics had been compiled. Recounting the losses at several of these branches and also several of the Bank's worst loans, he maintained that the Freedman's Bank could not be propped up by any legislation. "It is an edifice with crumbling walls and undermined foundations. A prolongation of its existence is not kindness but cruelty to the present depositors and colored people in general. The longer the day of its dissolution is put off the larger will be the number buried under its ruins when the inevitable crash shall come."[114] Bromberg's arguments elicited little support in the House, and a majority believed (or wished to believe) with Congressman Maynard of Tennessee that "These errors . . . were errors of judgment of men who were acting honestly, in good faith, and for the benefit of these people, who I have reason to assert have derived benefit from it, and thousands of them to-day have homes bought and paid for from these savings."[115]

The Senate, guided by its Committee on Finance (which had listened to the persuasive arguments of Douglass), was opposed to the House bill and amended it to require the Bank's closing ten days after the bill's approval.[116] But in the conference between the House and Senate, the Senate committee was almost completely won over to the House version, except for one amendment of great significance. The Senate committee urged and the House accepted a requirement that all new deposits be held as special deposits not subject to the company's previous debts and liabilities. In other words, the company's losses would not affect new deposits.[117] This change was crucial, for it enabled even the most despondent pessimists to try one last time to save the Bank without worrying that every new deposit, which the Bank certainly needed to survive, would be lost to the depositor should the Bank go under. Both houses passed the amended bill and sent it to the President, who signed it on June 20, 1874.[118]

113. The outcome of the legal proceedings is not known. *Ibid.*, p. 3900.

114. *Ibid.*, appendix, p. 288.

115. *Ibid.*, p. 3900.

116. *Ibid.*, June 3, 1874, p. 4490; *Evening Star*, June 6, 1874, p. 1.

117. *Evening Star*, June 6, 1874, p. 1, and June 13, 1874, p. 1; U.S., *Congressional Record*, 43rd Cong., 1st sess., June 13, 1874, p. 4936.

118. *Report of the Select Committee*, Senate, 1880, appendix, p. 1.

This legislative victory of the reformist trustees kindled a last glimmer of hope amid all the gloom of 1874. While the opposition newspapers continued to criticize the Bank in articles such as "Patching Up the Charter of the Freedman's Bank" and "Congress Regulating the Rotten Freedman's Bank," others that had previously defended the company again took up its cause.[119] For many, the Bank question was not a subject for rational inquiry but a test of faith in the purity of Republican efforts to help ex-slaves and to overcome the wicked Democrats.[120] Some papers thought the new loan policy would work wonders for the freedmen. Previously the *New National Era* had opposed such a radical change in the investment policy; now it reversed its position, observing that loans at southern branches would be the means of "vastly improving" the position of Negroes. Consequently, it advised, depositors should stand by the Bank and not panic.[121] On June 28 Louisville's *Courier-Journal*, a paper that had always viewed the Bank favorably, reported the proposed return of the local Bank's funds, stressing how Negroes would now be able to buy homes and in general "get ahead in the world."[122]

Frederick Douglass further increased the hopes of the optimistic (for only optimists still believed in the Bank) by issuing a reassuring circular to the public on June 25, 1874. The thrust of his argument was strongly for continuing the Bank, exactly the opposite of what he had told the senators in May. His circular followed the comptroller's report, acknowledging the deficit and a certain amount of previous mismanagement. Douglass, at least for public consumption, agreed with the comptroller that the deficit was caused by a high interest rate, nonpaying branches, and senseless runs, but in addition he ascribed a prominent place to race malignity. Because of the legislation of June 20, Douglass emphasized, past errors would not affect the new deposits, nor should they obscure the Bank's promising future. He assured new depositors that their money would be handled as a special fund, while to

119. Charleston *News and Courier*, May 9, 1874, p. 1; June 4, 1874, p. 1.

120. *Sunday Chronicle*, as reported in *New National Era*, May 21, 1874, p. 2; undated clipping from *New York Herald*, Letters Rec'd by the Commissioners, 1870–1914, FS&T Co.; *New Berne Times*, June 27, 1874, p. 4.

121. May 21, 1874, p. 2. Lewis and Frederick Douglass, Jr., were editing the paper. Upon Douglass's insistence, the *New National Era* of July 9, 1874, stated that the thoughts and ideas appearing in the editorial columns were not those of Frederick Douglass. "Hon. Frederick Douglass is not, nor has he been, editor of the *New National Era* for more than a year." See Foner, *Life and Writings*, IV, 223–226, 534, n. 13. Thus it was probably the Douglass sons who revised (between May 1, 1873, and May 24, 1874) the *New Era's* position on lending money at the branches.

122. June 28, 1874, p. 3.

old depositors he offered the hope that the trustees would now have time to realize interest from their investments and thus fill the chasm between liabilities and assets.[123] The long-standing, bitter complaints that the Bank withdrew money from southern Negro communities for the benefit of Washington could now be answered; half of the Bank's funds were to be available for blacks to borrow. The pride of black people was at stake, Douglass stressed.

> The history of civilization shows that no people can well rise to a high degree of mental or even moral excellence without wealth. A people uniformly poor and compelled to struggle for barely a physical existence will be dependent and despised by their neighbors, and will finally despise themselves. While it is impossible that every individual of any race shall be rich—and no man may be despised for merely being poor—yet no people can be respected which does not produce a wealthy class. Such a people will only be the hewers of wood and drawers of water, and will not rise above a mere animal existence. The mission of the Freedman's Bank is to show our people the road to a share of the wealth and well being of the world.[124]

Douglass had recently advocated closing the Bank because he believed it to be unsound. He would soon be accused of duplicity in encouraging blacks to support the Bank while allegedly knowing that in a few days, weeks, or months they would lose their money.[125] Although the evidence does not offer a complete explanation of Douglass's reversal in his June circular, there is no reason to suspect him of being dishonest or untruthful, for there is a perfectly reasonable alternative explanation for his actions. Bank officers, including Douglass, might consider the Bank unsound, but no one would know for months exactly how bad the situation was. Certainly some of the trustees believed it possible that, with a breathing spell and new safety measures, the Bank could be revived. Douglass may well have decided to give them the benefit of the doubt. He had originally decided to close the Bank because day by day more people were being hurt; between his meeting with the senators and the publication of his circular, the charter had been amended, and now at least no harm could come from a last attempt to save the Bank, for new deposits would be protected from the previous debts. If the reformers failed, he would only have raised false

123. *New National Era*, June 25, 1874, p. 2. Douglass's circular is also reprinted in *Report of the Select Committee*, Senate, 1880, appendix, pp. 42–44.

124. *Ibid.*

125. *Mobile Daily Register* (July 3, 1874, p. 2) charged that Douglass had been "deceitful."

hopes; but there could be no additional damage, for no new money could be lost.[126]

Douglass's three-month term as president was one of the unhappy experiences of his life. Later he claimed that his reputation suffered,[127] although evidence for this is scant. One southern paper charged that Cooke and Douglass ruined the Bank, and of course his June circular drew criticism.[128] But the black community, most whites, and even most southern newspapers realized that he had appeared in the president's chair after the damage was done and that his actions were aimed at reforming and then, reluctantly, closing the ill-fated institution.

The amendment of the charter, Douglass's circular, and the favorable newspaper stories failed to reverse the Bank's decline. Thousands of depositors no longer believed in the Bank, and the sixty-day notices given on May 1 and afterward were falling due. In mid-June the trustees released several employees, reduced salaries, and made tentative plans to enter into contract with their depositors to pay immediately 50 to 80 percent of their money and, hopefully, the remainder later.[129] By late June the Bank had run out of money, and legally it had to close or pay in full the depositors who had given proper notice. Reform had come too late.

On June 29, 1874, John Mercer Langston offered a resolution to close the Bank under the terms of the recent amendment. Only Dr. Alexander T. Augusta opposed it; those voting in favor were James Storum, Thomas L. Tullock, John Mercer Langston, O. S. B. Wall, John Alvord, Charles B. Purvis, Zalmon Richards, George W. Balloch, the Reverend Sampson Talbot, Frederick Douglass, and J. H. Ela.[130] But on July 1 Alvord had second thoughts and offered a motion to reconsider. Only Augusta, Balloch, and Talbot supported him; the other eight, plus trustee Sayles J. Bowen, a former mayor of Washington, voted to uphold the decision to wind up the Bank's affairs. The trustees then elected three commissioners to act as receivers under the supervision of the secretary of the treasury.[131] On July 2, 1874, a committee of trustees

126. When Douglass gave a "fair and unvarnished narration" of his connection with the Freedman's Bank in his *Life and Times* (p. 413), he made no mention of his June circular.

127. Douglass, *Life and Times*, p. 413. Frederick May Holland states that Douglass's efforts to close the Bank were unfortunate for his reputation, but offers no proof. Douglass retained his popularity among black Americans after the Bank's failure. See Frederic May Holland, *Frederick Douglass: The Colored Orator* (1891; reprinted, New York: Haskell House Publishers, 1969).

128. Louisville *Courier-Journal*, July 4, 1874, p. 1; July 16, 1874, p. 2.

129. Journal, June 17, June 23, and June 24, 1874.

130. *Ibid.*, June 29, 1874.

131. *Ibid.*, July 1, 1874.

informed the secretary of the treasury of the trustees' action, and the Freedman's Savings and Trust Company was officially closed.

As the doors were shut for the last time, the Bank owed $2,993,790 on 61,144 accounts. The Bank's vaults contained only $400 in United States bonds, and the branches counted only $31,689 in cash. Almost all the assets were in real estate security, personal loans, and land and buildings owned by the Bank (over $400,000 worth), which could be liquidated only with great delay and difficulty.[132] The commissioners appointed to wind up the Bank made a hasty investigation, and in December, 1874, they listed the total amount of real estate loans at the principal office as approximately $1,200,000. Six years later about one-fourth of this amount had not been collected.[133] The figure of $1,200,000 was questioned in 1880 by some experts who claimed that the total amount of loans would never be determined because of the Bank's shoddy bookkeeping. The available fund loans (including principal and interest) accounted for about $337,000 of the remaining assets. About half of these loans were on District of Columbia securities, which were then below par. "Of many of these loans," reported the commissioners, "the security is inadequate, of others utterly worthless, and in some cases the funds of the bank have been loaned upon mere personal notes without any security whatever." Six years later, three-fifths of the available fund loans, about $196,000, remained outstanding.[134] This terrible evidence of insolvency was a drastic indictment of the Bank's earlier managers and led many to conclude with Frederick Douglass that "bad loans and bad management have been the death of it."[135]

It is instructive to compare the fate of the Freedman's Bank with that of other savings banks during the financially troubled 1870's. Judged by the common standard, the Bank's record seems rather poor. Emerson Keyes, the nineteenth-century banking expert, and Weldon Welfling, his modern counterpart, are impressed by the soundness of mutual savings institutions and the paucity of disastrous failures. According to Welfling,

> Prior to the Panic of 1873, there were very few failures of savings banks and these few were generally attributed to "bad investments." Typically, depositors were paid 80 per cent or more of their deposits. In a few in-

132. *Report of the Commissioners,* 1874, p. 52; Fleming, *Freedmen's Savings Bank,* p. 98.
133. *Report of the Commissioners,* 1874, p. 32; *Report of the Select Committee,* Senate, 1880, p. 299.
134. *Report of the Select Committee,* Senate, 1880, p. 307; *Report of the Commissioners,* 1874, pp. 7, 40, 52.
135. Douglass to Gerrit Smith, July 3, 1874, Smith MSS, Syracuse University Library.

stances, defalcations led to failure or a savings bank failed along with a closely associated commercial bank. By Keyes' count, there were 11 failures before 1872. The losses to depositors, counted in terms of gross deposits made over the period, were minute.[136]

Welfling estimates that perhaps twenty savings banks failed, without being able to reopen, during or as a result of the Panic of 1873. Although savings banks faced turbulent conditions in the seventies and 123 suspended operations between 1875 and 1879, the number of savings banks actually increased slightly in that decade. Many of the 123 suspensions were only temporary; for those which were permanent, the process of liquidation was frequently carried out after a short period without loss to the depositors. All in all, mutual savings banks lost very little money.[137]

It is true that a number of the banks which failed exhibited many of the weaknesses of the Freedman's Bank. In some cases fraud and theft were evident, as at the Concord National Savings Bank, where the cashier embezzled $50,000 and the trustees treated the bank's investments as their own and appropriated the depositors' interest.[138] Heavy operating expenses, which resulted in speculative business ventures, led to the failure of the Third Avenue Savings Bank in New York in 1875.[139] The Freedman's Savings and Trust Company thus had no monopoly on ignorance, speculation, fraud, or tragedy. Nevertheless, the losses of the Bank were among the worst of that decade—and all the more tragic because they were the first savings of a recently freed people, symbolizing hopes for equal citizenship and economic security. Even with its special problems of structure and expense as a chain bank, competent management might have enabled the Freedman's Savings and Trust Company to weather the Panic of 1873 or at least to reimburse its depositors with only minimal losses.

136. *Mutual Savings Banks*, p. 47.
137. *Ibid.*, pp. 47–49.
138. *Evening Star*, August 21, 1874, p. 1. For other examples, see Richmond *Daily Enquirer*, February 26, 1874, p. 1; *Memphis Daily Appeal*, September 28, 1873, p. 1; *Evening Star*, September 25, 1873, p. 2; *Republican Banner*, September 26, 27, 1873, p. 1; *New York Times*, January 29, 1872, p. 2; February 1, 1874, p. 1; October 31, 1874, p. 1; November 28, 1875, p. 6; December 16, 1875, p. 1; December 23, 1875, p. 4; Welfling, *Mutual Savings Banks*, p. 47.
139. Keyes, *History of Savings Banks*, II, 550–553.

7

The Bank's Legacy

"... the poor Colored man must be ground between the upper mill stone of power and prejudice and the lower of government neglect and abandonment."—Anson Sperry to J. W. Purnell, August 19, 1874, Sperry Letters, Official Correspondence, FS&T Co.

The irony of the Bank's history was that the tragedy of its failure would not have been so severe if the Bank had not been so remarkably successful in its missionary crusade. It had set out to encourage ex-slaves to develop pride in themselves by working hard, saving their money, and investing their savings in their own bank. The response to this call had, within a surprisingly few years, built the Bank into a vast enterprise handling millions, operating in thirty-seven cities, and spread over half the nation. The influence of the Bank went well beyond its dealings with thousands of individual freedmen: dozens of Negro organizations had entrusted their money to the Bank and had made themselves active Bank promoters in the communities; hundreds of churches and schools were closely identified with the Bank's mission, and Negro leaders had responded to the invitation to become its employees, advisory committeemen, and unofficial partisans. The Freedman's Bank had become part of the very fiber of black community life across the South. Directly and indirectly, black America had made a massive investment of money, energy, and pride in the institution which now dragged everything down to failure.

To salvage their own self-respect and to explain the unbelievable cataclysm, many blacks came to believe the legend that from the beginning the whole operation had been a conspiracy to swindle the freedmen, to engage their trust by moral preachment the better to cheat them of their savings. It is hardly surprising that the legend took root; in fact, it is amazing that some Negroes did not believe this Bank legend.

The most avid purveyors of the conspiracy legend were the southern Democratic newspapers. For years they had regarded the Bank as just another element in the Reconstruction carpetbagger-missionary complex, and the failure with all its scandalous exposures simply vindicated their judgment. The *Daily Arkansas Gazette* declared: "The christian statesman Howard, the Young Mens Christian association, and the christian Cookes have gobbled all. It is merely 'forty acres and a mule' in another shape. 'When will a nigger ebber learn sense.' "[1] Some of the Democratic papers gloated over the tragedy with almost sadistic relish. The *Daily Memphis Avalanche* headlined its story, "Whar's Dat Money?" while the Charleston *News and Courier* chuckled, "A Colored Bubble Burst—How Cuffee's Money was Squandered."[2] The Richmond *Daily Enquirer* mocked the misery of the Negroes:

> Many of the colored people who put their "little all" in this now collapsed financial windbag, daily with sorrowing steps . . . pass down Tenth street and gaze with melancholy and languid air at the deserted office of the Richmond branch. Tears of anguish glisten on the protuding eyeballs of many who vainly hanker after buried treasure and sigh for the beautiful (greenback) that is vanished to return no more. . . . Is Sambo to be always a chattel slave to his ignorance, his fears and his prejudices? Alas, we fear so.[3]

The Bank quickly found its place in the Reconstruction mythology as another carpetbagger betrayal of the ignorant and trusting ex-slaves. The Freedman's Savings Bank thus became a byword for failure and scandal: when the *Savannah Morning News* described a particularly flagrant fraud perpetrated against Negroes in July, 1874, it commented that "this is equal to running a Freedman's savings bank."[4]

The initial notification of the failure caused excitement in all the branch communities; hundreds of freedmen ran directly to their branch offices, asking anxiously if the rumor were true. When told that the

1. May 3, 1874, p. 1. The reference to General Howard alludes to his close association with the trustees and the fact that he had borrowed from the Bank and had an account there which was overdrawn at the time of the failure. See *Report of the Select Committee*, Senate, 1880, pp. 106, 269.

2. Charleston *News and Courier*, July 3, 1874, p. 1; *Daily Memphis Avalanche*, July 3, 1874, p. 1.

3. July 9, 1874, p. 4. For similar accounts, see *Mobile Daily Register*, July 3, 1874, p. 2; *Richmond Dispatch*, July 3, 1874; *Savannah Morning News*, July 3, 1874, p. 3; *Baltimore American*, July 8, 1874, p. 2; *Richmond Daily Enquirer*, July 17, 1874, p. 4.

4. July 11, 1874, p. 2.

Bank had suspended and would begin repaying its depositors soon, almost all—with complaints and lamentation—acquiesced in the fait accompli, for there was little else they could do.[5] At Baltimore on July 10, for instance, Anson Sperry reported "much inquiry, but all quiet and undemonstrative."[6]

The Negro editors of the *New National Era* and the *Weekly Louisianian* (New Orleans) at first ignored the Bank's closing, as if they could not bear to discuss the tragedy of the failure.[7] Other black leaders angrily denounced those whom they held responsible for the Bank's faulty if not criminal management. Abe Smith, a member of the Nashville advisory board, placed the blame solely on the Washington officers; these men had brought sorrow and hardship to Nashville depositors —washerwomen, crippled soldiers, and "that class of people."[8] "Rotten as the devil" was the way Nelson Walker, another Nashville board member, described affairs at Washington. "I spent sometime last summer in Washington and got an insight into its management. The money of the bank has been habitually invested there contrary to the charter. It has been used in 'beautifying' the city. My confidence was then shaken in its management." Several depositors, Walker added, had resolved never again to "trust any bank to the extent of a dollar."[9]

A great many depositors seem to have shared Walker's distrust of banks. Anson Sperry's vigorous efforts to help some of the cashiers reorganize their branches as private banks failed dismally: in Louisville, Richmond, Augusta, Memphis, Norfolk, Macon, and St. Louis the cashiers' banks quickly withered under the communities' hostility or indifference. "It does not surprise me," Sperry wrote to the St. Louis cashier, "that our failure operates against your Bank. This is so all around. And the effect is cumulative. It will be worse before it is better."[10] Sperry himself, along with George T. Stickney, established

5. See the brief accounts in *Evening Star*, July 3, 1874, pp. 1, 4; *National Republican*, July 3, 1874, p. 1; *Washington Chronicle*, July 3, 1874, p. 8; *Savannah Morning News*, July 4, 1874, p. 3; *Daily Sentinel* (Raleigh), July 9, 1874, p. 1; *Daily Arkansas Gazette*, July 3, 1974, p. 1; *Richmond Daily Whig*, July 2, 1874, p. 4; *Philadelphia Inquirer*, July 9, 1874, p. 3.

6. A. M. Sperry to William H. Bishop, July 10, 1874, p. 12, Sperry Letters, Official Correspondence, FS&T Co.

7. *New National Era*, July, 1874; *Weekly Louisianian*, July, 1874. The latter printed Douglass's last circular without comment, while *New National Era* did not mention the Bank again until fall.

8. *Nashville Union and American*, July 3, 1874, p. 4.

9. *Ibid.*, July 3, 1874, p. 4.

10. Sperry to Charles Spencer, July 10, 1874, p. 21; Sperry to Horace Morris, July 21, 1874, p. 52; Sperry to D. A. Ritter, July 10, 1874, p. 11; Sperry to Thomas N. M. Sellers, July 15, 1874, pp. 31–32; Sperry to W. Brent, July 24, 1874, p. 68, Sperry Letters, Official Correspondence, FS&T Co.

the People's Savings Bank in Washington, which lingered feebly for a few months and then vanished without a trace.[11]

To establish another bank was impossible. The money which the poor and the well-to-do of the black community had been saving for months and years for homes, farm land, business improvements, insurance against sickness and unemployment, or for a sense of security and prosperity had vanished in one day by an order from Washington. Seventeen months elapsed before even a small portion was returned. "The great pity," wrote Sperry to the Huntsville cashier, "is the sorrow and anxiety caused our poor depositors who really need money to help them along. For these there is only hardship in suspension."[12] As the *New York Times* observed, the failure hurt the hard-working, industrious element the most—the artisans, laborers, servants, and farmers.[13] Societies too were injured by the collapse; nearly every black society in Richmond lost money in the failure. The *Richmond Daily Whig* noted that the First African Church temporarily lost $10,000 which had been destined for a new edifice, and thus every member of the congregation was affected.[14] Baltimore beneficial societies, it was later reported, lost nearly $50,000, which caused charitable work to be suspended for "want of means."[15]

Many of the depositors pleaded a special need to withdraw their money. Since some had lost all their ready cash in the failure, the pressure for a special advance was understandable, and in a few cases the cashiers relented.[16] The Columbia, Tennessee, cashier "loaned" money against the depositors' Bank claims: several depositors received money for meat, one received $8.50 for a school bill, one 75 cents to pay a minister for a wedding, and one 50 cents for medicine.[17] That the commissioners had to instruct the cashiers not to advance money even in cases of extreme necessity suggests that the cashiers had been following sentiment rather than Bank policy.[18]

---

11. Sperry to William Mann, July 25, 1874, p. 72; Sperry to Spencer, September 11, 1874, p. 190, *ibid.*; *Freedman's Bank*, House, 1876, p. 78.

12. Sperry to A. J. Hunt, July 9, 1874, p. 7, Sperry Letters, Official Correspondence, FS&T Co.

13. July 16, 1874, p. 4.

14. *Richmond Daily Whig*, July 4, 1874, p. 4; *Richmond Dispatch*, July 3, 1874, p. 1.

15. *New York Times*, September 15, 1874, p. 5.

16. Sperry to W. J. Bronaugh, July 9, 1874, p. 4, Sperry Letters, Official Correspondence, FS&T Co.

17. List of loans to depositors at Columbia, Tenn., Letters Rec'd by the Commissioners, 1870–1914, FS&T Co.

18. Commissioners to William Steward, July 17, 1874, p. 12; Commissioners to Morris, July 24, 1874, p. 75, Official Correspondence, I, FS&T Co.

There was hope in the first few days after the failure that all deposits would be repaid. The bank examiner spoke of returning 93 cents on the dollar, while at least two of the three commissioners, the Bank's receivers, hoped to repay dollar for dollar.[19] The *New York Times* surmised that the depositors would lose very little and that perhaps the Bank could even be reopened.[20] But as days lengthened into months and then a year, the Bank's hopeless insolvency was gradually recognized.

By the fall of 1874 all reports on repayment were pessimistic. The *Evening Star* said that the commissioners found it impossible to determine when a dividend could be declared, and later announced that the commissioners' report revealed larger losses than anyone had anticipated.[21] Numerous statements from the Tallahassee branch community contended that the Bank could pay only 20 to 40 cents on the dollar.[22] Even Anson Sperry, when asked when the first dividend would be paid, grumbled, "When all of our depositors are driven to despair and disgust."[23]

Lacking faith in the Bank and needing money, some depositors sought to sell their claims against the Bank at a discount. Nashville, Washington, New York, and Charleston papers had earlier warned depositors not to succumb to the blandishments of the speculators, since Bank Examiner Charles Meigs had declared they would receive 93 cents on the dollar.[24] Some speculation occurred in 1874, but how much is uncertain. A congressman declared that Negroes who needed groceries or other supplies sold their passbooks to storekeepers and merchants who then took up the freedmen's claims.[25] Two or three certificates of a later date attest to this practice.[26] An affidavit of another sort reveals that in 1881 one Richard Johnson surrendered his claim of

19. Commissioners to Morris, July 24, 1874, p. 76; R. H. T. Leipold to F. N. Gray, July 24, 1874, Official Correspondence, I, FS&T Co.; *New York Times*, July 2, 1874, p. 1. A Columbus, Miss., newspaper reprinted a Bank circular by S. L. Harris which stated that "it is the opinion of good financiers that there should be no deficit in closing up the affairs of the Institution." See clipping from a Columbus newspaper, Letters Rec'd by the Commissioners, 1870–1914, FS&T Co.

20. July 2, 1874, p. 1.

21. October 6, 1874, p. 4; November 14, 1874, p. 1.

22. Report on the Tallahassee branch, November 27, 1874, from William Lockwood, Agent, Letters Rec'd by the Commissioners, 1870–1914, FS&T Co.

23. Sperry to N. D. Smith, October 26, 1874, p. 247, Sperry Letters, Official Correspondence, FS&T Co.

24. *Nashville Union and American*, July 4, 1874, p. 1; *Washington Chronicle*, July 4, 1874, p. 5; *National Republican*, July 4, 1874, p. 1; *New York Times*, July 4, 1874, p. 1; Charleston *News and Courier*, July 4, 1874, p. 1.

25. House, Committee on Banking and Currency, *Hearings*, 1910, p. 3.

26. Affidavit of Hiram Brown, February 23, 1875; Power of Attorney of Martha Paine given to E. I. Magruder, Letters Rec'd by the Commissioners, 1870–1914, FS&T Co.

$352 at the New Orleans branch for $28.16.[27] By late 1874 and early 1875, however, even the speculators were abandoning hope. A Beaufort citizen declared: "I earnestly advise the depositors to wait and not sell their bank books to sharpers, though I've yet to learn of anyone now not sharp enough not to buy them."[28] Lacking conclusive evidence, one cannot estimate the number of depositors who sacrificed their claims for a pittance.

The mixture of hope and uneasiness gave way to despair and anger in the months following the failure. Mass protest meetings held in several cities in late 1874 and early 1875 absolved Frederick Douglass and the other black officials of blame for the failure and denounced the "rascals," "thieves," and "swindlers" who had caused the tragedy. For example, Washington Negroes gathered at the Union Bethel Church in September to hear Charles B. Purvis announce that friends of the Negro and "some grand rascals" had managed the Bank, and that the rascals and the panic had caused the failure.[29] At another meeting one week later, the depositors condemned those officials who had neglected their trust and defrauded them of their hard-earned savings.[30] Protest meetings held in Charleston resulted in the preparation of a memorial seeking relief from Congress. The Charleston petition emphasized the distress and economic paralysis which a poor laboring people had suffered through the failure of a bank established by "high officials of the Government of the United States."[31] At Philadelphia depositors were told that a vile ring had stolen their money and that their branch had been pulled down by corruption and extravagance at the central office.[32]

At a mass meeting in Savannah's St. Philip's Church, Negro speakers advised depositors and their friends not to lose faith in thrift or hide their money at home because of their unfortunate first experience in saving.[33] Savannah Negroes were very bitter about the Freedman's

27. Richard Johnson surrenders his claim to $352, *ibid.*

28. *Report of the Select Committee*, Senate, 1880, appendix, p. 29.

29. *Evening Star*, September 30, 1874, p. 4; *New York Times*, October 1, 1874, p. 1.

30. *Washington Chronicle*, October 7, 1874, p. 5; *New National Era*, October 8, 1874, p. 2.

31. *News and Courier*, January 5, 1875, p. 4; January 6, 1875, p. 4; *New York Times*, January 7, 1875, p. 5.

32. A clipping from a Philadelphia newspaper, September 9, 1874, Letters Rec'd by the Commissioners, 1870–1914, FS&T Co.

33. *Savannah Morning News*, July 9, 1874, p. 3; July 10, 1874, p. 3. At this meeting the depositors also elected a committee to find a proper depository for their money; they selected Henry McNeal Turner of the A.M.E. Church, a well-

Bank. The Bank and all its branches, argued one black minister, had been a "company of robbers and thieves"; it was a dead concern in which blacks were induced to invest their hard-earned money.[34] "While poor men have become victimized," wrote one Negro to the *Savannah Morning News*, "poor dry bones have become fat by crime and false representations."[35]

A particularly strong protest movement developed at Baltimore in the fall. Depositors met at the Ebenezer Methodist Church (which had lost over $1,000 in the Bank's collapse) to condemn the Bank and its managers. Although a few praised the Bank for its good work and good intentions, most agreed with one depositor who denounced it bitterly and spoke of the harm it had done to black people. The assembled depositors adopted resolutions accusing the Bank of being an "artful dodge to swindle poor colored people out of their hard-earned money."[36] A committee was appointed to interview the commissioners and discuss plans to hasten a settlement; one month later the committee presented its report to a meeting of four hundred depositors. The commissioners, who called the Baltimore committee's resolutions uncouth and "calvinistic," said they had found the Bank insolvent, could not predict how much the Bank would pay, and were unable to say when their trust would be completed.[37] Consequently, the Baltimore committee proposed that a permanent Freedmen's Rights Association be organized at every branch to guard the interests of the depositors and to press Congress to act on their behalf. Despite substantial opposition, which felt that the organization would cost too much and that poor depositors had lost enough already, the organization was approved by loud applause.[38]

Expressing their protest in the only other way feasible, depositors all

---

known minister, politician, and orator, to confer with the commissioners in Washington. It is not known whether Turner made the trip to Washington. Two months later, after debating whether to establish another black bank or adopt one of the city's white banks, the committee recommended that blacks open accounts with the Savannah Bank and Trust Company, where special care would be taken to meet the needs of a working people. The response to the committee's recommendation is unknown. See *Savannah Morning News*, September 12, 1874, p. 3.

34. *Ibid.*, September 29, 1874, p. 3.
35. *Ibid.*, December 2, 1874, p. 3.
36. *Baltimore American*, August 11, 1874, p. 4.
37. *Ibid.*, September 15, 1874, p. 4.
38. *Ibid.*; *New York Times*, September 15, 1874, p. 5. Unfortunately, there is no information about the Freedmen's Rights Association, other than S. L. Harris's laconic statement that no such association had been established in New York. See *Evening Star*, September 17, 1874, p. 1.

over the South rained petitions upon Congress, pleading that the government assume the company's assets and pay immediately the amounts
due them.[39] These petitions revealed that, by late 1874, the depositors
were becoming suspicious that the liquidation of the Bank was adding
yet another story of betrayal of trust to the dismal record. They suspected the commissioners of mismanagement. It seemed that the Bank
could not even die with dignity and honor.

The three commissioners, whose job under the amended charter was
to collect the Bank's assets and repay the depositors, were appointed
by the trustees on the day before the Bank closed. At first the appointees, Robert Purvis, John A. J. Creswell, and R. H. T. Leipold, seemed
unexceptionable. All were of high social position, excellent business
reputation, and commanding influence. Purvis was a distinguished
abolitionist and black leader from Philadelphia and the father of trustee
Dr. Charles Purvis; Creswell was a former postmaster general and a
skilled lawyer who was regarded as a friend of the freedmen; Leipold
was an expert accountant from the Treasury Department.[40] Their duties
were enormous. In addition to liquidating the Bank's assets and reimbursing the depositors, they also were instructed to repay as soon as
possible the special deposits (those made after June 20, 1874), to
ascertain the true condition of the Bank, and to reduce the company's
expenses by discharging the employees and closing the branches.[41]

The commissioners first attempted to prepare an accurate financial
statement—which, as they soon realized, was not easy.

> . . . the magnitude of the undertaking, the extent and diversified charac-
> ter of the company's affairs, the number of branches at which almost
> a separate and distinct banking business had been carried on, the de-
> fective system of book-keeping and the general confusion of accounts at
> some branches, soon convinced us that the preparation of such a state-
> ment would be a work of great difficulty.[42]

Preparation of the report, which included summaries of financial conditions at individual branches and schedules of loans and securities, took

39. See below, pp. 210–211, 216–221.
40. *Report of the Commissioners,* 1874, pp. 1–2; Langston, *From the Virginia
Plantation to the National Capitol,* p. 345; *Dictionary of American Biography,* II,
541–542; Fleming, *Freedmen's Savings Bank,* pp. 101–102. Not everyone was
pleased with the choice of these men. The *Savannah Morning News* (July 13, 1874,
p. 2) editorialized that they, like most radicals, have a "constitutional inaptitude
for finance."
41. *Report of the Commissioners,* 1874, pp. 1–2.
42. *Ibid.,* p. 4.

six months. Eventually the commissioners were able to show that the company was likely to suffer greater losses than anyone had anticipated, and that the Bank probably would not pay anything like 93 cents on the dollar.[43] Said the *New York Times*: "Altogether, the report gives a very bad account of the affairs of the bank, and its exhibit is so unfavorable that it seems impossible that more than fifty or sixty per cent will ever be realized by the creditors of the bank, and some years will be required to collect and distribute even so much as that."[44]

The commissioners began to call in the loans, almost all of which were overdue in principal and interest, and institute suits against those who proved obstinate.[45] The company's debtors, declared the Bank's attorney, "seem to think that the Freedman's Bank is bursted, and that they may as well get clear of it as anybody else."[46] The commissioners gradually took possession of a great deal of real estate, most of which had been grossly overpriced. Attempting to sell their real estate security at pre-panic prices in a declining market, the commissioners found few buyers and soon realized that with prices so low it was almost useless to try to sell.[47] For example, at public auction they received an offer of only $105,000 for the bank building.[48] Burdened with property, the failed Bank turned into an unsuccessful real estate company, and the commissioners had to delay their first dividend for seventeen months. The delay occasioned further anxiety and suffering.

The commissioners were not immediately able to reduce the company's staggering expenses. Because of the inaccuracy of the ledgers, caused by years of sloppy bookkeeping at the central office and the branches, they had to rely upon the depositors' passbooks to determine the Bank's liabilities. At each branch the cashier was ordered to verify the depositors' accounts and send the results to Washington.[49] The branches, thus still having an essential function, remained open for several months, and their substantial expenses continued even though the number of employees was reduced. Not until October 31 were the

43. *New York Times*, March 13, 1875, p. 1.
44. *Ibid.*, December 15, 1874, p. 4.
45. *Ibid.*; *Evening Star*, December 15, 1874, p. 1; Committee on Banking and Currency, *Freedman's Savings and Trust Company*, 1875, p. 7.
46. *Freedman's Bank*, House, 1876, p. 168.
47. Sperry to Mr. Blackburn, August 20, 1874, p. 162, Sperry Letters, Official Correspondence, FS&T Co.; "Great Bargains in Real Estate," Letters Rec'd by the Commissioners, 1870–1914, FS&T Co.; *New York Times*, December 15, 1874, p. 4; *Report of the Select Committee*, Senate, 1880, p. 38.
48. *New York Times*, June 24, 1877, p. 7.
49. *Evening Star*, December 15, 1874, p. 1; Committee on Banking and Currency, *Freedman's Savings and Trust Company*, 1875, pp. 4, 6–7.

branches closed, but even then agents were kept on in certain cities at nominal fees which totaled $2,600 for the month of December, 1874.[50]

The three commissioners had incurred criticism from the moment of their appointment. Some observers, such as John Mercer Langston, foreseeing the expense of the commission plan, had wanted to employ one official instead of three.[51] Others were slowly disillusioned by the commissioners' failure to pay a dividend promptly; later, the quarreling of the commissioners, the abrasive personality of Leipold and the feeling that he harbored anti-Negro sentiments contributed to the general dissatisfaction with the Bank's three appointees. But their generous salaries, totaling $9,000 a year, occasioned the most widespread censure.[52]

In 1875 Congress discussed a bill designed to limit expenses by substituting one official for the three-member commission. The bill was defeated, perhaps because of the arguments of black Congressman Joseph H. Rainey, a former depositor. Rainey, fearing fraud or mismanagement, was opposed to giving one man sole control over the company's assets. "I do not care who he is, whether he be colored or white, whether he be a German or an Irishman, it makes no difference to me. I want no one man to handle the assets of that bank."[53] Five years later the excessive costs of the three commissioners overrode Rainey's argument.

That the suspicions of the commissioners' handling of the Bank's affairs were well founded became evident in 1880, when a select committee of the Senate, chaired by Blanche K. Bruce, black senator from Mississippi, published a report. The committee revealed that the six-year cost of winding up the Bank had been $335,994.77, which was deducted, of course, from the depositors' dividends. There were heavy expenditures for advertising, maintenance of buildings and property,

50. *Evening Star*, August 8, 1874, p. 4; August 12, 1874, p. 1; *New York Times*, October 6, 1874, p. 1; Commissioners to the branches, July 18, 1874, pp. 30–33, Official Correspondence, I, FS&T Co.; Commissioners to Henry Montgomery, July 18, 1874, pp. 34–36, *ibid.*; Commissioners to the branches, September 21, 1874, p. 30, *ibid.*, II; pay roll of Commissioners of the Freedman's Savings and Trust Company, December 1874, Letters Rec'd by the Commissioners, 1870–1914, FS&T Co.; Committee on Banking and Currency, *Freedman's Savings and Trust Company*, 1875, pp. 6–7.
51. *From the Virginia Plantation to the National Capitol*, p. 344.
52. *New York Times*, September 15, 1877, p. 5; U.S., *Congressional Record*, 45th Cong., 2nd sess., February 25, 1878, p. 1312; *ibid.*, 46th Cong., 2nd sess., February 21, 1881, p. 1519; *Freedman's Bank*, House, 1876, pp. 117, 163–164, 166; *Report of the Select Committee*, Senate, 1880, pp. 62–63, 65, 74–75.
53. U.S., *Congressional Record*, 43rd Cong., 2nd sess., March 3, 1875, p. 2262.

taxes, office costs, and litigation. Almost $150,000 had gone for salaries of the commissioners and their agents and for attorneys' fees. Clearly the cost of winding up the Bank was unconscionable. The Senate committee discovered that Purvis and Creswell had each paid Leipold $500 to perform some of their work; it appears that Purvis and Creswell had lent their names to bring confidence and respect to the work of the commissioners, while Leipold performed most of the labor. The Bruce committee concluded that "if this expensive machinery were ever needed or expedient it is no longer so," and recommended passage of a bill to replace the commissioners.[54] Many critics commented on the commissioners with less restraint. William Wells Brown, a renowned fugitive slave who became an abolitionist and author, accused the three appointees of continuing an old Bank policy—that of pocketing the depositors' money. "Not satisfied with robbing the deluded people out of the bulk of their hard earnings, commissioners were appointed soon after the failure, with 'appropriate' salaries, to look after the interest of the depositors, and these leeches are eating up the remainder."[55] In 1881 Congress abolished the commission and turned over the affairs of the company to the comptroller of the currency, who was to conclude the Bank's business as speedily as possible.[56] Many blacks probably lost the last shred of trust in business ethics in this final episode of Bank mismanagement.

It took nine years, from 1874 until 1883, for the commissioners and then the comptroller of the currency to realize upon the assets of the defunct company and pay the depositors a substantial amount of their savings. Not until November 1, 1875, could the commissioners announce that the Bank would pay its first dividend: in this installment each depositor would receive 20 percent of his total deposits.[57] By newspaper advertisement, public circular, and letters to Negro ministers in the branch cities the commissioners informed the depositors of the event which they had expected momentarily for seventeen months.[58] To re-

54. *Report of the Select Committee*, Senate, 1880, pp. xi, 44–46, 50; *New York Times*, December 26, 1878, p. 4; U.S., *Congressional Record*, 46th Cong., 2nd sess., June 12, 1880, p. 4462; U.S., Congress, House, Committee on Ways and Means, *Freedman's Savings and Trust Company*, 46th Cong., 2nd sess., 1880, House Report No. 1571, pp. 1–2; *Annual Report of the Commissioner of the Freedman's Savings and Trust Company for the Year Ending December 1, 1883*, House, 1883, p. 16.
55. William Wells Brown, *My Southern Home*, 3rd ed. (Boston: A. G. Brown & Co., 1882), p. 201.
56. Fleming, *Freedmen's Savings Bank*, p. 123.
57. *Annual Report of the Commissioner*, House, 1883, p. 14.
58. *Colored Tribune* (Savannah), December 4, 1875, p. 2; *Report of the Select*

ceive his money, each depositor had to mail his passbook with return
address to Washington. The response at first seemed great: 1,500 to
2,000 books per day arrived from all over the country, and the commissioners set about writing the checks, a process which took approximately two months of steady work.[59] In all, the commissioners and the
comptroller of the currency declared five dividends, which paid off 62
percent of the Bank's indebtedness.[60]

By 1881, after the Bank had paid three dividends amounting to 40
percent, the funds seemed to be exhausted;[61] that the company paid
a fourth dividend the next year was due to congressional intervention.
In February, 1881, Congress barred all claims not made within six
months after the announcement of a dividend, and the money from
these barred claims served as a partial basis for a fourth dividend.[62] The
rest of the money for this dividend materialized when in early 1882 the
government decided to purchase the Bank building and adjacent property for $250,000. This was no philanthropic gesture: the government,
already renting the upper stories of the Freedman's Bank building, was
notoriously short of office space, and since investigative reports revealed that the building's construction had cost from $258,000 to
$325,000, congressmen believed they were purchasing a necessity at a
bargain price.[63] The government looked after its own interests and in-
cidentally helped the depositors receive another 15 percent of their
money.

Although the commissioners had spoken as if they were deluged
with deposit books, only 29,996 depositors of an eligible 61,131 sent
in their passbooks for the first dividend, and the statistics showed that

Committee, Senate, 1880, pp. 6, 7; U.S., Congress, Senate, *Report of the Commissioner of the Freedman's Savings and Trust Company*, 47th Cong., 1st sess., 1881,
Senate Miscellaneous Document No. 17, p. 7; circular from R. H. T. Leipold, August 21, 1880, Letters Rec'd from the Commissioners, 1870–1914, FS&T Co.

59. *New York Times*, November 4, 1875, p. 5; *Report of the Commissioner*, House,
1883, p. 15.

60. *Report of the Commissioner*, House, 1883, p. 14.

61. *Ibid.*, p. 6.

62. *Ibid.*

63. *New York Times*, February 13, 1878, p. 3; *Report of the Commissioner*,
Senate, 1881, pp. 12, 13; U.S., Congress, House, Committee on Banking and Cur-
rency, *The Freedman's Savings and Trust Company*, 47th Cong., 1st sess., 1882,
House Report No. 336, p. 1; Committee on Banking and Currency, *Freedman's
Savings and Trust Company*, 1875, p. 3; U.S., *Congressional Record*, 45th Cong.,
2nd sess., February 12, 1878, pp. 955–956; *ibid.*, 47th Cong., 1st sess., February 6,
1882, p. 911; *ibid.*, 47th Cong., 1st sess., March 8, 1882, pp. 1723–25. Senator
Blanche K. Bruce had been instrumental in arranging the purchase; *ibid.*, 46th
Cong., 2nd sess., April 2, 1880, p. 2053.

these were the wealthier depositors. To these depositors the commissioners paid $555,360.08 or, on the average, $18.51. Approximately 31,000 depositors—a majority—failed to request their dividends, which totaled only $32,624.96, or an average of $1.05 each.[64] The first dividend set the pattern for succeeding ones; each year the number of claimants declined, so that after the final dividend was paid in 1883, less than 18,000 depositors had received the full 62 percent.[65] Table 13 shows the number of claimants and the amounts paid for the five dividends.

Many holders of small balances collected little or nothing. Some died; some lost interest; some moved away and could not be located by Bank officials. Others concluded that the first dividend was all that the Bank would pay. Some depositors refused to mail their passbooks to Washington; having been deceived once, they were unwilling to surrender the only evidence of their bank account.[66] Furthermore, frequent swindles made the depositors overly cautious.[67] Many inexperienced depositors were unfamiliar with even simple business routine—some claimants, for example, did not cash their dividend checks because they thought the nicely inscribed paper was a receipt for their passbook.[68] Others were deterred by tiresome legal intricacies. In the event of a depositor's death, the family had to appear before a justice of the peace to obtain an affidavit swearing that they were the deceased's legal heirs, and then they had to communicate with the commissioners or the comptroller— no easy task for uneducated ex-slaves. Changing one's name (through marriage, for example) necessitated a similar procedure, and white officials were not always responsive or sympathetic to inquiries. The cost of claiming a very small dividend might be prohibitive. Churches and societies, whose titles, membership, and officers could change from year to year, frequently had trouble obtaining their money.[69]

64. *Report of the Commissioner*, House, 1883, p. 14; Committee on Finance, *Interview of the Committee . . . Trenholm*, April 24, 1888, p. 9.

65. *Report of the Commissioner*, House, 1883, p. 14; *Interview of the Committee . . . Trenholm*, 1888, p. 9.

66. *Report of the Commissioners*, House, 1874, p. 4; *Interview of the Committee . . . Trenholm*, 1888, p. 6.

67. Commissioner William B. Ridgely to Postmaster, Nashville, Tenn., September 29, 1903, Official Correspondence, XXXI, FS&T Co.; A. M. Paxton & Co. to Commissioners, March 22, 1878; Matilda Mitchell to Commissioners, February 14, 1878, Letters Rec'd by the Commissioners, 1870–1914, FS&T Co. The official correspondence and the miscellaneous papers of the commissioners provide ample evidence of fraud against the claimants.

68. Commissioner Ridgely to Giles B. Jackson, February 4, 1907, Official Correspondence, XXXI, FS&T Co.

69. A. J. Stirling, Jr., to the Hon. J. A. J. Creswell & other Commissioners, November 9, 1875; Edward W. C. Humphrey to Commissioner, October 7, 1882;

TABLE 13. Dividends of the Freedman's Savings and Trust Company

Dividends	Per-cent	Total claims			Actual total payments				Unclaimed sums		
		Total no. of claims	Total amt. due	Av. amt. due each depositor	Actual no. of claims paid	Amt. paid	Average payment	No. of failures to claim money	Actual amt. unclaimed	Av. amt. un-claimed	
Nov. 1, 1875	20	61,131	$587,985.04	$9.62	29,996	$555,360.08	$18.51	31,135	$32,624.96	$1.05	
March 20, 1878	10	"	$293,992.52	$4.81	26,063	$267,653.33	$10.27	35,068	$26,339.19	$ .75	
Sept. 1, 1880	10	"	$293,992.52	$4.81	23,276	$259,067.66	$11.13	37,855	$34,924.86	$ .92	
June 1, 1882	15	"	$440,988.78	$7.21	21,344	$382,032.50	$17.90	39,787	$58,956.28	$1.48	
May 12, 1883	7	"	$205,794.76	$3.37	17,893	$166,286.72	$ 9.29	43,238	$39,508.04	$ .91	

SOURCE: *Report of the Commissioner*, 1883, p. 14.

Although the final dividend was paid in 1883, the affairs of the Bank were not concluded for many years. In the 1880's and 1890's the comptroller of the currency still collected sums due the company and provided Congress with annual financial reports. He also answered the voluminous correspondence from depositors and their relatives who inquired incessantly about future dividends.[70] In 1899 Congress removed the bar against those who had not originally claimed their money, and from then until 1919 dividends were paid to those who could prove with their passbook that they had not received the full 62 percent.[71] In the peak year of 1903 about $1,500 was paid, but after 1910 payments had dwindled to almost nothing—in 1918 the comptroller's office paid $2.49. The final report in 1919 showed that of $2,939,925.22 due depositors when the company failed, $1,733,475.71 had been repaid and only $1,153.66 remained to the Bank's credit in the United States Treasury.[72] The comptroller closed the Bank's account by paying $153.66 for clerical work and appropriating the remaining $1,000 as his salary.[73]

As early as the autumn of 1874, when it was becoming apparent that the Bank's assets were far too small to enable full repayment, the disgruntled depositors began to press the federal government to reimburse them out of the national treasury. A host of petitions asked Congress to recognize that the government had a moral if not a legal duty to save the freedmen from becoming the victims of a catastrophe

---

Joseph C. Calvert to J. W. Burke, November 13, 1882; letter to the Commissioner, February 10, 1883; John Medley, Richard Gray, & Jeremiah Pinckney to Commissioners; release of the dividends of Richmond Lodge of New Orleans to Ludie G. Polk, Letters Rec'd by the Commissioners, 1870–1914, FS&T Co.; Commissioner Ridgely to Miss Sylvia Thomas, August 19, 1903, Official Correspondence, XXXI, FS&T Co.

70. The correspondence is scattered throughout the records of the Freedman's Bank in the National Archives.

71. U.S., Congress, House, *Annual Report of the Commissioner of the Freedman's Savings and Trust Company*, 56th Cong., 1st sess., 1899, House Document No. 128, p. 7.

72. U.S., Congress, House, *Annual Report of the Commissioner of the Freedman's Savings and Trust Company*, 66th Cong., 2nd sess., 1919, House Document No. 499, pp. 1, 2; "Report of Funds in Freedman's Savings and Trust Company from December 1900 to Present Date"; Commissioner of FS&T Co. to the Hon. T. P. Kane, Deputy Comptroller of the Currency, November 29, 1920, Letters Rec'd by the Commissioners, 1870–1914, FS&T Co.; Cole, *Development of Banking*, p. 346.

73. "Annual Report of the Commissioner for the Year Ended December 1, 1920," Letters Rec'd by the Commissioners, 1870–1914, FS&T Co. The comptroller was entitled to a salary of $1,000 per year for his Bank work, but he had had no compensation in the previous seven years.

which was not of their making. From Charleston, Nashville, Richmond, Baltimore, Lexington, Louisville, and Wilmington came pleas for federal assumption of the Bank's debts.[74]

The depositors called Congress's attention to the Bank's misleading advertising, which had contrived in many ways to convey the impression that the Bank was an official governmental institution. Both explicitly and implicitly Bank officials had led depositors to believe that their deposits were guaranteed by the credit of the U.S. government. In addition, the government had failed to live up to the terms of its own legislation, since it had neglected to carry out the charter-prescribed inspections of the books. The Nashville depositors' petition neatly summarized the issues:

> . . . the principal, and in fact *the effective*, argument used by the managers and agents of the institution to induce that poor, unlettered, and trusting class to deposit their small earnings—the fruit of their toil—in the institution was, that it was an institution chartered by the Government, with its principal office at the seat of Government, and that its funds, by express direction of Congress, (which the class appealed to believed was a guarantee by *Congress*) were to be invested in Government securities. It is easy to see that the colored people, for whose benefit Congress chartered this institution, would readily conclude that the Government was bound or under some pledge which secured their deposits. This may not be the law of the case, but it is certain that such representations were made by the agents of the institution, and that the people who placed their deposits in the bank believed that the Government was bound for the deposits.[75]

For many years the depositors, encouraged by Frederick Douglass's support, continued to hope for federal payments, and every sign of congressional interest evoked another sheaf of petitions.[76] Certainly Congress's persistent curiosity about the history of the Bank encouraged these hopes.

At the insistence of southern Democrats and the Negro members of Congress, two congressional investigations explored the Bank's activities and its failure. In 1876 a politically motivated House investigating committee, composed of B. B. Douglas, chairman and Democrat from Virginia; Taul Bradford, Democrat from Alabama; W. S. Stenger, Democrat from Pennsylvania; H. Y. Riddle, Democrat from Tennessee; Charles E. Hooker, Democrat from Mississippi; J. H. Rainey, a Negro

74. Committee on Banking and Currency, *Freedman's Savings and Trust Company*, pp. 4–11.

75. *Ibid.*, pp. 4–5.

76. For Douglass's position, see Foner, *Life and Writings*, IV, 387–388, 534.

Republican from South Carolina; and Rufus S. Frost, Republican from Massachusetts, reported on the causes of the Freedman's Bank's failure. With only Rufus Frost dissenting on minor points, the committee concluded that the Bank had been little more than an enormous swindle. This "new confidence game called the Freedman's Bank" had been the brainchild of the "friends of the Negro." The poor freedmen, the report asserted, were a people "almost literally stabbed under the fifth rib with a hug and the salutation 'How is it with thee to-day, my brother?' " The summary was equally vituperative: "It is believed that if not originally conceived in fraud it will be easy to discern how naturally it degenerated into a monstrous swindle and justifies a suspicion that it was, almost from the start, merely a scheme of selfishness under the guise of philanthropy, and to its confiding victims an incorporate body of false pretenses."[77]

In 1880 Senator Blanche K. Bruce secured the appointment of a Senate committee to inquire into all aspects of the Freedman's Savings Bank. Because Bruce was the chief backer of the inquiry, he was appointed chairman. Other members were Angus Cameron, Republican from Wisconsin; John B. Gordon, Democrat from Georgia; Robert E. Withers, Democrat from Virginia; and A. H. Garland, Democrat from Arkansas. The Bruce committee questioned the surviving Bank employees, examined the company's records, and investigated the work of the commissioners.[78] Though less aggressively biased than the House committee, the Bruce committee essentially covered the same ground. Both committees concentrated on bad loans, scandals, irregularities, and fraud. Concerned only with these limited objectives, the lengthy investigative reports—covering more than six hundred pages of testimony and documents—provide the principal published sources for the Bank's history, revealing more than enough damaging information to "prove" that the Freedman's Bank was fully as evil as its worst enemies maintained. The reports of the House committee and the Senate Select Committee are source books for the legend of the Freedman's Savings Bank.

Several congressmen responded to the committees' disclosures and the depositors' petitions by sponsoring bills to reimburse the depositors. Some congressmen were motivated by generous indignation, others by

77. *Freedman's Bank*, House, 1876, pp. i, x.
78. U.S., *Congressional Record*, 46th Cong., 1st sess., April 7, 1879, p. 286; *Report of the Select Committee*, Senate, 1880, p. xi and *passim*. When the Bruce Committee findings were disclosed the *New York Tribune* (May 28, 1880, p. 1) asserted that "the entire report is a straightforward statement of the facts, as ascertained by the investigation, without any attempt to produce a sensational document, and it reflects great credit upon Senator Bruce."

a desire to obtain black votes or to return a substantial sum of money to their home districts. Southern white representatives introduced relief bills in 1875, 1879 (two bills), 1881, and 1910. Two black congressmen—Senator Bruce in 1880 and Representative John R. Lynch in 1882—introduced bills for reimbursement, while Senator John Sherman presented bills which passed the Senate in 1887 and 1888.[79] None, however, became law.

Although the cause of reimbursement never had enough backing to sway both houses of Congress, it did win considerable support. Most of those favoring action argued that the government had a moral obligation concerning the Freedman's Bank. Senator Justin Morrill, for example, said in 1878 that since Congress ultimately was responsible for the company's management, some relief should be provided.[80] While the government had no legal obligation, said the House Committee on Education and Labor in discussing Congressman Lynch's bill, it was "morally and equitably" responsible to the Bank's creditors because of the circumstances connected with the company's inauguration and management. It would be embarrassing if not cruel to deny this assistance when the government enjoyed an overflowing treasury.[81]

In 1888 the House Committee on Banking and Currency declared that Congress had been derelict in its duty because it had never bothered to inspect the company's books and had amended the charter in 1870 "without the knowledge or consent of those who had entrusted their savings to its custody." The close connection with army officers and the Bureau, and the pictures, symbols, and quotations on the passbooks all suggested a governmental tie. "It seems plain," said the com-

79. *New York Times*, March 14, 1876, p. 4; "Resolutions of a convention of colored citizens held in Chatham County in the State of Georgia endorsing the Bill, . . ." 1880, records of the Committee on Ways and Means, Legislative Records, NA, RG 233; "Joint Resolution of the General Assembly of the State of Louisiana Relative to the Freedman's Savings Bank," 1880, *ibid.*; U.S., *Congressional Record*, 43rd Cong., 2nd sess., February 15, 1875, p. 1272; *ibid.*, 44th Cong., 1st sess., December 8, 1875, p. 186; *ibid.*, 45th Cong., 3rd sess., January 30, 1879, p. 850; *ibid.*, 46th Cong., 2nd sess., December 4, 1879, p. 27; *ibid.*, April 12, 1880, p. 2303; *ibid.*, 47th Cong., 1st sess., December 13, 1881, p. 106; *ibid.*, 60th Cong., 1st sess., March 3, 1908, p. 2851; *ibid.*, 47th Cong., 1st sess., May 15, 1882, p. 3946; Fleming, *Freedmen's Savings Bank*, pp. 127–128; U.S., Congress, House, Committee on Banking and Currency, *Reimbursement of Depositors of Freedman's Savings and Trust Company*, 61st Cong., 2nd sess., 1910, House Report No. 1282 (Private Calendar No. 532), pp. 18–19.

80. *New York Times*, December 6, 1878, p. 2.

81. U.S., Congress, House, Committee on Education and Labor, *Reimbursing Depositors of Freedman's Savings Bank*, 47th Cong., 2nd sess., 1883, House Report No. 1991, pp. 1–4; U.S., Congress, House, Committee on Banking and Currency, *Depositors of the Freedman's Savings and Trust Company*, 50th Cong., 1st sess., 1888, House Report No. 3139, pp. 1–2.

mittee, "that the honor of the Government became involved in this undertaking."[82]

Until 1890 every comptroller of the currency recommended passage of a relief bill. "The Government," said John Jay Knox in 1881, "has assumed a quasi-moral responsibility."[83] "Under such circumstances, with an overflowing Treasury, it would be little more than just for Congress to make an appropriation for the payment in full of all the creditors of the Freedman's Bank, instead of allowing them to lose 40 per cent. of the scanty means which they had deposited in an institution organized, as they believed, for their benefit, and some of whose branches were controlled by officers of the government."[84] In 1906 another comptroller again recommended reimbursement, pointing out the fact that in spite of the passage of thirty-two years, many applications for dividends and pathetic appeals for relief were still being received.[85]

Even President Grover Cleveland became concerned with the plight of the freedmen. In December, 1886, in his second annual message to Congress, he called attention to the "plain duty which the Government owes to the depositors" of the Freedman's Bank. Chartered by Congress for the benefit of "the most illiterate and humble of our people," the Bank, said Cleveland, was established to encourage industry and thrift. Since it was reasonable to assume that the Bank was a government enterprise, Cleveland argued that it was only fair to repay the remaining 38 percent, about $1,000,000.[86]

All this favorable sentiment never secured a nickel of federal money for reimbursement. In the late 1870's and 1880's the country was backing away from its commitments to the freedmen, and it was easy to find arguments to refute the depositors' case. Those who opposed reimbursement insisted that the government had no legal responsibility

82. House, Committee on Banking and Currency, *Depositors of the Freedman's Savings and Trust Company*, 1888, pp. 2–3.

83. U.S., Congress, House, *Annual Report of the Commissioner of the Freedman's Savings and Trust Company*, 49th Cong., 1st sess., 1885, House Miscellaneous Document No. 18, p. 12; U.S., Congress, House, *Annual Report of the Commissioner of the Freedman's Savings and Trust Company*, 51st Cong., 1st sess., 1889, House Miscellaneous Document No. 33, p. 10; U.S., Congress, House, *Annual Report of the Commissioner of the Freedman's Savings and Trust Company*, 59th Cong., 2nd sess., 1906, House Document No. 394, pp. 1–2.

84. *Report of the Commissioner*, Senate, 1881, p. 13.

85. *Annual Report of the Commissioner of the Freedman's Savings and Trust Company*, House, 1906, pp. 1–2.

86. J. D. Richardson, ed., *Compilation of the Messages and Papers of the Presidents, 1789–1897*, 53rd Cong., 2nd sess., 1907, House Miscellaneous Document No. 210, pts. 1–10, 10 vols. (Washington, D.C.: Government Printing Office, 1907), VIII, 528.

in the matter; it had never directed or authorized its officers to act as agents of the company.[87] A minority report of the Committee on Education and Labor in 1883 denied that the government should guarantee "ignorant investors against the results of their business incapacity or the incapacity or dishonesty of their agents."[88] Alarmists predicted that to repay the depositors of this defunct bank would provoke endless demands by the depositors of other insolvent banks. Others believed that the government had already, with genuine liberality, provided sufficient relief by purchasing the bank building. Many no doubt felt that a 62 percent refund was an adequate settlement—one which would be gladly accepted by thousands of white depositors who had lost large sums in dubious banking schemes.[89] The reputed paternalism of a relief bill occasioned further criticism, as did the belief that speculators instead of former depositors would be benefited by reimbursement.[90]

The government's refusal to shoulder the Bank's debts must have been a sickening disappointment to the freedmen. Shocked by the Bank's failure, enraged by the revelations of the management's frauds, and disgusted by the commissioners' apparent mismanagement of the receivership, the depositors finally found appeals to the United States government, their last resort, quite fruitless. It is tempting to indulge in the somewhat heartless speculation that it would have been better all around if the Bank's affairs had been wound up in a year or two at whatever cost to the depositors. A straight, once-and-for-all monetary loss might have been less scarring than the interminable decades of promises and disappointments, the hopes raised only to be dashed. Thousands of pathetic letters and petitions, accumulating in the files of government offices and politicians over half a century, express the heartbreak.[91] In 1910 a congressional hearing on a bill to reimburse the depositors revealed just how little the intervening years had diminished the sense of sadness, disillusionment, bitterness, and outrage that had

87. *Reimbursing Depositors of Freedman's Savings Bank*, House, 1883, pt. 2, pp. 1–2; U.S., Congress, House, Committee on Banking and Currency, Views of the Minority, *To Reimburse Depositors of the Late Freedman's Savings and Trust Company*, 60th Cong., 1st sess., 1908, House Report No. 1637, pt. 2, pp. 1–2.

88. *Reimbursing Depositors of Freedman's Savings Bank*, House, 1883, pt. 2, pp. 1–2.

89. *Ibid.*

90. *Ibid.*; U.S., *Congressional Record*, 49th Cong., 2nd sess., February 26, 1887, pp. 2323–28.

91. These letters are scattered throughout the records of the commissioners of the Bank in the National Archives. See also "Petitions on Legislation to Secure the Savings of Depositors in the Freedmen's Savings and Trust Company," 1880, records of the Committee on Ways and Means, Legislative Records, NA, RG 233. Other petitions are in the *Congressional Record* of January and February, 1880.

attended the Bank's closing. It was as though the Bank had failed only recently, not thirty-six years ago.[92] Petitions again flooded Congress, and former depositors traveled from Richmond, Augusta, and Tennessee to urge Congress to act. One petition, voicing the support of thousands of Negroes, was endorsed by the National Baptist Convention, the African Methodist Episcopal Zion Church, the National Negro Business League, and other organizations whose names covered over twelve pages.[93] Appeals continued even into the 1920's. One woman wrote to President Warren G. Harding that her late husband had appealed for relief to president after president, but the replies, though encouraging, always proved unproductive. Still hopeful of "getting back the money he labored so hard to earn and saved in vain," she pleaded, "I, his widow, am in sore need of the money this rich country is withholding from a poor citizen."[94] Another letter to Harding said, "Mr. President I pray you to consider us old People after all these years our best life spent in slavery And sir our Bal of 38 per ¢ coming to us now in our old age Would be a God send to us old one who lives after all these years. . . . we still believe that help will come though all these years Just asking for what we worked for." A postscript concluded the letter: "I am writing this my self not a days schooling."[95]

Founded to encourage saving and economic enterprise, the Freedman's Bank left an entirely different legacy. Observers of every type recorded their impression that many black depositors and their friends, who had accepted the maxims of work and thrift, lost faith in frugality and accumulation as a means toward improvement. The New Orleans *Louisianian* doubted whether blacks could ever again be persuaded to be frugal, and in 1879 it declared that the Bank's failure "has caused on the part of our people, not only a feeling of distrust for other moneyed corporations, but has created a feeling of apathy in regard to saving and intensified the desire to spend in a round of pleasure, the earnings of a week, after the expenses of the household have been met!"[96] *Banker's Magazine* reported that depositors became disheart-

---

92. House, Committee on Banking and Currency, *Hearings*, 1910, *passim*.

93. *Ibid.*, p. 17; Papers concerning the Freedman's Bank, Committee on Banking and Currency, 61st Cong., Legislative Records, NA, RG 233; Petitions concerning S 48, Papers of the Committee on Education and Labor, 60th Cong., 1st sess., Legislative Records, NA, RG 233.

94. Mary M. Brown to President Harding, December 19, 1921, Letters Rec'd by the Commissioners, 1870–1914, FS&T Co.

95. Henry L. Thomas to President Harding, March 27, 1921, *ibid.*

96. Cited in John W. Blassingame, *Black New Orleans* (Chicago: University of Chicago Press, 1973), pp. 67, 68.

ened and discouraged. "Many of them, it is said, have ceased to save, and are spending their earnings as fast as they get them. Thus disastrously has resulted Mr. Sumner's philanthropic scheme to teach the colored wards of the nation the virtues of economy and forethought, which are so essential to their new position as free citizens."[97] The banking expert Emerson W. Keyes concluded in 1876 that only if the government reimbursed the depositors in full could the memory and the consequences of the failure be erased.[98] A "paralysing effect upon the blacks everywhere" was the way William Wells Brown described the effects of failure.[99] Although he exaggerated the consequences, Brown accurately conveyed the sense of disgust, disillusionment, and desperation felt by so many.

> Large numbers quit work; the greater portion sold their bankbooks for a trifle, and general distrust prevailed throughout the community. Many who had purchased small farms, or cheap dwellings in cities and towns, and had paid part of the purchase money, now became discouraged, surrendered their claims, gave up the lands, and went about as if every hope was lost. It was their first and their last dealing with a bank.[100]

And in 1890 John Mercer Langston recognized the still harmful results of that sudden collapse:

> Perhaps the failure of no institution in the country, however extended its relations, however generally it enjoyed popular confidence and popular patronage, has ever wrought larger disappointment and more disastrous results . . . than . . . the Freedmen's [*sic*] Savings and Trust Company. Nor was there ever found in the population of any, at any time, under any circumstances, persons who could so ill afford to be thus disappointed. . . . The day is distant even now when they will lose entirely their sense of disappointment and their consciousness of loss in its failure.[101]

As late as the 1890's and 1900's the Bank's failure probably had deleterious effects on black economic enterprise, although this impact cannot be measured with exactness. True, there were other important obstacles to the rise of black businesses, but the near unanimity of contemporaries concerning the disastrous effect of the failure, and the fact that the Bank was still a live issue in black communities for thirty

97. "The Freedman's Savings Bank," *Banker's Magazine*, XXIX (June, 1875), 939.
98. Keyes, *History of Savings Banks*, II, 564.
99. Brown, *My Southern Home*, p. 200.
100. *Ibid.*
101. Langston, *From the Virginia Plantation to the National Capitol*, p. 345.

or forty years, suggest that the Bank's failure cannot be ignored in assessing the difficulties faced by the black businessman.

Historian Abram Harris in an important book, *The Negro as Capitalist*, dissented from this interpretation. He was impressed that in 1888, only fourteen years after the failure, blacks in Richmond and Washington established their own banks, and on this evidence he concluded that the failure had not resulted in a damaging legacy.[102] Many black historians and commentators did not share Harris's belief.[103] A fourteen-year hiatus in black banking in Richmond and Washington seemed to indicate that the failure had stunned and discouraged the black community. In none of the other branch cities were black banks established until after 1900—twenty-six years after the failure,[104] despite the fact that black communities in such cities as Washington, Richmond, Charleston, Savannah, Philadelphia, New Orleans, Nashville, and Louisville were fully capable of sustaining a flourishing bank on the very day the Freedman's Savings Bank closed. Evidence, though scanty, indicates that when banking did revive, the depositors at first did not patronize these banks as they had the Freedman's Bank in the early 1870's. At Charleston in 1886, Negroes had $125,000 on deposit in the only (white) banks available, as opposed to $350,000 in the Charleston branch in 1873.[105] In 1907 the relatively new black savings banks at Nashville, Memphis, Natchez, Vicksburg, Columbus (Mississippi), and Jacksonville contained deposits much smaller than those held by the respective branches of the Freedman's Bank in the 1870's.[106] While it may be unfair to compare these new black enterprises with the Freedman's Bank in its greatest period, it seems clear that the later bankers had to contend with a less enthusiastic clientele. The early history of

102. Harris, *Negro as Capitalist*, pp. 42–44. E. Franklin Frazier's interpretation follows Harris closely. See *The Negro in the United States*, rev. ed. (Toronto: Macmillan, 1957), p. 391, and *Black Bourgeoisie* (New York: Free Press, 1957), pp. 37–38.

103. See, among others, Benjamin Brawley, *A Short History of the American Negro* (New York: Macmillan, 1913), pp. 126–127; Taylor, *Negro in Tennessee*, p. 164; Quarles, *Frederick Douglass*, p. 270; Asa Gordon, *Sketches of Negro Life and History in South Carolina*, 2nd ed. (1929; reprinted, Columbia: University of South Carolina Press, 1971), pp. 152–153.

104. W. E. B. Du Bois, ed., *Economic Co-operation among Negro Americans* (Atlanta: Atlanta University Press, 1907), p. 138; Booker T. Washington, *The Negro in Business* (Boston: Hertel, Jenkins, & Co., 1907), p. 110.

105. *News and Courier*, May 7, 1886, p. 4; George Brown Tindall, *South Carolina Negroes, 1877–1900* (Columbia: University of South Carolina Press, 1952), p. 142.

106. Du Bois, *Economic Co-operation among Negro Americans*, pp. 136–138; Richmond is an exception. By 1907 the business of the savings banks of Richmond had surpassed that of the old branch of the Freedman's Bank.

Nashville's One-Cent Savings Bank and Trust Company, which had as its primary goal the establishment of confidence in black institutions, supports this conclusion. In 1913, on the ninth anniversary of the bank's opening, its first president spoke about the persistent distrust among Tennessee blacks: "Some of the elder citizens still living remember and often refer to the lamented calamity of the so-called Freedman's Savings bank. They have transmitted this lamented tradition to their children. And for years throughout the length and breadth of the State of Tennessee, and many other parts of the South, whenever a Negro banking institution was referred to the cry was always raised by them . . . 'Remember the Freedmen's Bank.' "[107]

For blacks the failure of the Freedman's Bank was a denial of the American promise. It ruined the hopes of thousands and cast doubt upon their ability to achieve social and economic status in white America. Ironically, the freedmen had accepted the philanthropists' panaceas and had made the Bank a success by working and saving in order to earn the rewards of middle-class America. The record of the Bank in the branch communities shows that the heritage of slavery was not all-pervasive, and that the transition from slavery to a secure economic position need not have been delayed so long.

Black leaders as diverse as Booker T. Washington and W. E. B. Du Bois agreed upon the tragic impact of the Freedman's Bank. Du Bois believed that the Bank's corruption and mismanagement had widespread influence in discouraging the saving habit, and that it was difficult to overestimate the psychological effects of the failure.[108] In 1903 he wrote:

> Then in one sad day came the crash,—all the hard-earned dollars of the freedmen disappeared; but that was the least of the loss,—all the faith in saving went too, and much of the faith in men; and that was a loss that a Nation which to-day sneers at Negro shiftlessness has never yet made good. Not even ten additional years of slavery could have done so much to throttle the thrift of the freedmen as the mismanagement and bankruptcy of the series of savings banks chartered by the Nation for their especial aid.[109]

And in 1909 Washington, who like Du Bois was then promoting the development of black business, said of the freedmen:

107. Cited in Lester C. Lamon, "Negroes in Tennessee, 1900–1930," Ph.D. dissertation, University of North Carolina 1971, p. 227.
108. W. E. B. Du Bois, *Black Reconstruction* (New York: Russell & Russell, 1935), p. 600.
109. W. E. B. Du Bois, *The Souls of Black Folk* (1903; reprinted, Greenwich, Conn.: Fawcett Publications, 1970), p. 39.

When they found that they had lost, or been swindled out of all their little savings, they lost faith in savings banks, and it was a long time after this before it was possible to mention a savings bank for Negroes without some reference being made to the disaster of the Freedman's Bank. The effect of this disaster was the more far-reaching because of the wide extent of territory which the Freedmen's [*sic*] Bank covered through its agencies.[110]

The collapse left a legacy of suspicion and failure which carried into the twentieth century. When Washington and Du Bois and others spoke of black economic enterprise, the legacy of the Freedman's Bank was still very real for black Americans in many southern communities.

110. Booker T. Washington, *The Story of the Negro* (New York: Doubleday, Page & Co., 1909), II, 214.

Appendix A
Founders of the Freedman's Savings and Trust Company, January 27, 1865

Peter Cooper, manufacturer, inventor, and philanthropist, and William Cullen Bryant, poet, editor of the New York *Evening Post*, and abolitionist, were the best known. Abraham Baldwin, R. R. Graves, Walter T. Hatch, and A. S. Hatch were engaged in business and owned or directed their own companies. A. S. Barnes was a publisher who was much involved in railroad, banking, and insurance ventures; Hiram Barney was a well-known attorney, Republican politician, and collector of the Port of New York. Others excelled in various professions, businesses, or social services: Charles Collins was a dry-goods commission merchant and ruling elder of the Madison Square Presbyterian Church; Thomas Denny, banker, lawyer, and founder of the Society for Improving the Condition of the Poor; Walter S. Griffith, merchant and president of the Home Life Insurance Company; E. A. Lambert, Commission merchant and president of the Craftsmen's Life Insurance Company; Roe Lockwood, book merchant and formerly a member of the New York Kansas (free-soil) League; R. H. Manning, merchant and abolitionist; R. W. Ropes (probably one of the Ropes brothers, either Reuben or Ripley, merchants and philanthropists); A. H. Wallis, lawyer and educator; and the Reverend George Whipple, secretary of the American Missionary Association. The remaining four members (excluding John Alvord) were William Allen, S. B. Caldwell, W. G. Lambert, and Albert Woodruff. For biographical sources, see the *Dictionary of American Biography; National Cyclopedia of American Biography; Appleton's Cyclopedia of American Biography; New York Times*; Philip S. Foner, *Business and Slavery* (Chapel Hill: University of North Carolina Press, 1941); *Freedman's Savings and Trust Company* (pamphlet), 1865; and Journal, January 12, 1872.

Appendix B
A Note on Branch Banking

Branch banking in the United States dated from the establishment of the First Bank of the United States in 1791, and proved successful during the Bank's twenty-year existence. At one time the Second Bank of the United States had twenty-five branches in operation. Before the Civil War, branch banking was common in most states, except for those in the Northeast. In 1848 there were twenty-seven banks averaging 5.3 branches. The State Bank of Ohio, for example, had thirty-six branches, although it had no central bank and its so-called branches were practically independent. In South Carolina and other southern states the modern type of branch system emerged; branches were strictly controlled and were conducted primarily as agencies of a principal office. The Freedman's Bank system was to reflect the pattern of branching typical in the ante-bellum South.

After the Civil War, however, branch banking was practically nonexistent. Some of the southern systems had been destroyed by the Civil War and Reconstruction turmoil. In other cases, writes Shirley Donald Southworth, "the state authorities chose to dissolve the state institutions rather than to allow their conversion into national banks." The North Carolina, South Carolina, and Tennessee systems disappeared in this way. In Indiana, Iowa, Ohio, and other northern states, branch banks entered the national banking system as separate banks. Only four or five branch banks—and these were all *intrastate* systems—survived the war; by 1890 there were hardly a dozen branches.

Branch banking ceased for a variety of reasons having little to do with branches per se. Two authorities on American banking structure have concluded that "branch banking had been killed by 'free banking' legislation, both state and national, by the spread of the bond-secured note scheme, by the prohibitory tax on state bank notes, by the decline in importance of the state banks and the rise of the national banks, and by the collapse of the South during and after the Civil War—a region where branch banking had been common." The decline of branching clearly had little to do with the fear of monopoly or centralization of capital. See John M. Chapman and Roy Westerfield, *Branch Banking* (New York: Harper & Bros., 1942), pp. 29–31, 47, 61; Shirley Donald Southworth, *Branch Banking in the United States* (New York: McGraw-Hill, 1928), pp. 6–7, 14, 22.

Appendix C
Cashiers of the Freedman's Savings and Trust Company

The cashiers are listed in the order of their employment at each branch bank. Where only one cashier is listed for a branch, it should be assumed that he served from the branch's organization until the Bank's failure. All cashiers have been included, though it is possible that one or two who served only briefly may have been omitted. The cashiers who played a prominent role in their branch's development, at least according to this writer's interpretation of bank records and letters, are marked with an asterisk. This does not necessarily imply that they were capable as cashiers or were entirely honest. A double asterisk indicates those branches which were closed before the Bank failed in July, 1874.

The sources for the cashiers' backgrounds are too numerous to list individually, but among the most important documents or collections of documents are the following: the two congressional investigations (*Freedman's Bank*, House, 1876; and *Report of the Select Committee*, Senate, 1880); *Report of the Commissioners*, 1874; the letters of John Alvord in the Freedmen's Bureau records; the letters of the Educational Division of the Freedmen's Bureau; the letters of the AMA; minute books of the Freedman's Bank; city directories; Richard Drake, "The American Missionary Association"; *Biennial Register: Register of Officers and Agents . . . in the Service of the United States*, I, 1865; II, 1867 (Washington: Government Printing Office, 1865, 1867); and *New Era* and *National Savings Bank*. Also, various books on blacks during Reconstruction were very helpful.

Branch	Cashier and year appointed	Race	Background and employment or associations
Alexandria, Va.**	Charles Whittlesey Fields Cook	White Black	Minister, Alexandria & Richmond; member of Republican State Convention in 1867
Atlanta, Ga. Jan., 1870	Philip D. Cory* C. S. Johnson (late 1873 or early 1874)	White Black	Congregational minister; AMA teacher Former assistant cashier at Augusta
Augusta, Ga. March, 1866	C. H. Prince David A. Ritter*	White Black	Native of Maine; state superintendent of education; Republican elected to Congress in 1868 Son of the Charleston cashier
Baltimore, Md. March, 1866	Nathaniel Noyes* Samuel Townsend* W. L. Van Derlip H. H. Webb (acting cashier)	White White White Black	Baltimore resident in 1860; owner of mercantile & law agency; AMA superintendent of schools Quaker; produce commission merchant; former chairman of advisory board
Beaufort, S.C. Oct., 1865	Nelson Scovel* William Lockwood	White White	Freedmen's Bureau agent; closely associated with AMA; temperance advocate Freedmen's Bureau official from North; later a Beaufort banker
Charleston, S.C. Jan., 1866	J. H. Jenks Nathan Ritter*	White White	Paid bounties under Bureau direction Aided the AMA but turned down a position with the association, because cashiership at Charleston was a full-time position; father of Augusta cashier
Chattanooga, Tenn. May, 1869	Rev. E. O. Tade*	White	Congregational minister; AMA principal of Howard School in Chattanooga
Columbia, Tenn. Jan., 1870	G. W. Blackburn*	White	

Location/Date	Name	Race	Description
Columbus, Miss. Aug, 1870	George W. VanHook	White	Principal of Columbus Union Academy (AMA); county superintendent of education for AMA
	J. N. Bishop*	White	
Houston, Texas**	- - Fayle	White	Presiding elder of the Methodist Episcopal Church, north
Huntsville, Ala. Dec., 1865	Lafayette Robinson*	Black	Free before the war; involved in Republican party
Jacksonville, Fla. Mar., 1866	N. C. Dennett	White	Paid bounty money for the Freedmen's Bureau
	Rev. William L. Coan*	White	Minister; assistant treasurer of Staunton Normal Institute (AMA); AMA missionary
	J. W. Swain	White	
Lexington, Ky. Nov., 1870	J. G. Hamilton*	White	AMA teacher; educated at Oberlin; helped build Sabbath schools; worked as Indian agent after Bank closed
Little Rock, Ark. Nov., 1870	William Colby*	White	Bureau superintendent of education
	A. J. Thompson	White	
Louisville, Ky. Sept., 1865	Dr. William H. Goddard (1865)	White	Dentist; resigned cashiership in 1866 because of insufficient time for the position
	Col. L. A. Porter (1866)	White	Worked closely with the Bureau; died in 1868
	H. H. Burkholder	White	
	Horace Morris* (1868 or 1869)	Black	Born and raised in Louisville; free before the war; steward on the river; educated in Ohio; worked in Underground Railroad; secretary of advisory board for colored schools in Louisville; former member of Louisville branch's advisory board
Lynchburg, Va. June, 1871	W. F. Bronaugh*	Black	Former bookkeeper at Washington; protested against discrimination
Macon, Ga. Oct., 1868	T. G. Stewart*	Black	
	Thomas N. M. Sellers* (1871)	Black	Pastor of one of the largest black churches in the city

Branch	Cashier and year appointed	Race	Background and employment or associations
Martinsburg, W.Va.**	H. H. Mathews	White	
Memphis, Tenn. Dec., 1865	A. L. Rankin	White	
	A. M. Sperry	White	Former major and paymaster in army; former agent of Freedman's Bank and later inspector
	N. D. Smith*	White	Very well acquainted with AMA teachers
Mobile, Ala. Jan., 1866	C. A. Woodward*	White	Paid bounty for Freedmen's Bureau; involved in temperance movement; involved in local politics as Republican; wrote history of the Bank (1869)
Montgomery, Ala.** June, 1870	Edwin Beecher*	White	From Illinois; former major and paymaster in army; Bureau assistant commissioner and superintendent of education; very cognizant of AMA school affairs
Nashville, Tenn. March, 1870	John J. Cary*	Black	Spent early years in Canada; teacher in Cincinnati in 1830's was John W. Alvord; trustee of Fisk University; chairman for Nashville's celebration of ratification of Fifteenth Amendment
Natchez, Miss. Oct., 1865	Fred Jordan	White	
	J. M. Hawksworth	Black	
New Bern, N.C. Jan., 1866	Edward Woag	White	
	A. A. Ellsworth* (1867)	White	Congregational minister from Maine
	C. A. Nelson	White	Harvard graduate; former Freedmen's Bureau clerk in Mississippi
	William Steward (1874)	Black	Probably pastor of a Negro church
New Orleans, La. Jan., 1866	C. S. Sauvinet*	Black	Creole who challenged racial discrimination in Reconstruction period; brought suits against civil rights violators; elected to position of civil sheriff; special agent for the Bureau
	C. D. Sturtevant* (1871)	White	Freedmen's Bureau clerk and businessman; probably from North
New York, N.Y. July, 1866	John J. Zuille*	Black	Worked on Underground Railroad; member of New York African Society for Mutual Relief

Location/Date	Name	Race	Description
Norfolk, Va. June, 1865	Jonathan Dickinson H. C. Percy* (1866–74 except for a brief period)	White White	New Englander; AMA superintendent of schools; temperance crusader; paid bounty for the Bureau; trustee of Hampton Institute (1870)
Philadelphia, Pa. Jan. 1870	William Whipper*	Black	Wealthy coal and wood merchant; active in antislavery movement; helped found the American Moral Reform Society; tried to promote Negro education, press, and history
Raleigh, N.C. Jan., 1868	G. W. Brodie*	Black	One of Alvord's pupils in Cincinnati in 1830's
Richmond, Va. Oct., 1865	Charles Spencer*	White	Born in England; Freedmen's Bureau clerk
Savannah, Ga. Jan., 1866	I. W. Brinckerhoff*	White	Congregational minister; agent for Bureau; author of a temperance pamphlet; aided AMA in Savannah
St. Louis, Mo. Nov., 1870	Willis N. Brent*	Black	Free before the war; in 1860, occupation was whitewasher
Shreveport, La. June, 1868	Samuel Peters* (1870–73)	Black	Not a Southerner; appointed by acting Governor P. B. S. Pinchback as division superintendent of education for Fourth Congressional District; died in 1873
	J. W. Purnell (acting cashier)	Black	Former Philadelphia bookkeeper
Tallahassee, Fla. Aug., 1866	F. W. Webster (1866–69) William Stewart (1870)	White Black	Involved in school affairs of AMA
Vicksburg, Miss. Dec., 1865	J. A. Hawley Benjamin Lee*	White White	Minister; former army chaplain and Bureau officer Captain in army; later mayor of Vicksburg; paid bounties for Bureau
Washington, D.C. Aug., 1865	William J. Wilson*	Black	Born and raised in Washington; worked in pay department of army in 1865; trustee of Howard University (1869); AMA teacher in Washington

Branch	Cashier and year appointed	Race	Background and employment or associations
Wilmington, N.C. Oct., 1868	Rev. S. S. Ashley*	White	Congregational minister; native of Maine; Oberlin graduate; worked in churches and schools; founder of Williston School in Wilmington (AMA)
	Rev. R. B. Hunt	White	Minister; member of AMA mission community
	B. G. Bryan (1870)	White	Former AMA teacher in Virginia
	Van D. Macumber	Not known	
	John A. Smythe (1873)	Black	Free before the war; educated in Philadelphia; entered Howard University Law School (1869); clerk in Freedmen's Bureau; clerk in government offices and the Freedman's Bank (1870–73); later entered politics in North Carolina; appointed minister resident and general consul to Liberia (1878)

Brief Summary of Occupational Backgrounds of Cashiers

	White	Black
Ministers	8	2
Teachers, principals, superintendents of education for AMA, Freedmen's Bureau, or state	11	2
Bureau workers (excluding teachers, principals, and superintendents)	14	2
AMA workers (excluding teachers, principals, and superintendents)	4	1
Cashiers who became involved in politics	3	3
Businessmen	3	1
Professional	1	0
Army personnel	4	1
Temperance workers	4	0

Note: It should be remembered that several cashiers had a variety of occupations and/or associations: a few of them were teachers and Bureau workers who had been in the army. The backgrounds of seventeen cashiers are unknown, while the backgrounds of others do not fit into any particular category. This is especially true of several black cashiers who were educated in the North and elected to certain honorary positions. At least three black cashiers (Whipper, Zuille, and Morris) had worked on the Underground Railroad.

Bibliography

PRIMARY SOURCES

ARCHIVAL MATERIALS AND MANUSCRIPTS

Alexander Shepherd Papers. Library of Congress.
Archives of the American Missionary Association. Amistad Research Center, Dillard University.
Blanche Kelso Bruce Papers. Moorland-Spingarn Collection, Howard University.
Christian Fleetwood Papers. Library of Congress.
Frederick Douglass MSS. Library of Congress.
Gerrit Smith Papers. Syracuse University Library.
Miscellaneous Documents Concerning the Freedman's Savings and Trust Company. Washingtoniana Collection, District of Columbia Public Library.
Miscellaneous Papers Relating to the Freedman's Savings and Trust Company. Legislative Records, Record Group 233, National Archives.
Oliver Otis Howard Papers. Bowdoin College Library.
Records of the Bureau of Refugees, Freedmen, and Abandoned Lands. Record Group 105, National Archives.
Records of the Freedman's Savings and Trust Company, 1865–1920. Record Group 101: Records of the Bureau of the Comptroller of the Currency, National Archives.

ARTICLES AND BOOKS

Alvord, John W. *Letters from the South Relating to the Condition of the Freedmen.* Washington: Howard University Press, 1870.
———. *Semi-Annual Reports on Schools and Finances for Freedmen, 1866–70.* 10 Reports. Washington: Government Printing Office, 1866–70.
"Banking and Financial Items." *Banker's Magazine,* XXIX (August, 1874), 154–161; XXIX (September, 1874), 234–240; XXIX (October, 1874), 315–319; XXIX (February, 1875), 641–646.
Barnes, Gilbert H., and Dumond, Dwight L., eds. *Letters of Theodore Dwight Weld, Angelina Grimké Weld, and Sarah Grimké 1822–1844.* New York: D. Appleton-Century Co., for American Historical Association, 1934.
Brown, William Wells, *My Southern Home.* 3rd ed. Boston: A. G. Brown & Co., 1882.

Douglass, Frederick. *Life and Times of Frederick Douglass.* 1892. Reprinted, New York: Macmillan, 1962.
Du Bois, W. E. B. *The Souls of Black Folk.* 1903. Reprinted, Greenwich, Conn.: Fawcett Publications, 1970.
"Five Years of Freedmen's Education as Seen in the Bureau Reports." *Freedmen's Record,* V, 7 (January, 1871), 91.
Foner, Philip S. *The Life and Writings of Frederick Douglass.* 4 vols. New York: International Publishers, 1955.
"The Freedman's Savings Bank." *Banker's Magazine,* XXIX (June, 1875), 936–939.
"The Freedmen's Savings." *Freedmen's Record,* IV, 2 (February, 1868), 22–23.
"Freedmen's Savings Bank." *Old and New,* II, 2 (August, 1870), 245–247.
Howard, General O. O. "The Freedmen's Savings Banks." *American Missionary,* XIII (November, 1869), 243–245.
Langston, John Mercer. *From the Virginia Plantation to the National Capitol.* Hartford: American Publishing Co., 1894.
Macrae, David. *The Americans at Home.* 2 vols. Edinburgh: Edmonston & Douglas, 1870.
Siegfried, Reverend W. D. *A Winter in the South.* Newark: Jennings Bros., 1870.
Somers, Robert. *The Southern States since the War, 1870–71.* New York: Macmillan, 1871.
"The South as It Is." *Nation,* I, 25 (December 21, 1865), 779–780.
"The Story of the Freedman's Bank." *Nation,* XX, 511 (April 15, 1875), 253–254.
"The Winding-Up of the Freedmen's Savings Bank." *Nation,* XX, 540 (November 4, 1875), 289–290.
Woodward, C. A. *Savings Banks: Their Origin, Progress and Utility, with a History of the National Savings Bank for Colored People.* Cleveland: Fairbanks, Benedict & Co., 1869.

GOVERNMENT PUBLICATIONS

Heitman, Francis B. *Historical Register and Dictionary of the United States Army.* 2 vols. Washington: Government Printing Office, 1903.
Register of Officers and Agents . . . in the Service of the United States 1865. Washington: Government Printing Office, 1865.
Richardson, J. D., ed. *Compilation of the Messages and Papers of the Presidents, 1789–1897.* 10 vols. (53rd Cong., 2nd sess., House Miscellaneous Document No. 210, Pts. 1–10). Washington: Government Printing Office, 1907.
U.S. Bureau of the Census. *Negro Population 1790–1915.* Washington: Government Printing Office, 1918.
———. *The Statistics of the Population of the United States.* Vol. I. 1870.
U.S. *Congressional Record.* Vols. I–XX.
U.S. *Congressional Globe.* Vols. XXXV–XL.
U.S., Congress, House of Representatives. *Annual Report of the Commissioner of the Freedman's Savings and Trust Company for the Year Ending December 1, 1883.* House Miscellaneous Document No. 10. 48th Cong., 1st sess., 1883.

————. *Annual Report of the Commissioner of the Freedman's Savings and Trust Company.* House Miscellaneous Document No. 7. 48th Cong., 2nd sess., 1884.

————. *Annual Report of the Commissioner of the Freedman's Savings and Trust Company.* House Miscellaneous Document No. 18. 49th Cong., 1st sess., 1885.

————. *Annual Report of the Commissioner of the Freedman's Savings and Trust Company.* House Miscellaneous Document No. 34. 49th Cong., 2nd sess., 1886.

————. *Annual Report of the Commissioner of the Freedman's Savings and Trust Company.* House Miscellaneous Document No. 33. 51st Cong., 1st sess., 1889.

————. *Annual Report of the Commissioner of the Freedman's Savings and Trust Company.* House Document No. 128. 56th Cong., 1st sess., 1899.

————. *Annual Report of the Commissioner of the Freedman's Savings and Trust Company.* House Document No. 394. 59th Cong., 2nd sess., 1906.

————. *Annual Report of the Commissioner of the Freedman's Savings and Trust Company.* House Document No. 330. 61st Cong., 2nd sess., 1909.

————. *Annual Report of the Commissioner of the Freedman's Savings and Trust Company.* House Document No. 499. 66th Cong., 2nd sess., 1919.

————. *Charges against General Howard.* House Report No. 121. 41st Cong., 2nd sess., 1870.

————. *Freedman's Bank.* House Report No. 502. 44th Cong., 1st sess., 1876.

————. *Freedmen's Affairs in Kentucky and Tennessee.* House Executive Document No. 329. 40th Cong., 2nd sess., 1868.

————. *Freedmen's Branch of the Adjutant General's Office for Year Ending June 30, 1875.* House Executive Document No. 144. 44th Cong., 1st sess., 1875.

————. *Freedmen's Bureau.* House Executive Document No. 70. 39th Cong., 1st sess., 1866.

————. *Letter from the Commissioner of the Freedman's Savings and Trust Company.* Miscellaneous Document No. 43. 45th Cong., 2nd sess., 1878.

————. *Letter from the Secretary of the Treasury.* Executive Document No. 10. 45th Cong., 3rd sess., 1878.

————. *Report of the Commissioner, Bureau of Refugees, Freedmen, and Abandoned Lands.* House Executive Document No. 11. 38th Cong., 1st sess., 1865.

————. *Report of the Commissioner of the Freedman's Savings and Trust Company.* House Miscellaneous Document No. 16. 43rd Cong., 2nd sess., 1874.

————. *Resolution of the Legislature of South Carolina.* House Miscellaneous Document No. 29. 43rd Cong., 2nd sess., 1875.

————, Committee on Banking and Currency. *Depositors of the Freedman's Savings and Trust Company.* House Report No. 3139. 50th Cong., 1st sess., 1888.

————, Committee on Banking and Currency. *Freedman's Savings and Trust Company.* House Report No. 58. 43rd Cong., 2nd sess., 1875.

————, Committee on Banking and Currency. *The Freedman's Savings and Trust Company.* House Report No. 336. 47th Cong., 1st sess., 1882.

————, Committee on Banking and Currency. *Hearings in January, 1910, on*

House Bill 8776 to Reimburse Depositors of the Freedman's Savings and Trust Company. 1910.

————, Committee on Banking and Currency. *Reimbursement of Depositors of Freedman's Savings and Trust Company.* House Report No. 1282, Private Calendar No. 532. 61st Cong., 2nd sess., 1910.

————, Committee on Banking and Currency. *Report from Committee on Banking and Currency.* House Report No. 1282, Pt. 1. 61st Cong., 2nd sess., 1910.

————, Committee on Banking and Currency. *To Reimburse Depositors of Late Freedman's Savings and Trust Company.* House Report No. 1637, Pts. 1 and 2. 60th Cong., 1st sess., 1908.

————, Committee on Banking and Currency. *Views of the Minority of the Committee on Banking and Currency.* House Report No. 1282, Pt. 2. 61st Cong., 2nd sess., 1910.

————, Committee on Education and Labor. *Reimbursing Depositors of Freedman's Savings Bank.* House Report No. 1991, Pts. 1 and 2. 47th Cong., 2nd sess., 1883.

————, Committee on Ways and Means. *Freedman's Savings and Trust Company.* House Report No. 1571. 46th Cong., 2nd sess., 1880.

U.S., Congress, Senate. *Annual Report of the Commissioner of the Freedman's Savings and Trust Company.* Senate Miscellaneous Document No. 10. 47th Cong., 2nd sess., 1882.

————. *Freedman's Savings and Trust Co.* Senate Document No. 759. 62nd Cong., 2nd sess., 1912.

————. *Report of the Commissioner of the Freedman's Savings and Trust Company.* Senate Miscellaneous Document No. 17. 47th Cong., 1st sess., 1881.

————. *Report of the Commissioners of the Freedman's Savings and Trust Company.* Senate Miscellaneous Document No. 36. 44th Cong., 1st sess., 1876.

————. *Report of the Comptroller of the Currency upon the Condition of the Savings Banks of the District of Columbia.* Senate Miscellaneous Document No. 88. 42nd Cong., 3rd sess., 1873.

————. *Report of the Select Committee to Investigate the Freedman's Savings and Trust Company.* Senate Report No. 440. 46th Cong., 2nd sess., 1880.

————. *Resolution of the Legislature of North Carolina.* Senate Miscellaneous Document No. 24. 43rd Cong., 2nd sess., 1874.

————, Committee on Education and Labor. *Report from Committee on Education and Labor.* Senate Report No. 434. 61st Cong., 2nd sess., 1910.

————, Committee on Education and Labor. *To Reimburse Depositors of Late Freedman's Savings and Trust Company.* Senate Report No. 211. 60th Cong., 1st sess., 1908.

————, Committee on Finance. *Interview of the Committee on Finance with Hon. W. L. Trenholm.* April 24, 1888.

————, Committee on Finance. *Payment of Dividends of Freedman's Savings and Trust Company.* Senate Report No. 1884. 55th Cong., 3rd sess., 1899.

U.S. *Statutes at Large.* Vol. XIII.

U.S., War Department. *The War of the Rebellion. A Compilation of the Official Records of the Union and Confederate Armies.* 70 vols. Washington: Government Printing Office, 1880–1901.

NEWSPAPERS

Alabama State Journal (Montgomery). June 19, 1870; September, 1873.
Atlanta Constitution. September 24, 26, 27, 1873; February 17, 1874.
Baltimore American. July 8, August 11, September 15, 1874.
Baltimore *Sun.* April 28, 29, 30, May 2, 1874.
Charleston Daily Courier. April–December, 1866; 1868; 1870.
Charleston Daily News. January–June, 1873.
Charleston Daily Republican. June 11, 1870.
Charleston *News and Courier.* July, 1873–December, 1874; May 7, 1886.
The Colored Tribune (Savannah). December 4, 1873; January 1, 1876.
Daily Arkansas Gazette (Little Rock). September, 1873; May 3, July 3, 1874.
Daily Critic (Washington). September, 1873; July, 1874.
Daily Enquirer and Examiner (Richmond). January–June, 1869.
Daily Memphis Avalanche. July 3, 1874.
Daily Sentinel (Raleigh). July 9, 1874.
Daily Union-Herald (Columbia, S.C.). July 3, 4, 8, 1874.
Evening Star (Washington). 1867; 1869; May, 1870–May, 1871; February–December, 1874.
Little Rock Daily Republican. April 29, 1874.
The Louisianian (New Orleans). 1870–74.
Louisville *Courier–Journal.* 1868; 1870; September, 1873; 1874.
Memphis Daily Appeal. September 26, 28, 1873.
Mobile Daily Register. April, July, 1874.
Nashville *Republican Banner.* September, 1873; July, 1874.
Nashville Union and American. March, 1873; July, 1874.
National Republican (Washington). September, 1873; July, 1874.
National Savings Bank. January 1, February 1, June 1, 1868.
The Nationalist (Mobile). 1865–68.
New Berne Times. September, 1873; June, 1874.
New Era (*New National Era, New National Era and Citizen*) (Washington). 1870–74.
New South (Jacksonville, Fla.) July 22, 1874.
New York Herald. April 28, 1874.
New York *Sun.* April–July, 1874.
New York Times. 1864–80.
New York Tribune. 1865–80.
People's Advocate (Washington). January 3, 1880.
Philadelphia Inquirer. July, 1874.
Philadelphia *Press.* July, 1874.
Richmond *Republic.* June 1, October 11, 1865.
Richmond *Daily Enquirer.* February–June, 1871; January–June, 1872; January–May, July, 1874.
Richmond Daily Whig, July, 1874.
Richmond Dispatch. July, 1874.

Savannah Morning News. 1870–75.
South Carolina Leader (Charleston). December, 1865–66.
U.S., Works Projects Administration. *Annals of Cleveland.* 1818–1935.
————. *Annals of Savannah, 1850–1937.* Vols. 18–26, covering 1867 through 1875.
Vicksburg Daily Times. September, 1873; July, 1874.
Vicksburg Weekly Republican. October 3, 1869.
Washington Chronicle. 1874.
Washington Post. June, 1899.

PAMPHLETS

Adams, F. C. *The Washers and the Scrubbers: The Men Who Robbed Them.* Washington: Judd & Detweiler, 1879. Toner Collection, Library of Congress.
Banks, Nathaniel P. *Emancipated Labor in Louisiana.* New York: n.p., 1865.
The Charter and By-Laws of the Freedman's Savings and Trust Company. 1872. Library of Congress.
Freedman's Savings and Trust Company. 1865 and 1869. Library of Congress.
National Savings and Trust Company. 1867. Library of Congress.
Proceedings, Findings, and Opinion of the Court of Inquiry . . . in the Case of Brigadier General Oliver O. Howard. Washington: Government Printing Office, 1874.
Statement of Br. Maj. Gen. O. O. Howard before the Committee on Education and Labor in defense against the charges presented by Hon. Fernando Wood, and Argument of Edgar Ketchum, Esq. New York: Bradstreet Press, 1870.

SECONDARY SOURCES

ARTICLES AND BOOKS

Abbott, Martin. *The Freedmen's Bureau in South Carolina, 1865–1872.* Chapel Hill: University of North Carolina Press, 1967.
Ames, Charles Edgar. *Pioneering the Union Pacific.* New York: Appleton-Century-Crofts, 1969.
Appleton's Cyclopedia of American Biography. 7 vols. Ed. J. G. Wilson and John Fiske. New York: Appleton, 1887–1900.
Bentley, George R. *A History of the Freedmen's Bureau.* Philadelphia: University of Pennsylvania Press, 1955.
Biographical Directory of the American Congress, 1774–1961. Washington: Government Printing Office, 1961.
Blassingame, John W. *Black New Orleans, 1860–1880.* Chicago: University of Chicago Press, 1973.
Bolles, Albert S. *Bank Officers: Their Authority, Duty and Liability.* New York: Homans Publishing Co., 1890.
Boyd's Directory of Richmond City. 1869.
Brawley, Benjamin. *A Short History of the American Negro.* New York: Macmillan, 1913.

Bremner, Robert H. *American Philanthropy*. Chicago: University of Chicago Press, 1960.

Carpenter, John A. *Sword and Olive Branch*. Pittsburgh: University of Pittsburgh Press, 1964.

Chapman, John M., and Westerfield, Ray. *Branch Banking*. New York: Harper & Bros., 1942.

City Directories, 1870. Baltimore, Charleston, New Orleans, Richmond, Savannah, Washington.

Cole, David M. *The Development of Banking in the District of Columbia*. New York: William-Frederick Press, 1959.

Coulter, E. Merton. *The South during Reconstruction, 1865–1877*. Vol. 8 of *A History of the South*, ed. Wendell Holmes Stephenson and E. Merton Coulter. Baton Rouge: Louisiana State University Press, 1947.

Dew, Charles B. "Disciplining Slave Ironworkers in the Antebellum South: Coercion, Conciliation, and Accommodation." *American Historical Review*, LXXIX, 2 (April, 1974), 393–418.

Dictionary of American Biography. 20 vols. New York: Charles Scribner's Sons, 1928–36.

Du Bois, W. E. B. *Black Reconstruction*. New York: Russell & Russell, 1935.

———, ed. *Economic Co-operation among Negro Americans*. Atlanta: Atlanta University Press, 1907.

———. *The Souls of Black Folk*. 1903. Reprinted, Greenwich, Conn.: Fawcett Publications, 1970.

Dyson, Walter. *Howard University*. Washington: Graduate School of Howard University, 1941.

Emeka, Mauris L. P. *Black Banks, Past and Present*. Kansas City, Mo.: By the Author, 1971.

Fischer, Gerald C. *American Banking Structure*. New York: Columbia University Press, 1968.

Fleming, Walter L. *Civil War and Reconstruction in Alabama*. New York: Peter Smith, 1949.

———. *The Freedmen's Savings Bank; A Chapter in the Economic History of the Negro Race*. Chapel Hill: University of North Carolina Press, 1927.

Fletcher, Robert Samuel. *A History of Oberlin College from Its Foundation through the Civil War*. 2 vols. Oberlin: Oberlin College, 1943.

Fogel, Robert William. *The Union Pacific Railroad*. Baltimore: Johns Hopkins Press, 1960.

———, and Engerman, Stanley L. *Time on the Cross: The Economics of American Negro Slavery*. Boston: Little, Brown, 1974.

Foner, Philip S. *Business and Slavery*. Chapel Hill: University of North Carolina Press, 1941.

Franklin, John Hope. *From Slavery to Freedom*. 3rd ed. rev. New York: Alfred A. Knopf, 1967.

Frazier, E. Franklin. *Black Bourgeoisie*. New York: Free Press, 1957.

———. *The Negro in the United States*. Rev. ed. Toronto: Macmillan, 1957.

Galloway, Thomas J. "The Negro as a Business Man." *World's Work*, XVI (June, 1908), 10349–51.

Gaston, Paul. *The New South Creed*. New York: Alfred A. Knopf, 1970.

Gilbert, Abby L. "The Comptroller of the Currency and the Freedman's Savings Bank." *Journal of Negro History*, LVII, 2 (April, 1972), 125–143.

Gordon, Asa H. *Sketches of Negro Life and History in South Carolina*. 2nd ed. Reprint, Columbia: University of South Carolina Press, 1971.

Green, Constance McLaughlin. *The Secret City*. Princeton: Princeton University Press, 1967.

————. *Washington*. 2 vols. Princeton: Princeton University Press, 1962–63.

Harris, Abram L. *The Negro as Capitalist*. Philadelphia: American Academy of Political and Social Science, 1936.

Hoffman, Frederick L. *Race Traits and Tendencies of the American Negro*. New York: Macmillan, 1896.

Holland, Frederic May. *Frederick Douglass: The Colored Orator*. 1891. Reprinted, New York: Haskell House Publishers, 1969.

Jones, Louis C. "A Leader Ahead of His Times." *American Heritage*, XIV, 4 (June, 1963), 59, 83.

Keyes, Emerson Willard. *A History of Savings Banks in the United States*. 2 vols. New York: Bradford Rhodes, 1878.

Kniffin, William H., Jr. *The Savings Bank and Its Practical Work*. New York: Bankers Publishing Co., 1918.

Kolchin, Peter. *First Freedom: The Responses of Alabama's Blacks to Emancipation and Reconstruction*. Westport, Conn.: Greenwood Press, 1972.

Larson, Henrietta M. *Jay Cooke, Private Banker*. Cambridge: Harvard University Press, 1936.

Lindsay, Arnett G. "The Negro in Banking." *Journal of Negro History*, XIV (April, 1929), 156–201.

Litwack, Leon F. *North of Slavery*. Chicago: University of Chicago Press, 1961.

McFeely, William S. *Yankee Stepfather: General O. O. Howard and the Freedmen*. New Haven: Yale University Press, 1968.

McPherson, James M. *The Struggle for Equality*. Princeton: Princeton University Press, 1964.

National Cyclopedia of American Biography. New York: J. T. White & Co., 1893–1919.

Oates, Stephen B. *To Purge This Land with Blood*. New York: Harper & Row, 1970.

Oberlin College. *Alumni Register: Graduates and Former Students, Teaching and Administrative Staff*. 1833–1960.

Ottley, Roi, and Weatherby, William J., eds. *The Negro in New York*. New York: Praeger, 1967.

Pease, William H., and Pease, Jane H. "Antislavery Ambivalence: Immediatism, Expedience, Race." *American Quarterly*, XVII (Winter, 1965), 682–695.

Peirce, Paul Skeels. *The Freedmen's Bureau: A Chapter in the History of Reconstruction*. Iowa City: State University of Iowa, 1904.

Prince, Richard E. *Steam Locomotives and History: Georgia Railroad and West Point Route*. Green River, Wyo.: By the Author, 1962.

Quarles, Benjamin. *Black Abolitionists*. New York: Oxford University Press, 1969.

————. *Frederick Douglass*. Washington: Associated Publishers, 1948.

Richardson, Joe M. *The Negro in the Reconstruction of Florida, 1865–1877*. Tallahassee: Florida State University Press, 1965.

Rose, Willie Lee. *Rehearsal for Reconstruction.* Indianapolis: Bobbs-Merrill, 1964.

Simmons, Reverend William J. *Men of Mark.* Cleveland: George M. Rewell & Co., 1887.

Southworth, Shirley Donald. *Branch Banking in the United States.* New York: McGraw-Hill, 1928.

Statistical History of the United States from Colonial Times to the Present. Stamford, Conn.: Fairfield Publishers, 1965.

St. Louis City Directory, 1860.

Swint, Henry Lee. *The Northern Teacher in the South, 1862–1870.* Nashville: Vanderbilt University Press, 1941.

Taylor, Alrutheus Ambush. *The Negro in the Reconstruction of Virginia.* Washington: Association for the Study of Negro Life and History, 1926.

———. *The Negro in South Carolina during Reconstruction.* Washington: Association for the Study of Negro Life and History, 1924.

———. *The Negro in Tennessee, 1865–1880.* Washington: Associated Publishers, 1941.

Tindall, George Brown. *South Carolina Negroes, 1877–1900.* Columbia: University of South Carolina Press, 1952.

Trescott, Paul B. *Financing American Enterprise.* New York: Harper & Row, 1963.

Trow's New York City Directory. Vol. LXXVI. New York: John F. Trow, 1863.

Washington, Booker T. *The Negro in Business.* Boston: Hertel, Jenkins & Co., 1907.

———. *The Story of the Negro.* 2 vols. New York: Doubleday, Page & Co., 1909.

Weeden, H. C. *Weeden's History of the Colored People of Louisville.* Louisville: By the Author, 1897.

Welfling, Weldon. *Mutual Savings Banks: The Evolution of a Financial Intermediary.* Cleveland: Case Western Reserve University Press, 1968.

Wesley, Charles H. *Negro Labor in the United States, 1850–1925.* New York: Vanguard Press, 1927.

Wharton, Vernon Lane. *The Negro in Mississippi, 1865–1890.* Chapel Hill: University of North Carolina Press, 1947.

Whyte, James H. *The Uncivil War: Washington during the Reconstruction, 1865–1878.* New York: Twayne Publishers, 1958.

Williams, George Washington. *History of the Negro Race in America from 1619 to 1880.* 2 vols. New York: G. P. Putnam's Sons, 1883.

Williamson, Joel. *After Slavery.* Chapel Hill: University of North Carolina Press, 1965.

Wilson, Joseph T. *The Black Phalanx.* 1890. Reprinted, New York: Arno Press & New York Times, 1968.

MISCELLANEOUS

Andrews, W. T., and Cromwell, J. W. *Eulogies: In Memoriam.* Ed. Tally R. Holmes of South Carolina and Colonel Joseph T. Wilson of Virginia. Washington: Bethel Literary and Historical Society [1891].

Banks, Charles. *Negro Banks of Mississippi.* [1909].
Drake, Richard Bryant. "The American Missionary Association and the Southern Negro 1861–1888." Ph.D. dissertation, Emory University, 1957.
Lamon, Lester C. "Negroes in Tennessee, 1900–1930." Ph.D. dissertation, University of North Carolina, 1971.

Index

1873, 176–180; efforts to reform, 180–186, 193–194, 196, 197, 198; charge of duping black leaders, 184–185; and Comptroller's reports, 171, 180, 187–188, 190; telegraphic correspondence of, 192; Senate wants to close, 195; closed, 198–199; financial condition at closing, 199; and other savings banks, 199–200; legend of, 199, 200; reaction to failure, 202–208; dividends after failure, 211–215; Congress investigates, 216–217; Congress and reimbursement, 217–220; legacy of failure, 221–225
—Agency Committee: and advisory boards, 19–20, 108, 109, 110; and crisis at branches, 37–39; advertises in black newspapers, 48; resolves to merge with Freedmen's Bureau, 69; importance, 151; mentioned, 11, 46
—Finance Committee: established, 11; reduced in membership, 142; reports, 142n; loans, 145, 152, 153–165 *passim*; rejects higher interest rate, 146; dominated by Henry D. Cooke, 151, 152; restrictions on, 182; mentioned, 180. *See also* Cooke, Henry D.; Huntington, William
—Trustees: board of fifty, 6–7; changes in membership, 10–11, 141–142, 183; and concentration of power, 11, 142, 151; negligence of, 139, 140, 143; and loans, investments, and fraud, 139–166 *passim*; blacks as, 142, 183–185; return to conservative management, 182. *See also* Advisory boards; Branch banks; Cashiers; Depositors
Freedmen: financial condition and needs of, 36, 37, 124; make Bank a success, 135–136; reaction to failure, 202–208. *See also* Depositors
Freedmen's Bureau: and bounty money, 26; and close cooperation with Bank, 27, 28, 34, 40, 63–70, 139; scandals surrounding, 163; mentioned, 10, 13, 40, 56, 57, 59, 61, 73
"Freedmen's Bureau Ring," 163
Freedmen's Rights Association, 207
French, E. G., 142
Frost, Rufus, 217

Galveston branch, 28
Ganson, John, 5
Garland, A. H., 217
Garnet, Henry H., 46
Garnet, Mrs. Henry H., 18
Gibbs, Joseph M., 79
Gibbs, Oscar, 98
Gillem, General, 66
Goddard, William H., 231
Goodall, William P., 75
Gordon, John B., 217
Grant, Ulysses S., 55
Graves, R. R., 227
Gregory, D. S., 141
Gregory, General, 48
Griffith, Walter S., 12, 227
Gwathney, Scott, 116

Hadley, B. J., 116
Hall, R. M., 162
Hamilton, John G.: works for AMA and Bank, 63, 231; and incompetence or fraud, 169; mentioned, 62, 120, 169
Hamilton College, 7
Harding, Henry, 113
Harding, Warren G., 221
Harris, Abram, 223
Harris, Edward, 6
Harris, Samuel L.: and bounty policy, 27; and Memphis branch, 40–41; publicity work of, 45, 46; and runs, 178; writes circular against sale of deposit books, 205n; mentioned, 38, 41, 59, 83, 95, 102, 104, 106, 179, 186
Harwood, Edward, 143
Hatch, A. S., 227
Hatch, Walter T., 227
Hawksworth, J. M., 232
Hawley, J. A., 233
Hayden, Charles W., 157, 158
Hayes (of Richmond), 117
Hewitt, Mahlon T.: term as vice-president and president, 12, 141; active in Bank's expansion, 15, 18; on Negro industry, 35; urges change of cashiers, 36; observes conditions at Mobile, 37; and financial crisis (1866–1867), 38–39, 41, 43; and quarrel with Freedmen's Bureau at Vicksburg, 65, 66; and race, 71; favors black